The Cuisine of
ALAIN
SENDERENS

The Cuisine of
ALAIN SENDERENS
LA CUISINE RÉUSSIE

adapted for this edition by Caroline Conran

MACMILLAN
LONDON

Originally published in French under the title *La Cuisine Réussie* 1981 by
Editions Jean-Claude Lattès

This edition published in the United Kingdom 1986 by
Macmillan London Limited
4 Little Essex Street London WC2R 3LF and Basingstoke

Associated companies in Auckland, Delhi, Dublin, Gaborone, Hamburg,
Harare, Hong Kong, Johannesburg, Kuala Lumpur, Lagos, Manzini,
Melbourne, Mexico City, Nairobi, New York, Singapore and Tokyo

British Library Cataloguing in Publication Data
Senderens, Alain
The cuisine of Alan Senderens:
la cuisine réussie.
I. Cookery, French
I. Title   II. Senderens, Eventhia
III. Conran, Caroline   IV. La cuisine
réussie. *English*
641.5944   TX719.S4413

ISBN 0-333-42281-3

Typeset by Bookworm Typesetting, Manchester
Printed and bound in Great Britain by Anchor Brendon Limited, Tiptree

Contents

List of Illustrations

Foreword

Alain Senderens is a chef well used to the limelight; enthusiastic Parisian devotees have followed his career avidly from the time that he opened the doors of l'Archestrate, his first small restaurant in the rue de Varennes, and started, in 1968, to produce his amazingly innovative cuisine. Ten years later, with a worldwide reputation, and much written about in *Gourmet*, he won his third and most coveted Michelin star.

In 1985, having outgrown l'Archestrate, Senderens moved to the famous Lucas Carton restaurant, opposite the Madeleine. He already knew and loved that grand old Belle-Epoque restaurant, having worked there as *chef-rôtisseur* during his apprenticeship. Now he is well established as its hard-working and thoughtful owner-*patron* and has completely changed the tone of what was formerly a quiet old-fashioned backwater. He is often to be seen emerging at high speed from his kitchen, in his sparkling chef's whites, for a quick consultation at the 'front-of-the-house', noticing every detail of the service and, with Eventhia his wife, sorting out the small problems that occur in his crowded dining room. He takes such details very seriously. Eventhia, *la patronne*, who greets their glossy clients, is also completely involved in the smooth running of the restaurant – an invaluable ally to the chef.

Husband and wife have also worked as a team on this book and, in order to make it easier for home cooks to succeed with the sometimes complex recipes, Mme Senderens has tested them all at home in her domestic kitchen.

One of the most important things to recognise is that many of these recipes require a lot of last-minute preparation, although many of the stages can, in fact, be done in advance. However, provided, as Eventhia suggests, you have a perfect *mise en place*, with every ingredient to hand and all preliminary preparations done, and with teatowels, oven-gloves, heated dishes and peppermills at the ready, the final stages can be accomplished smoothly and fairly rapidly. But if you are the sort of person who gets flustered easily, perhaps it is best to keep certain recipes, such as the Salmon, Bass and Turbot with White Wine Sauce (see page 126) for your immediate family, or people you know extremely well and who might like to give you a bit of assistance. Also, make a point of not having more than one complicated recipe in any menu for dinner or lunch.

As far as ingredients are concerned, there are some things that do make a tremendous difference to the end result. Many of these recipes use quantities of fresh herbs, which have a profound effect on the finished flavours – dried herbs will not do. Fortunately, most good supermarkets now stock a very good selection, including such things as dill, basil and chervil.

It is just possible to use frozen puff pastry instead of freshly home-made for such recipes as Salmon Tarts with Beurre Blanc (see page 46), but if you take the trouble to make your own you will be well rewarded, as the flavour and texture will be incomparably better.

A very great number of the sauces rely on butter for colour, flavour and liaison – no flour is used. Often the butter is introduced gradually into a smallish quantity of concentrated liquid – usually reduced cooking juices and reduced cream. Sauce made in this way is both rich and delicate, but all depends on the flavour of the butter; much EEC butter tastes old and rancid and is not particularly fresh, so be careful to buy best-quality butter and make sure it tastes fresh.

If you have the time to make *crème fraîche* (see page 290), you will have a much better flavour than can be obtained simply by using ordinary cream. Incidentally, it is possible to boil double cream and whipping cream, but single cream does not have a high enough fat content to boil successfully, so do not try to use it as a substitute. If you cannot get whipping cream, use a mixture of single and double cream, half and half; this can be boiled and also rises lightly to a very good volume when it is whipped.

Sauce-making is of supreme importance in the excellent fish chapter. Bass, salmon, monk fish and brill all appear, but fillet of turbot is Senderens' favourite fish. For these recipes you will have to ask the fishmonger to prepare fillets specially for you, as fish shops in this country sell turbot in steaks and slices only. (The tail end makes particularly good fillets.)

Many of the shellfish in these recipes should, ideally, be dealt with while they are still alive. I recommend that you ask your fishmonger to kill them for you and that you then go straight home and do the first stages of the cooking at once, before the fish have time to waste away. Freshwater crayfish, which appear frequently in Senderens' cooking, are available in season only, from May to autumn (try Richards (SOHO), 11 Brewer Street, London W1), and are sold live. It is best to carry crayfish home live as they deteriorate extremely quickly.

In Senderens' restaurant, both fish and meat are famously underdone by many people's standards and very much appreciated for their succulence. However, if you prefer duck, for example, a bit better cooked, just increase the cooking time given in the recipe by a couple of minutes.

It is true to say that French butchers have an attitude to their customers unknown in this country: nothing is too much trouble and the meat is lovingly trimmed and presented. Apart from the care lavished on presenting the meat, they offer for sale all sorts of offal, giblets and oddities such as cauls and feet, which we find it difficult to obtain. If you can, find a butcher who buys whole animals (many nowadays just buy the particular cuts they want to sell, already butchered) and come to some arrangement with him. If that is impossible, the Boucherie Lamartine, 229 Ebury Street, London SWI, is as French as a butcher can be (the shop is owned by Albert and Michel Roux) and can usually help with difficult ingredients, including fresh *foie gras* and fresh black truffles. Goose fat in tins, called 'Graisse d'Oie Pure Filtrée', packed by Aux Ducs de Bourgogne, is available from Hobbs & Co., 29 South Audley Street, London WI, who also have very interesting fruit and vegetables.

Many of the salads in the book are served slightly warm, which makes them delicious, but take care not to overheat them or the delicate leaves will quickly wilt. Frizzy and Batavian are the two types of endive that stand up best to heating. When shopping for salads, pick only the freshest and use only the tender parts – the outside leaves are never included, although they can be used to make soup. Oil of arachide (refined peanut oil) is used as a salad oil in some recipes because its flavour is less pronounced than that of olive or nut oil. It is also used by Senderens and many other chefs as a cooking oil, as it has little taste or smell and can be heated to a higher temperature without burning than most other oils.

The vegetables used in this sort of cooking should always be fresh, and are usually best young, tender and small. When cutting them into julienne, slice them thinly and then cut the slices a few at a time into strips of the required size. If you don't have time to make them as small as the recipe suggests, it will not alter the flavour of the dish. In Lucas Carton the julienne resemble hair rather than matchsticks or pine needles, while the diced vegetables look like a doll's-house mosaic.

As far as equipment is concerned, most people who are interested in food of this standard enjoy doing some things by hand, but probably have a food processor, kitchen thermometer and all the utensils, forcing bags and different kinds of sieves necessary. It is also extremely useful to have a selection of individual moulds, soufflé dishes and tart tins, as many of the recipes such as Chicken Liver Mousse with Bacon and Cream Sauce (see page 88) or Hot Apple Charlottes (see page 272) are cooked and served individually – a form of presentation that most chefs favour and which gives a very professional look to even quite simple dishes.

A very great deal can be learned by cooking the dishes of someone as skilled as Senderens, with the recipes carefully adapted for home cooks, as these are. So do not be daunted if you are still a beginner: persevere if they do not come quite right at the first attempt, because many of them – particularly the fish recipes with their excellent sauces – are in fact quite simple once you have the knack and are well worth mastering.

Caroline Conran
London, 1986

Author's Preface

This book is dedicated to those who love to cook and who cook at home. All of my recipes presented here have been adapted for home use by my wife, Eventhia, in our home kitchen. In this book, you will find chef's recipes made accessible to you. The instructions are as clear and precise as possible, as are measurements and cooking times. But remember that cooking is an inexact art, so be relaxed when you cook. Once you understand the basic principles, don't be afraid to adapt, to use other products (they are sometimes suggested), to invent new recipes – in short, to use what you learn here to develop your own personal style of cooking.

Introduction

by Eventhia Senderens

One of the first things I learned when I started to adapt these recipes for my own kitchen was how important it is to be perfectly organised and to have every ingredient called for in a recipe within arm's reach.

Before starting any cooking, the work surfaces, stove-top and oven need to be completely in order. *La mise en place* – the preparation, measuring, and 'lining-up' of ingredients in advance – must be thought through by reading the recipe carefully to understand the steps that lie ahead. Such mundane things as teatowels and oven gloves should be at hand the moment they are needed. Avoid the exasperation of having to search for things, whether tools or ingredients.

The success of a meal cooked at home depends, much more than when you are ordering in a restaurant, on the way the menu is planned. If a dish you choose is time-consuming, see how much of it can be prepared in advance, and precede or follow it with simpler dishes. This not only means that you will not spend too much time in the kitchen when your guests arrive; it will also help you to ensure the excellence of each part of the menu.

I have carefully tested all these recipes. Many of them I have found demanding at home without the help of a kitchen staff, but all of them have worked well if I did not try to do too many things at once – essentially, to repeat, if I have planned my menus carefully. The measurements are given as specifically as they can be. Do try the recipes as they are before attempting to improvise. The subtle balance of flavours is calculated in each one of them, but later, with experience, you can make your own adjustments and variations.

Next, there are some techniques of cooking that present themselves repeatedly for ingredients you will use often. It is good to remember them as general methods, even though they are described in each recipe.

First, of course, always use fresh products. The cooking techniques used in the cuisine of Alain Senderens aim at preserving the maximum flavour of each food (and the vitamins too). Therefore, cooking times tend to be short: vegetables should be tender but still slightly crunchy, and meat (except for pork and veal) should be served rare.

Vegetables
You will notice that vegetables are rarely boiled if they are to be served as a garnish. Generally, they are cooked in very little butter, over low heat; the water they contain is usually sufficient to cook them. If not, a spoonful or two of water is added so that there will be enough steam to allow them to become tender without scorching.

Meat
Meat for roasting is often seasoned before it is cooked. Large pieces of meat, however, will not be sufficiently seasoned this way, so salt and pepper will have to be added when the meat is sliced and served.

The best method of ensuring a nice crust on meat is to brown it rapidly in a mixture of butter and oil; a teaspoon of each is often enough because the meat itself contributes its own fat to the browning process. Once the meat has browned, pour off the fat in the pan. If it is heavily glazed with fat, pat the pan with paper towels, being careful to leave the caramelised meat juices. These juices give a wonderful flavour to sauces, so don't wash the pan after browning meat unless the contents have burned and blackened – which can happen; do discard anything that has scorched in a pan.

Fish
The same simple method is used throughout this book for the initial cooking of most fish. Chopped shallots and mushrooms are allowed to soften in a gratin dish or roasting tin. Fish fillets are laid on top of them, white wine, or a mixture of white wine and water, is added, and the pan is placed in a hot (425°F/220°C/Reg. 7) oven to bake. Cooking times are short, generally between 7 and 10 minutes (there is nothing worse than overcooked fish). The fish are served with sauces, made either separately or with the cooking liquid, which is reduced and enriched with cream, simmered to thicken it, and seasoned in different ways to give each recipe its particular quality.

Sauces
Alain Senderens follows a hard and fast rule for sauces: they are never thickened with flour. Cream (boiled down to a velvety consistency) or egg yolk whisked in at the last minute make for lighter sauces that are not only easier to digest but much more delicate in flavour than sauces thickened with flour.

Salads
I have noticed that many people do not season salads enough. The first thing to remember about them is that lettuce leaves should be as dry as possible. After washing (very thoroughly), dry them in a salad spinner or

pat each leaf carefully in a towel. Then remember that the dressing you make will taste stronger alone than it will when mixed with the salad. For variety, try mixing oils or vinegars. There are many different ones available today, each with its distinctive taste. Some are very strong: but combinations can modulate them in pleasant and surprising ways.

Last but not least, think about
Your butcher and fishmonger   They will be glad to prepare your meat or fillet your fish for you. All it takes is clear instructions … and a smile.

Organising your menu   Plan carefully so that you spend the least time possible in the kitchen once your guests arrive.

Your budget   You can splurge on one part of a meal and save on another. For example, if you want to serve a lobster salad as a first course, follow it with a main dish of chicken or pork.

Serving and presentation   Very often I have suggested serving directly on to individual plates rather than from a serving dish. This saves time and makes for the best presentation to each guest. However, it may be inconvenient if you have limited space on which to arrange the plates. If you do present something on a serving dish, divide it first into serving portions. In either case, remember that plates and serving dishes must be heated.

And now, in conclusion, we wish you all … *Bon appétit*!

Publisher's Note

The recipes in this edition have been tested for English-speaking cooks by the translators. This produced information that does not appear in the original French, including substitutes for ingredients that might not be readily available to most cooks outside France. All such material not contained in the French text is given under the heading 'Notes'.

Alain and Eventhia Senderens themselves propose substitutes and variations in their 'Suggestions', which precede the translators' Notes.

APPETISERS

Smoked Eel Butter on Toast
Beurre d'anguille

For 6–8 people

125g *(4 oz)*	smoked eel fillets (see Note on purchasing)
70g *(3 oz)*	softened butter
3 tbsps	*crème fraîche* (see p.290) or thick double cream
½	loaf of white bread, very thinly sliced
	butter (for the toast)

Equipment
liquidiser or food processor · bowl
To serve: small bowl and plate or serving dish

The butter
Place the smoked eel in the liquidiser or food processor and blend to a purée. Blend in the butter, add the cream and blend until smooth and glossy. Transfer the smoked-fish butter to a bowl, beat for a minute more with a wooden spoon, then place in a small serving bowl and chill until ready to serve.

To serve
Heat the grill. Cut the crusts off each slice of bread and cut it into little pieces of any shape you like: squares, circles, triangles and so on. Spread them with butter, transfer them to a baking sheet and toast lightly for a minute or two.

Serve the toast on a plate with the bowl of eel butter, or spread each little piece of toast with the eel butter and serve on a serving dish.

Suggestion
Smoked salmon or any other smoked fish may be prepared in the same way.

Note
The weight of fish given in the list of ingredients is for smoked eel fillets. Often smoked eel is sold whole with skin and bones still attached; in this case you will need to buy about 175g *(6 oz)* and remove the skin and bones, in order to have the 125g *(4 oz)* needed for this recipe.

Wine
Accompany this dish with a well-chilled young white wine – Sancerre or Pouilly-Fumé, for example.

Little Asparagus Tarts
Tartelettes aux asperges

For 8 people

300g *(11 oz)*	puff pastry (see p.242)
2.3 litres *(4 pints)*	water
2 tsps	coarse salt
450g *(1 lb)*	asparagus
4	egg yolks
200ml *(7 fl. oz)*	double cream or thin *crème fraîche* (see p.290)
	salt, freshly ground pepper
	a pinch of cayenne pepper
	a pinch of nutmeg

Equipment
8 tartlet moulds, 8cm *(3 in)* in diameter · rolling pin · large saucepan · mixing bowl · wire whisk · baking sheet
To serve: large serving dish

The pastry
Lightly butter the tartlet moulds.

On a lightly floured worktop roll out the puff pastry into a rectangle about 22 × 44cm *(9 × 18 in)* and cut it into 8 squares about 12 × 12cm *(4½ × 4½ in)*. Line each mould with a square of dough, cutting off any excess with a knife. Chill for 45 minutes.

The asparagus
Meanwhile, place the water and coarse salt in the large saucepan and bring to the boil.

Break off the tough ends of the asparagus and cut off the tips. Peel the lower ends of the stems and cut them in half. Drop the stems into the boiling water, bring back to a boil and boil for 4 minutes. Add the tips and boil for 5 minutes longer. Drain the asparagus, cool briefly under cold running water and drain thoroughly on a cloth.

Cut the asparagus stems and tips in half lengthwise, then across into 1cm *(½-in)* cubes. Reserve.

To bake and serve
Pre-heat the oven to 425°F/220°C/Reg. 7.

Beat the egg yolks, cream, salt, pepper, cayenne and nutmeg together in a bowl until you have a completely smooth mixture.

Place equal amounts of asparagus cubes in each tartlet, then spoon the egg–cream mixture into each one until full. Place on a baking sheet and bake for 16 minutes, or until the surface of the tartlets is golden brown.

Remove from the oven, allow to cool for about 5 minutes, then serve on a large serving dish.

Wine
Sherry is excellent with these little tarts.

Miniature Spring Rolls
Crêpes de riz farcies

For about 50 small spring rolls, serving 8–10

650g *(1lb 7oz)*	boneless chicken breasts
1 tbsp	butter
4 tbsps	onion, finely chopped
4 tbsps	apple, finely chopped
4 tsps	mild curry powder
2 tsps	tomato paste
	salt, freshly ground pepper
6 tbsps	dry white wine
14	large round spring-roll wrappings (see Note)
	cooking oil

Equipment
food processor (optional) · small frying pan, with lid · large teatowel · large frying pan or wok
To serve: serving dish or 8–10 small plates

The stuffing
Chop the chicken breast finely by hand or with a food processor.

Melt the butter in a small frying pan, add the onion and apple and cook gently over a moderate heat for about 30 seconds. Sprinkle in the curry powder, cook for 30 seconds more, add the tomato paste, lower the heat and cook for 1 minute. Add the chopped chicken, salt, pepper and white wine. Cover and simmer very slowly for 20 minutes, stirring frequently. Remove from the heat and set aside.

The spring rolls

Dampen a large teatowel and spread it on a table. Separate the spring-roll wrappings and cover half the towel with them, then fold the towel over to cover them. Pat the towel lightly and leave for about 3 minutes or until the wrappings have softened and become flexible.

Cut each wrapping into quarters. Place a heaped teaspoon of the stuffing on each piece and fold it to enclose the stuffing. Fold the curved side over the stuffing. Fold the right side over the top and then the left side, then fold the pointed end opposite over this. Press gently to seal. Continue in this manner until all the stuffing has been used up.

To cook and serve the spring rolls

Heat 3 tablespoons of oil in a large frying pan or wok. When it is very hot, place some of the spring rolls in the pan (do not crowd), and brown over a moderate heat for about 2 minutes. Turn them over and brown for 2 minutes on the other side. Remove from the pan, drain on kitchen paper and remove to a serving dish or plate. Add another tablespoon of oil to the pan and cook another batch of spring rolls in the same manner. Continue until they are all cooked. Serve hot with drinks or as a first course.

Note

Spring-roll wrappings are sold in Oriental groceries. They are very thin, white, crêpe-like sheets of dough made from rice flour. They are generally sold in packets containing from 10–25 skins, and they can be kept refrigerated in their original packet or a plastic bag for several days without drying out.

Blue Cheese Wafers
Palets de Bleu d'Auvergne

For 16 appetisers

100g *(4 oz)*	Bleu d'Auvergne or other soft blue cheese
100g *(4 oz)*	softened butter
1	egg yolk
140g *(4½ oz)*	plain flour

Equipment

liquidiser or food processor · mixing bowl · spatula · baking sheet
To serve: serving dish

To mix and shape

Remove any hard outer rind from the cheese, then cut it into slices and place it in the liquidiser or food processor. Blend to break up the cheese, add the butter and egg yolk and blend until smooth and creamy. Place the mixture in a bowl and stir in the flour to make a soft, sticky dough.

Spoon the mixture on to a large sheet of aluminium foil. Using the back of a spoon or a spatula, spread it into a rectangle about 15 × 20cm *(6 × 8 in)*. Lift up one end of the foil; the dough should start to roll on to itself. (It may be necessary to detach the edge from the foil with a spatula; after that, push on the foil, behind the dough, to make it roll up.) When the dough has been shaped into a thick cylinder, wrap it in the foil, rolling it round and pressing on it lightly, and seal the ends. Refrigerate for 2–3 hours to stiffen before baking.

To bake and serve the wafers

Pre-heat the oven to 425°F/220°C/Reg. 7. Lightly butter a baking sheet.

Unwrap the roll of dough and cut it into 16 slices a little more than ½cm *(¼ in)* thick. Place them on the baking sheet with plenty of space between them.

Bake for 15 minutes or until golden brown, place on a serving dish and serve immediately.

Monkfish Fritters
Beignets de lotte

For 4 people

For the batter

15g *(½ oz)*	fresh baker's yeast or ¼ tsp active dried yeast
½ tsp	salt
125ml *(5fl. oz)*	beer
100g *(4 oz)*	plain flour
250g *(9 oz)*	monkfish fillets, cut into 1cm *(½-in)* cubes
	juice of half a lemon
3 tbsps	olive oil
1 tbsp	chopped parsley
	salt, freshly ground pepper
	oil for deep frying

Equipment

small mixing bowl · large saucepan or deep fryer · deep-frying thermometer · slotted spoon
To serve: serving dish or several small plates

The batter

Make the batter as described for Fritter Batter (see p.238), using the measurements given here.

To marinate

Put the pieces of fish into a small bowl with the lemon juice, olive oil, parsley, salt and pepper. Mix with your hands, then marinate in the refrigerator for at least an hour before frying.

To fry and serve

Heat the oil to 385°F/194°C in a large saucepan or deep fryer.

While the oil is heating, remove the fish from the marinade and pat it dry with a cloth or kitchen paper. Drop the pieces of fish into the fritter batter, stir to coat each piece well, and carefully place them, one by one, in the hot oil. Fry for about 2 minutes, then, using a wooden spoon, turn the fritters over and cook for 2 minutes more or until each one is an even golden brown. Lift the fritters out of the oil with a slotted spoon, drain on kitchen paper for a minute or two, sprinkle with salt and serve at once on a serving dish or individual plates.

Suggestion

Any firm-fleshed fish may be used for this recipe – or, for that matter, you could use chicken livers, which are excellent cooked this way. Serve them with drinks or as a first course.

Note

The fritters will puff up in the oil, so don't crowd them in the pan. Cook them in several batches if necessary.

SOUPS

Arab Soup
Soupe arabe

For 4–6 people

100g *(4 oz)*	dried chick-peas
100g *(4 oz)*	dried haricot beans (see Note)
	salt, freshly ground pepper
750g *(1¾ lb)*	breast of lamb, cut into 12 short ribs
3 tbsps	olive oil
2 litres *(3½ pints)*	cold water
2 tsps	salt
	bouquet garni of parsley, bay leaf, thyme and a leek leaf
3 tbsps	olive oil
1	large onion, diced
2	small peppers (1 red, 1 green), seeded and diced
1	medium courgette, diced
3	cloves of garlic, diced
2	tomatoes, weighing 250g *(9 oz)*, skinned, seeded and chopped
	salt, freshly ground pepper
	a generous pinch of saffron
½ tsp	thyme leaves
5	mint leaves, cut into strips

Equipment
large bowl · 2 large pans, 1 with lid · ladle
To serve: large soup tureen

The beans and lamb
Soak the chick-peas and beans overnight.
Season the lamb generously with salt and pepper. Heat 3 tablespoons of olive oil in a large pan and brown the meat briskly over a high heat. Remove the lamb from the pan and drain on kitchen paper. Discard the fat from the pan, then add the chick-peas, beans, cold water, salt, *bouquet garni* and pepper. Bring to the boil, lower the heat and simmer for 1 hour. Add the lamb and simmer for 45 minutes longer, skimming off any fat that rises to the surface.

The vegetables
Heat the remaining 3 tablespoons of olive oil in another pan, add the onion and soften over a medium heat, then add the garlic and all the remaining vegetables. Season lightly with salt and pepper and add the saffron, thyme and mint. Stir well, cover the pan and simmer slowly for 30 minutes without adding any liquid (the vegetables will cook in their own juices); if necessary, a little more olive oil may be added.

To finish and serve the soup

Pour the cooked vegetables into the pan with the lamb and beans and bring to the boil. Simmer for 5 minutes. Add salt and pepper if needed. Remove the *bouquet garni* and skim all the fat from the surface of the soup. Ladle the soup into a large soup tureen and serve immediately.

Suggestions

Duck or chicken may be used instead of lamb, and 450g *(1 lb)* of green peas instead of the chick-peas. Broad beans, rosemary or basil may all be added to this soup.

Note

Instead of dried beans, 450g *(1 lb)* of fresh white beans may be used. Simply bring the seasoned water to a boil, add the lamb and fresh beans and cook for 45 minutes. If using fresh peas, cook them for the last 20 minutes only.

This very meaty soup could easily be turned into a main dish by doubling the ingredients listed here. If served as a soup, you will find it easier to eat if you bone the pieces of lamb just before serving.

Wine

Drink a light wine that can be swigged down, such as a white Provençal – Bandol, Palette or Cassis or a red Pinot d'Alsace.

Cold Cucumber Soup with Mint and Chives
Crème de concombre aux herbes

For 4 people

3	large cucumbers
2 tsps	butter
1	onion, finely chopped
200ml *(7 fl. oz)*	water
150ml *(¼ pint)*	double cream or *crème fraîche* (see p.290), lightly whipped
10	fresh mint leaves, cut into thin slivers
1	heaped tsp chives, finely chopped
	salt, freshly ground pepper

Equipment
large saucepan · liquidiser or food processor · 2 mixing bowls
· wire whisk
To serve: chilled soup tureen or 4 chilled soup bowls

The cucumber purée
Peel the cucumbers and cut in half lengthwise. Using a sharp teaspoon, scoop out all the seeds. Dice one-quarter of the cucumber and reserve for garnishing the soup. Chop the remaining cucumber coarsely ready for the purée.

Heat the butter in a large saucepan, add the onion and soften without browning over a moderate heat for about 4 minutes. Add the chopped cucumber and continue cooking over a low heat for 2 minutes. Add the water, season lightly with salt and pepper and bring to a boil, then lower the heat and simmer for 10 minutes. Purée in the liquidiser or food processor until smooth, then transfer to a bowl and chill, stirring occasionally, for about 35 minutes, or until the purée is completely cold.

To finish and serve the soup
Carefully stir the diced cucumber, mint and chives into the lightly whipped cream. Slowly pour the cold cucumber purée into the cream, stirring gently until smooth. Add salt and pepper to taste and chill the soup for at least an hour before serving. Serve in a chilled soup tureen or in individual soup bowls.

Suggestion
Yoghurt may be used instead of whipped cream, in which case add diced raw button mushrooms to the soup with the diced cucumber and herbs.

Wine
A light, chilled wine – a rosé or a very young Sauvignon, for example – would be delicious with this soup.

Brazilian Mussel Soup
Soupe de moules brésilienne

For 4 people

1	whole coconut (see Note)
400ml *(¾ pint)*	single cream

For the mussels

1.5kg *(3¼ lb)*	mussels (see Suggestion)
1½ tbsps	butter
5	shallots, finely chopped
150ml *(¼ pint)*	dry white wine

For finishing the soup

3	small tomatoes, peeled, seeded and chopped
½	green pepper, seeded, chopped, boiled for 1 minute and cooled under running water
½	red pepper, prepared like the green
1 tsp	fresh ginger, finely chopped
4 tsps	canned sweetcorn, drained
	salt, freshly ground pepper
1 tsp	fresh coriander leaves

Equipment
knife or ice-pick · 2 large bowls · hammer · grater or food processor · 2 clean teatowels · 2 large saucepans
To serve: 4 heated soup plates

The coconut
Prepare the coconut the night before making the soup. With a knife or ice-pick, puncture the 3 indentations in the top of the coconut and pour the 'milk' that comes out of it into a bowl. Break the coconut in half with a hammer, then use a knife to pry the flesh away from the shell of the nut. Grate the coconut, or chop it in a food processor, and place it in the bowl with the 'milk'. Add the cream, cover and chill overnight in the refrigerator.

Next day, line a bowl with a clean cloth and pour the coconut–cream mixture into it. Lift up the corners of the towel and twist them together, squeezing and pressing on the towel to extract as much liquid as possible. Discard the contents of the towel and reserve the liquid for the soup.

The mussels
Clean and cook the mussels as described for Mussels with Tomato and Basil (see p.60), using the measurements given here. Once the mussels have opened, remove them from the pan and take each one out of its shell. Place in a bowl and reserve.

To finish and serve the soup

Strain the mussel cooking liquid through a clean cloth into a large saucepan. Boil to reduce it to about 125ml *(4 fl. oz)*. Add the coconut liquid, simmer for 2 minutes, add the tomato, green and red peppers and ginger, and simmer for 2 minutes more. Add the sweetcorn, simmer for 4 minutes, then add the mussels, season with salt and pepper to taste, and simmer for a final 3 minutes.

Ladle the soup into hot soup plates, sprinkle each serving with a little fresh coriander leaves and serve.

Suggestion

Clams may be used instead of mussels.

Note

If a fresh coconut is unavailable, use 225g *(8 oz)* of desiccated (grated) coconut. Add 200ml *(7 fl. oz)* of boiling water and use this mixture as described for the fresh coconut and its 'milk'.

If you do have a fresh coconut but it has no 'milk' inside, add 6 tablespoons of water to the coconut–cream mixture.

Wine

Serve with a cool Provençal white or rosé – Cassis, Bandol or Palette.

Vichyssoise of Courgettes
Vichyssoise de courgettes

For 4 people

1kg *(2 lb)*	courgettes
1	large potato
2 litres *(3½ pints)*	water
2 tsps	coarse salt
	salt, freshly ground pepper
200ml *(7 fl. oz)*	whipping cream or *crème fraîche* (see p.290)
4 tsps	mixed chopped parsley, chervil and chives

Equipment

large saucepan · liquidiser or food processor · large bowl
To serve: soup tureen

To make and serve the soup

Peel the courgettes, cut them in half lengthwise and scoop out the seeds with a spoon. Cut each half into pieces about 5cm *(2 in)* long.

Peel the potato and cut it into 1cm *(½-in)* cubes.

Salt the water and bring it to the boil in a large saucepan. Add the courgettes and potato and boil for 13 minutes once the water comes back to the boil.

Drain the vegetables and save the cooking liquid. Allow to cool for 5 minutes, then place the vegetables and 250ml *(8 fl. oz)* of the cooking liquid in a liquidiser or food processor, season with salt and pepper, and blend to a smooth purée. Pour the purée into a bowl and allow to cool for 10 minutes.

Whisk the cream lightly. Fold the whipped cream into the purée, as you would beaten egg whites. Taste for salt and pepper, pour the mixture into a soup tureen and chill for at least 2 hours.

Serve chilled, sprinkled with the chopped herbs.

Wine

It is better not to serve any wine with this particular soup.

SALADS

Skate Salad
with Italian Parsley
Salade de raie au persil simple

For 4 people

For the vinaigrette

6 tbsps	oil of arachide (refined peanut oil)
3 tsps	red wine vinegar
	salt, freshly ground pepper

For the court bouillon

3 litres *(5 pints)*	water
2 tsps	sea salt
2	large carrots, thinly sliced
2	medium onions, thinly sliced
6	whole peppercorns
	bouquet garni (thyme, bay leaf, parsley stalks)
800g *(1¾ lb)*	skate (for substitutes, see Suggestions)

For the garnish

2	medium tomatoes, skinned, seeded and diced
300g *(11 oz)*	lamb's-lettuce, well washed and dried
2 tsps	parsley, finely chopped
2 tsps	chives, finely chopped
2 tsps	chervil, finely chopped
1 tbsp	capers
2	shallots, finely chopped
	salt, freshly ground pepper
6 or 7	sprigs of Italian flat parsley, leaves only

Equipment
small bowl · wire whisk · *sauteuse* or large saucepan, 6-litre *(10-pint)* capacity · skimmer or slotted spoon · large saucepan
To serve: 4 salad plates

The vinaigrette
Whisk the oil, vinegar, salt and pepper together in a bowl and reserve.

The skate
In a large *sauteuse* or saucepan wide enough to hold the skate, make the following *court bouillon*: bring the water to the boil, add the salt, carrots, onions, peppercorns and *bouquet garni*, bring back to the boil and simmer, uncovered, for 30 minutes, skimming off any foam that appears. Wash the skate thoroughly in cold water to remove any slime, then place it in the *court bouillon*. Cover the pan and poach the fish in the gently simmering liquid for 17 minutes.

The garnish

Five minutes before serving, place the finely diced tomatoes in a large saucepan, warm over a low heat, then add the lamb's-lettuce, herbs, capers and shallots. Toss gently, barely warming the salad; do not allow to wilt. Whisk the vinaigrette. Add 3 tablespoons of vinaigrette and a little salt to the salad, toss again and place equal amounts on each plate.

To serve

Lift the skate out of the *court bouillon*. Using a fork, remove the skin, then lift the meat off the bone. Divide the fish into 4 equal portions.

Whisk the remaining vinaigrette, dip the pieces of skate into it and place a piece on top of each salad. Dip the flat parsley leaves into the vinaigrette and place them on top of the skate. Season the pieces of skate lightly and serve immediately.

Suggestions

A mixture of lettuces of your choice may be used instead of lamb's-lettuce, and lemon sole, mackerel or whiting may be used instead of skate. A little lemon, cut into small dice, may also be sprinkled on the fish just before serving.

Wine

Accompany with a dry white wine such as Muscadet, Gros Plant or Palette.

Salad of Calf's Liver with Leeks
Salade de foie de veau aux blanc de poireau

For 4 people

For the vinaigrette

l tsp	Dijon mustard
	salt, freshly ground pepper
l tbsp	sherry vinegar
6 tbsps	oil of arachide (refined peanut oil)

For the salad

2–3	large leeks, weighing 450g *(1 lb)*, white only
275g *(10 oz)*	calf's liver in one piece
l ½ tbsps	butter
	salt, freshly ground pepper
4	slices streaky bacon, cut into thin strips
l tbsp	red wine vinegar
200g *(7 oz)*	salad leaves (lamb's-lettuce, Batavian endive, raddichio, rocket, etc.)

Equipment

small bowl · wire whisk · saucepan · 2 frying pans · large saucepan
To serve: 4 heated salad plates

The vinaigrette:

Place the mustard and a little salt and pepper in a mixing bowl and whisk gently, adding first the sherry vinegar, then the oil. Reserve.

The leeks

Cut the white of each leek into sections 5cm *(2 in)* long. Cut each section in half lengthwise, then separate the layers from each other. Wash them carefully and drop them into a saucepan of rapidly boiling salted water, boil for 3 minutes, drain, cool under running water and drain again.

The bacon

Heat the strips of bacon in a frying pan without any fat for about 4 minutes to brown lightly, add the red wine vinegar to the pan, remove from the heat and reserve.

The liver

Pre-heat the oven to 250°F/130°C/Reg. ½. Trim the calf's liver and season it with salt and pepper.

In a frying pan, melt the butter over a moderate heat. When very hot, add the liver. Cook for 3 minutes on one side and 2 minutes on the other; the liver should be pink inside when done. Cover and keep it warm in the oven while preparing the garnish.

The garnish

Place the leeks on a plate in the oven to warm slightly.

Place the salads in a large saucepan, toss with 4 tablespoons of the vinaigrette, and barely warm the leaves over a very low heat, tossing constantly; do not allow to wilt

Pile some of the salad on each of the warm salad plates. Scatter the leeks over the salad.

Cut the liver into thin slices, sprinkle with the vinaigrette and arrange on the salad. Lightly season with salt and pepper, sprinkle the bacon over the salad and serve. (If necessary, reheat the bacon before serving.)

This salad should be barely warm when served. If need be, place the garnished plates in a hot oven for several seconds before serving.

Suggestions

Chicken livers may be used instead of calf's liver; sauté them for about 2 minutes over a high heat.

Belgian endive, boiled or sautéed, may be used instead of leeks.

Note
Also very good without the leeks or any other cooked vegetable.

Wine
A dry white wine – perhaps a Sauvignon.

Salad of Scallops with Fried Celery Leaves
Salade de coquilles Saint-Jacques au céleri frit

For 4 people

12	unopened scallops in their shells; if unavailable, buy 12 shelled scallops (see Note)

For the stock

1 tsp	butter
6 tbsps	dry white wine
4 tbsps	water
	salt, freshly ground pepper
1 tsp	fresh dill, chopped

For deep frying

450g (1 lb)	goose fat (preferably) or lard
	leaves from 8 sticks of celery

For the scallops

15g (½ oz)	butter
	salt, freshly ground pepper

Equipment
saucepan · skimmer or slotted spoon · bowl · saucepan, with lid · deep fryer · deep-frying thermometer   *To serve:* 4 heated plates

The stock
If using scallops in their shells, open them yourself. Cut off the frilly strip surrounding each, wash it, chop it coarsely and reserve on a plate. Wash, clean and dry each scallop, then place it with its bright orange coral on another plate and reserve. (See Note if using shelled scallops.)

Melt 1 teaspoon of butter in a small pan and add the chopped scallop strips. Stir and simmer, uncovered, for 3 minutes. Add the white wine, water, salt and pepper. Bring to the boil, add the dill and simmer for 20 minutes, skimming off any foam that appears with a skimmer or slotted spoon. Strain the stock into a bowl and reserve.

24

The scallops and celery leaves

Wash the celery leaves, keeping only the pale ones (the darker ones taste too strong). Pat the leaves dry in a clean towel.

Heat the 15g *(½ oz)* butter in a saucepan. When it is very hot, add the scallops (they should all fit in one layer) and season with salt and pepper. Shake the pan or stir the scallops with a wooden spoon, add 5 tablespoons of strained stock, bring to the boil, then cover and simmer for 2 minutes (see Note).

In a deep fryer, heat the fat to 375°F/190°C. Cook the celery leaves in 2 batches, dropping them into the hot fat for 2–3 minutes. Drain them thoroughly on kitchen paper.

To serve

Place some of the fried celery leaves on each plate and salt them lightly. Remove the scallops from the pan with a slotted spoon and cut each one into thin slices. Salt and pepper lightly, place them on top of the celery and serve immediately

Note

This recipe really calls for sea scallops, but queen scallops may be used. Cook these for 1 minute only and serve them whole. In Britain scallops are usually sold out of their shells with the orange coral, but with the frilly strips that are the gills and are used for making the stock, removed. When this is the case, buy 120g *(¼ lb)* extra scallops (or fish) for making the stock.

Wine

A young white Côtes du Rhône or white Mâcon.

Salad of Artichokes, Crayfish and Preserved Duck

Salade d'écrevisses aux fonds d'artichauts et confit de canard

For 4 people

For the vinaigrette

9 tbsps	oil of arachide (refined peanut oil)
3 tbsps	wine vinegar
	salt, plenty of freshly ground pepper
2 tsps	parsley, finely chopped
2 tsps	chives, finely chopped
2 tsps	chervil, finely chopped

For the salad

20	live crayfish (for substitute, see Note)
4 tbsps	oil of arachide (refined peanut oil)
2	legs of preserved duck (see p.196) or 1 leg and 1 breast
2 tbsps	duck fat from the preserved duck
225g *(8 oz)*	lamb's-lettuce or spinach
4	artichoke hearts, cooked or tinned, cut into thin slices
	salt, freshly ground pepper.

Equipment

mixing bowl · wire whisk · large frying pan, with lid · skimmer or slotted spoon · small frying pan · large saucepan · small saucepan
To serve: 4 heated salad plates

The vinaigrette

In a bowl whisk together the vinegar, salt, pepper and herbs, then gradually whisk in the oil. Reserve.

The crayfish

Remove the central fin from the tail of each crayfish as described in Lamb with Crayfish (see p.166). Heat 2 tablespoons of cooking oil in a large frying pan, add half the crayfish, cover the pan and cook over a moderate heat for 4 minutes, turning the crayfish frequently. The crayfish should turn completely red all over; if they do not, cook for a few minutes longer. Remove the crayfish from the pan with a skimmer or slotted spoon, heat the remaining oil and cook the rest of the crayfish in the same way. When the crayfish are cool enough to handle, detach the tails from the heads and remove the tail meat from the shell. Reserve the shelled tails on a plate.

The duck

Bone the pieces of duck and cut the meat into fine slices. Heat the duck fat in a frying pan, add the slices of duck and brown on each side for 2–3 minutes. Drain on kitchen paper and keep hot.

To finish and serve

Place the lettuce or spinach in a large saucepan, add all but 1 tablespoon of the vinaigrette and toss over a low heat until barely warm; do not allow to wilt. Remove from the heat and add the artichoke hearts, toss to mix, then arrange a quarter of the salad in a little pyramid on each plate.

Place the crayfish tails in a small saucepan with the remaining vinaigrette, salt and pepper, heat to lukewarm, then arrange them around the salad on each plate. Place the slices of duck on top of the salad, sprinkle with freshly ground pepper and serve.

Suggestions

Cooked asparagus or French beans may replace the artichokes. If French beans are used, sprinkle each plate with a julienne of raw carrot just before serving to make it look pretty.

Note

If necessary, the garnished salad plates can be placed in 350°F/180°C/ Reg. 4 oven for a minute or two to reheat the salad just before serving; the salad should be served barely warm, not hot.

Prawns may be used instead of crayfish.

Wine

A young Givry, a dry white wine or a red Loire wine.

Salad of Scallops and Lamb's-Lettuce
Salade de Saint-Jacques et de mâche

For 4 people

For the vinaigrette

1 tbsp	lemon juice
2 tbsps	olive oil
1 tbsp	oil of arachide (refined peanut oil)
	salt, freshly ground pepper

For the salad

175g (6 oz)	lamb's-lettuce, well washed and dried
1	shallot, finely chopped

For the scallops

1 tbsp	fresh dill, chopped, or 1 tsp powdered dill
	salt, freshly ground pepper
8	large scallops (for substitute, see Note)
2 tbsps	butter
3 tbsps	dry white wine

Equipment

small mixing bowl · wire whisk · large mixing bowl · large frying pan slotted spoon
To serve: 4 heated salad plates

The vinaigrette

In a bowl whisk together the lemon juice, olive oil and oil of arachide, season with salt and pepper and reserve.

The salad

Place the lamb's-lettuce in a large bowl with the shallot, add 3 tablespoons of the vinaigrette and toss. Place in a very low oven to warm while cooking the scallops.

The scallops

Season the scallops with salt, pepper and dill. In a large frying pan heat the butter until very hot, add the scallops and brown lightly for 1–2 minutes, then turn them over and brown for a further 1–2 minutes. Lower the heat, add the wine, cook for 1 minute more on each side, then remove the scallops with a slotted spoon. Cut each into 5 thin slices and sprinkle them with the remaining vinaigrette.

To serve

Remove the lamb's-lettuce from the oven, place some on each plate, make sure the scallops are bathed with the vinaigrette and arrange the slices on the salad. Serve immediately.

Suggestions

You can vary the salad by sprinkling finely chopped herbs (parsley, chives, etc.) or thin strips of truffle over the scallops just before serving. The lamb's-lettuce can be replaced with dandelion salad or spinach and the scallops with fillets of trout or brill.

Note

Queen scallops may be used instead of sea scallops in this recipe.

Wine

Drink a Condrieu or Pouilly-Fumé with this dish.

Salad with Truffles
Salade de truffes

For 4 people

4	truffles, fresh or tinned, weighing 100g *(3½ oz)* altogether
4 tbsps	oil of arachide (refined peanut oil)
1 tsp	sherry vinegar
½ tsp	wine vinegar
	salt, freshly ground pepper

For the salad (see Note)

50g *(2 oz)*	lamb's-lettuce
50g *(2 oz)*	red raddichio
75g *(3 oz)*	chicory leaves
1	frizzy endive, heart only
1	Batavian endive, heart only
3 tbsps	chives, finely chopped
2 tbsps	chervil, finely chopped
2 tbsps	parsley, finely chopped
	salt, freshly ground pepper

Equipment
2 small mixing bowls · wire whisk · large salad bowl
To serve: 4 salad plates

The truffles
Brush fresh truffles clean, or drain canned ones. Place them in a bowl with the oil of arachide and roll them around to coat them with the oil. Cover the bowl with plastic film and leave to marinate overnight.

To make and serve the salad
Drain the oil from the truffles into a small mixing bowl. Whisk the two vinegars, salt and pepper, then gradually whisk in the truffle-flavoured oil.

Cut the truffles into thin slices, place them on a plate, season lightly with salt and pepper and spoon 1½ tablespoons of the vinaigrette over them. Place all the different lettuces and herbs, well washed and picked over, in a salad bowl. Add the remaining vinaigrette, toss, and add salt and pepper to taste.

Place some of the salad on each serving plate, arrange the slices of truffle over the salad and serve.

Suggestion
Instead of the salad 450g *(1 lb)* of potatoes can be peeled, boiled, sliced, seasoned with the herbs and vinaigrette while still warm and served with the truffles – a really splendid combination!

Note
A variety of fresh greens may be used instead of those listed: spinach, cos lettuce, watercress or Belgian endive, for instance.

Wine
Drink a Pomerol or Côte Rôtie with the truffles.

Sweetbread Salad
with Fresh Ceps
Salade de ris de veau aux cèpes frais

For 4 people

400g *(14 oz)*	sweetbreads
3 tbsps	oil of arachide (refined peanut oil)
I tbsp	olive oil
2 tbsps	red wine vinegar
	salt, freshly ground pepper
I	generous tbsp parsley, finely chopped
I	generous tbsp chervil, finely chopped
I	generous tbsp chives, finely chopped
2	shallots, finely chopped
275g *(10 oz)*	fresh ceps (boletus mushrooms), cut into thick strips (for substitute, see Suggestion)
I tbsp	cooking oil (for the sweetbreads)
100g *(4 oz)*	lamb's-lettuce or spinach
50g *(2 oz)*	heart of frizzy endive
25g *(I oz)*	red raddichio

Equipment
large bowl · small mixing bowl · wire whisk · small saucepan · frying pan (preferably non-stick) · large saucepan
To serve: 4 heated salad plates

Preliminary preparations
Soak the sweetbreads in a large bowl of cold water for 5 hours before cooking, changing the water several times. Drain, and use a knife to remove any gristle, fat and outside skins or membranes. Cut the sweetbreads into ½cm *(¼-in)* slices and reserve.

The vinaigrette
Put the vinegar into a small bowl, season lightly with salt and pepper, gradually whisk in the oils, stir in one-third of the fresh herbs and shallots, and reserve.

To make and serve the salad
Place the ceps, cut into strips, in a small saucepan with one-third of the vinaigrette. Add half of the remaining herbs and shallots, and reserve.

Heat I tablespoon of cooking oil in a non-stick frying pan. Season the slices of sweetbread lightly, brown them quickly (about 2–3 minutes on each side) and drain on paper towels. Keep them warm.

Place the salads and the remaining herbs and shallots in a large saucepan over a very low heat and toss until barely warm; do not allow to wilt. Add the remaining vinaigrette, toss to mix, and divide the salad between 4 plates, piling it up lightly.

Heat the ceps, stirring, until barely warm (not hot), then sprinkle them over the salad on each plate.

Place the slices of sweetbread around the edges of the salad and serve immediately.

Suggestion

You could replace the sweetbreads with brains, and crisp, white ordinary mushrooms may replace the ceps used here.

Wine

A white Burgundy or Graves, or a chilled red Graves.

Salad of Crawfish and Mango with Duck and Basil

Salade de langouste à la mangue, au canard et au basilic

For 4 people

For the vinaigrette

2 tbsps	wine vinegar
1 tbsp	sherry vinegar
8 tbsps	oil of arachide (refined peanut oil)
	salt, freshly ground pepper
1	medium carrot (for the garnish)
	pepper
	zest of ⅓ of a medium orange, cut into fine julienne strips (about 1 tbsp of strips)

For the court bouillon

3 litres *(5 pints)*	water
1 tbsp	coarse salt
3	medium carrots, finely sliced
2	medium onions, cut in half
½	a stick of celery
8	whole peppercorns
	bouquet garni (including the green of a small leek, thyme and a bay leaf)
1	live crawfish, weighing about 1¼kg *(2¾ lb)* (see Note)

For the garnish

300g *(12 oz)*	lamb's-lettuce, fresh spinach or other lettuce
2 tbsps	chives, finely chopped
I tbsp	parsley, finely chopped
I tbsp	chervil, finely chopped
20	medium basil leaves, cut into thin strips
I tbsp	shallot, finely chopped
2	duck legs, boned and diced; leave skin attached (see Note)
	salt, freshly ground pepper
I	ripe mango, weighing about 350g *(¾ lb)*, peeled, stone removed and cut into ½ cm *(¼-in)* julienne strips

Equipment

small bowl · wire whisk · medium saucepan · large pan, with lid · tongs · large saucepan · frying pan, preferably non-stick
To serve: 4 heated salad plates

Preliminary preparations

Make a vinaigrette by whisking together in a small bowl the 2 vinegars, salt and pepper, then gradually whisking in the oil. Cut the carrot in half lengthwise, remove the core and slice the halves very finely.

Sprinkle the carrot crescents with pepper and drop them into a saucepan of lightly salted boiling water. Cook for 10 seconds and drain. Cool under running water, drain again and reserve.

Place the julienne of orange in the rinsed saucepan, cover with cold water, bring to a boil, then drain immediately. Cool under running water, drain again and reserve.

The crawfish

In a large pan bring the water and coarse salt to a boil. Add the carrots, onions, celery, peppercorns and *bouquet garni*, lower the heat and simmer, uncovered, for 12 minutes. Bring the liquid back to a rolling boil, drop in the live crawfish, cover, return to the boil and cook for 9 minutes. Lift out the crawfish with tongs, place it in a colander and make a little hole between its eyes with a knife. Place it head down in the colander and allow to drain for 5 minutes. Remove all the meat from the tail and claws. Remove the blackish intestine, then cut the tail into thin escalopes.

The garnish

In a large saucepan combine the lamb's-lettuce or other salad, herbs, shallot, orange julienne, carrot strips and one-third of the basil over a very low heat. Add 8 tablespoons of vinaigrette and toss until the garnish is barely warm; do not allow to wilt. Remove from the heat, toss to mix, and arrange the salad on the warm plates. Keep warm in a very low oven.

To finish and serve the salad

Heat a frying pan with no fat in it. Lightly salt and pepper the diced duck and fry quickly until brown and crisp – about 2–3 minutes. Drain on paper towels and sprinkle over the salad on each plate.

Place the rest of the vinaigrette and the crawfish slices in a clean saucepan and warm for 2 minutes over a low heat. Arrange the crawfish around the edges of the plates.

Place the strips of fresh mango in the centre of each salad, sprinkle with the remaining basil and serve immediately.

Note

Instead of duck, 120g *(¼ lb)* of diced salt pork may be fried and used.

You can use lobster or several freshwater crayfish instead of the crawfish, or perhaps Dublin Bay or Mediterranean prawns.

If necessary, the plates garnished with salad may be placed in a very low oven to keep warm while preparing the duck and crawfish.

Wine

A white Burgundy, such as Rully, or a Côtes du Rhône – perhaps the latter: Condrieu, Domaine de Beaucastel or Châteauneuf-du-Pape.

Oxtail Salad
Salade de queue de boeuf

For 4–6 people

For the oxtail

1kg *(2¼ lb)*	oxtail, cut into joints
2½ tsps	coarse salt
1	large carrot, quartered
1	large onion, stuck with a clove
1	large stick of celery, quartered
	large *bouquet garni* of thyme, bay leaf, parsley stalks and a leek leaf

For the garnish

1	large or 2 small leeks, white only, cut into julienne strips
1	large or 2 small carrots, cut into julienne strips
1	medium turnip, cut into julienne strips

For the vinaigrette

l–2 tsps	Dijon mustard
l tbsp	sherry vinegar
6 tbsps	oil of arachide (refined peanut oil)
	salt, freshly ground pepper

For the salad (see Note)

150g *(5 oz)*	lamb's-lettuce
50g *(2 oz)*	red raddichio
150g *(5 oz)*	frizzy endive (heart only)
l tsp	parsley, finely chopped
l tsp	chervil, finely chopped
l tsp	chives, finely chopped
2	shallots, finely chopped
	salt, freshly ground pepper

Equipment

large pan · slotted spoon · large saucepan · small mixing bowl · wire whisk

To serve: 4–6 heated salad plates

The oxtail

Place the oxtail in a large pan, add enough warm water to cover completely, and bring to a boil. Skim off any foam with a skimmer or slotted spoon, boil the oxtail for 10 minutes, drain, and cool under running water. Return the oxtail to the rinsed pan, cover again with warm water – about 2 litres *(3½ pints)* – add the salt and bring to a boil, skimming off any foam. When boiling, add the vegetables and *bouquet garni*, skim if necessary, cover the pan, and simmer for 3 hours or until the meat detaches easily from the bone.

The garnish

Bring a large pan of lightly salted water to a boil, add the leeks and boil for l minute, add the carrots and boil for l minute, then add the turnip and boil for l minute. Drain, cool under running water, drain again and reserve.

The vinaigrette

Place the mustard in a small bowl, add a little salt and pepper and the sherry vinegar, whisk to combine, then gradually whisk in the oil. Taste for salt and pepper, and reserve.

To finish and serve the salad

When the oxtail is cooked, remove from the pan with a slotted spoon and allow to cool enough to handle. Remove the meat from the bones while warm, dice and reserve.

Place the salads in a large saucepan with the herbs, shallots and half of the julienne vegetables. Season with salt and pepper, add 4 tablespoons of vinaigrette and place over a very low heat to warm, tossing constantly; do not allow to wilt. Remove from the heat and toss the salad again. Place some on each plate.

In the same saucepan, stir the remaining julienne strips and 1½ teaspoons of vinaigrette over a low heat. Arrange the julienne strips on top of the salad. Pour the remaining vinaigrette over the meat, season well with salt and pepper, stir, and place the pieces of oxtail on top of the salad. Serve immediately.

Suggestions

The cooking liquid from the oxtail can be strained and used as stock in many of the recipes in this book, or can be served alone as *bouillon* or with vegetables as a soup.

A pressure cooker may be used for cooking the oxtail. Proceed as described above, but cook for only 1 hour once the pressure has risen.

Note

If the salads mentioned are not available, use a mixture of spinach, watercress and a little finely sliced red cabbage.

The oxtail can be cooked and de-boned well ahead of time. Reheat the meat in a little of its cooking liquid, drain, and finish as described above.

Wine

A young Côtes-du-Jura, served chilled, Passe-Tous-Grains or Madiran.

Lentil Salad
Salade de lentilles

For 6 people

For the lentils

450g (1 lb)	lentils, soaked overnight if necessary
1 tbsp	coarse salt
2	onions, stuck with a clove
2	carrots, cut in half
16	whole peppercorns, tied in a cloth
	bouquet garni of thyme and a bay leaf

For the garnish

4	medium carrots, finely diced
2	medium turnips, finely diced
3	medium leeks, white only, finely diced

For the vinaigrette

2 tbsps	Dijon mustard
200ml *(7 fl. oz)*	oil of arachide (refined peanut oil)
2 tbsps	wine vinegar
	salt, freshly ground pepper
4–5	shallots, finely chopped
120g *(¼ lb)*	boiled pork rind, finely diced (for substitute, see Suggestion)
2	boiled pig's trotters, boned and finely diced (fo. substitute, see Suggestion)
2 tbsps	chervil or parsley, finely chopped

Equipment

large saucepan · skimmer or slotted spoon · large mixing bowl · medium saucepan · 4 small mixing bowls · wire whisk
To serve: 6 salad plates

The lentils

Wash and drain the lentils. Place them in a large saucepan with 2 litres *(3½ pints)* of cold water, add the coarse salt and bring to a boil. Skim off any foam that appears, then add the onions, carrots, peppercorns and *bouquet garni.* Lower the heat and simmer for 30–45 minutes or until the lentils are just tender. Strain the lentils and remove the onions, peppercorns, carrots and *bouquet garni.* Place the lentils in a large bowl and keep them warm while preparing the garnish.

The garnish

Cook the finely diced carrots for 3 minutes in a saucepan of lightly salted boiling water. Drain and reserve the water. Bring the water back to the boil and cook the turnips for 2 minutes. Drain the turnips and again reserve the water. Place the turnips in a bowl separate from the carrots. Cook the leeks for 5 minutes in the same water, drain and reserve in a third bowl. Cover each vegetable with foil to keep warm.

To season and serve the salad

Make a vinaigrette by whisking together in a bowl the mustard, oil, vinegar, and a little salt and pepper. Stir in the chopped shallots.

Season the warm lentils with 200ml *(7 fl. oz)* of the vinaigrette and place some of the lentils on each plate.

Spoon a tablespoon of the remaining vinaigrette over each of the 3 vegetables used as garnishes and place a little pile of each one around the lentils on each plate.

Place the remaining vinaigrette in a bowl with the boiled pig's trotters and rind, stir, and arrange on top of the lentils. Finally, sprinkle each salad with chopped chervil or parsley and serve warm.

Suggestion
Instead of the pork rind and pig's trotters, 225g *(½ lb)* bacon, cut into thick 'lardons' and fried just before serving, may be used. Drain the fat from the pan the bacon has been cooked in, deglaze the pan with 2 tablespoons of vinegar, and pour this over the salad with the bacon just before serving.

Wine
Accompany with a light, young wine. Use red or white, although red might be better – a Saint-Pourçain, for example.

Partridge and Cabbage Salad
Salade de perdrix au chou

For 2 people

For the vinaigrette

5 tsps	oil of arachide (refined peanut oil) or walnut oil
1 tsp	sherry vinegar
	salt, freshly ground pepper

For the partridge

2 litres *(3½ pints)*	water
2 tsps	salt
1	carrot, quartered
1	leek
1	turnip, quartered
1	small onion, stuck with a clove
1	stick of celery
	bouquet garni
1	chicken stock cube
1	partridge, weighing about 350g *(¾ lb)* (for substitutes, see Suggestions)
1	medium green cabbage
	salt, freshly ground pepper
2	thin slices of fresh *foie gras* (optional; for substitute, see Suggestions)

Equipment
wire whisk · medium bowl · large saucepan · skimmer or slotted spoon
To serve: 2 heated salad plates

The vinaigrette
Whisk the oil, vinegar, salt and pepper in a bowl and reserve.

The partridge

Bring the water and salt to a boil in a large saucepan. Add the vegetables, stock cube and *bouquet garni* and boil gently for 20 minutes. Add the partridge, lower the heat and poach for 10 minutes, skimming off any foam. Remove the bird from the pan with a skimmer or slotted spoon and leave to cool on a cutting board. Strain the cooking liquid and pour it back into the pan.

With a sharp knife cut the legs off the partridge and carefully remove the 2 sides of the breast. Cut the carcass into pieces, add it to the cooking liquid and raise the heat. Boil for 5 minutes, lower the heat, return the legs to the pan and simmer very gently for 5 minutes more, skimming; remove the legs and reserve on a plate with the breast meat.

Strain the liquid once more and pour it back into the saucepan.

The cabbage

Remove the dark outside leaves of the cabbage and use only the light-coloured inner ones. Cut the cabbage in half from top to bottom, remove the core, separate the leaves and remove the thick central rib from each one.

Bring the partridge cooking liquid to a boil, add the cabbage leaves and boil slowly for a few minutes (the cabbage should be slightly crisp when done). Remove the cabbage from the pan with a skimmer or slotted spoon and drain.

To finish and serve the salad

Pre-heat the oven to 425°F/220°C/Reg. 7.

Place the warm cabbage in the bowl with the vinaigrette and toss to mix.

Quickly reheat the pieces of partridge by dropping them into their hot cooking liquid for 2 minutes to warm through. Drain.

Cut the breast meat into thin slices. De-bone the legs and slice them finely. Season lightly with salt and pepper.

Pile the cabbage in a mound on each salad plate, place the slices of partridge on and around it, and lay a slice of *foie gras* on top.

Put the plates into the oven for 1 minute to warm through, then serve immediately.

Suggestions

Quails or poussins could be used instead of partridge (poach either bird for 15 minutes).

Leeks or spinach (spinach can be served either raw or cooked) may be used instead of cabbage.

A thin slice of calf's liver may be used instead of *foie gras*. Sauté it rapidly in a little butter, sprinkle it with salt and pepper, cut it into strips and arrange it around the salad.

Wine
A well-chilled Sauternes or velvety Jurançon, a late-picked Gewürztraminer or a young Volnay.

Salad of Preserved Duck with Lamb's-Lettuce
Salade de mâche au confit de canard

For 4 people

For the vinaigrette

½ tsp	salt
	freshly ground pepper
2 tsps	wine vinegar
4 tsps	sherry vinegar
5 tbsps	oil of arachide (refined peanut oil)

For the salad

380g *(14 oz)*	preserved duck (see p.196), leg and breast
300g *(12 oz)*	lamb's-lettuce or spinach
2 tbsps	parsley, finely chopped
2 tbsps	chervil, finely chopped
2 tbsps	chives, finely chopped
5	shallots, finely chopped
1	medium apple, peeled, cored and cut into fine julienne strips
1	young turnip, cut into fine julienne strips
1	truffle, cut into fine julienne strips (optional)

Equipment
small bowl · wire whisk · large frying pan · skimmer or slotted spoon · large saucepan
To serve: 4 heated salad plates

The vinaigrette
Place the 2 vinegars in a small bowl with the salt and pepper. Whisk in the oil gradually and reserve.

The preserved duck

Put the pieces of duck and their fat into a large frying pan and place over a low heat for about 9 minutes to warm through; do not allow to brown. Remove the duck from the pan with a skimmer or slotted spoon, de-bone the leg and thigh, and cut the meat into julienne strips. Cut the breast into 12 slices, cover with aluminium foil to keep warm, and reserve.

To make the salad and serve

Place the lamb's-lettuce, herbs, shallots, apple, turnip and truffle, and the julienne strips of duck in a large saucepan and toss over a very low heat to warm; do not allow to wilt. Remove from the heat, add 4 tablespoons of the vinaigrette, toss to mix and place some of the salad in a pyramid on each of the heated salad plates. Quickly dip the 12 slices of breast meat in the remaining vinaigrette and arrange 3 of them on top of each mound of salad. Serve immediately.

Suggestion

Julienne strips of beetroot and celery may be used instead of turnip.

Wine

Choose a red wine – Saumur, Champigny, chilled Bourgueil, Madiran or Cahors.

FIRST
COURSES

Poached Eggs
with Beurre Rouge
Oeufs pochés, beurre rouge

For 4 people

For the garnish

120g (¼ lb)	smoked streaky bacon, cut into short, thick strips (lardons)
2 tbsps	butter
16	button onions
	salt, freshly ground pepper
½ tsp	sugar
225g (8 oz)	crisp white mushrooms, each cut into 6 equal pieces

For the sauce

1 tbsp	butter
5	shallots, finely chopped
300ml (½ pint)	red wine
3 tbsps	water
225g (8 oz)	butter, cut into pieces
	salt, freshly ground pepper

For the eggs

1½ litres (2½ pints)	water
1½ tbsps	vinegar
1½ tsps	salt
8	very fresh free-range eggs

Equipment
2 small saucepans · small frying pan, with lid · skimmer or slotted spoon · wire whisk · large *sauteuse* or deep frying pan · clean cloth
To serve: 4 heated plates

The garnish
Place the bacon in a small saucepan with cold water to cover, bring to a boil and drain immediately. Rinse under running water, drain again and reserve.

In a small frying pan melt 1 tablespoon of butter, add the onions, salt, pepper and sugar. Add enough water almost to cover the onions (they should not float), bring to a boil over a moderate heat, cover the pan and cook for 10 minutes. Remove the lid and boil to evaporate all the water. Shake the pan to roll the onions around in the brown butter–sugar glaze, remove them from the pan and reserve in a clean saucepan.

43

Rinse the pan used for cooking the onions, place over a moderate heat and melt another tablespoon of butter. Add the mushrooms, salt and pepper, and brown over a high heat for about 3 minutes, shaking the pan often. Remove the mushrooms with a skimmer or slotted spoon and place them in the saucepan with the onions. Add the blanched bacon to the frying pan, brown for about 5 minutes and drain on a paper towel. Add the bacon to the pan with the onions and mushrooms.

The *beurre rouge* sauce

Melt 1 tablespoon of butter in a saucepan, add the shallots and cook for 2 minutes or until soft. Add the red wine and boil for about 15 minutes or until it has evaporated almost completely and only the moist shallots are left in the pan. Whisk in 3 tablespoons of cold water, bring to a boil and whisk in the remaining butter little by little, as described for the *beurre blanc* in the recipe for Hot Fish Terrine (see p.71). The finished sauce should be smooth and velvety. Taste for salt and pepper, remove from the heat and reserve.

The eggs

Heat the water in a large pan or frying pan. When simmering, add the vinegar and salt and bring to a gentle boil.

Break each egg first into a small saucer or cup, then slide them one by one into the boiling water, spinning each one round with a wooden spoon for a few seconds to keep the whites together. Poach for 3 minutes, lift the eggs out of the water with a skimmer or slotted spoon and drain on a clean cloth.

To serve

Reheat the garnish. If necessary, gently reheat the *beurre rouge*, whisking constantly.

Lift the edge of the cloth to roll an egg on to the slotted spoon, then place it on a plate. Place 2 eggs in the centre of each plate, spoon the garnish around them, spoon the sauce over the top and serve.

Suggestions

The eggs can be poached in red wine instead of water. If desired, fried *croûtons* and slices of poached bone marrow may be placed on top just before serving.

Wine

A fresh young red wine such as Beaujolais.

Eggs Rosemonde
Oeufs brouillés Rosemonde

For 4 people

For the hollandaise

220g *(½ lb)*	smoked salmon, thickly sliced
200g *(7 oz)*	softened butter
3	egg yolks
3 tbsps	cold water
	salt, freshly ground pepper
l tbsp	double cream or *crème fraîche* (see p.290), whipped until stiff
	juice of ½ lemon

For the toast and eggs

l tbsp	butter
4	slices brioche or sandwich bread
8	eggs
	salt, freshly ground pepper
2 tbsps	butter
l tbsp	*crème fraîche* or double cream
	salt, freshly ground pepper

Equipment

liquidiser or food processor · fine sieve · 2 small saucepans · 2 medium saucepans · wire whisk · large frying pan · 2 mixing bowls
To serve: large ovenproof dish or 4 plates

The *hollandaise*

In a liquidiser or food processor purée together half the salmon and the softened butter. Then work the mixture through a sieve with a wooden spoon to eliminate any stringy fibres from the salmon. You should have a smooth, rosy-pink mixture.

Place the salmon butter in a small saucepan and heat gently to boiling, then strain the butter through a fine sieve into another saucepan. Stir once or twice, but do not press on the solids. Leave until all the butter has dripped into the saucepan, reserve the butter and discard the solids left in the sieve.

Place the egg yolks and water in a saucepan, whisk until foamy, then place over a low heat and whisk for 2–3 minutes, moving the pan on and off the heat to warm the eggs but not to cook them. When the eggs begin to thicken, remove the saucepan from the heat and little by little whisk in the melted salmon butter (reheated to warm, but not hot, if necessary). Season with a little salt, pepper and lemon juice, and reserve.

The toast and eggs

Pre-heat the grill. Melt the tablespoon of butter in a large frying pan; when very hot, add the slices of bread and brown on both sides (if using sandwich bread it may be necessary to add more butter). Remove the fried bread from the pan, cover with a cloth and keep warm.

Dice the remaining salmon.

Whisk the whole eggs lightly in a bowl with a little salt and pepper.

Melt 1 tablespoon of butter over a moderate heat in a medium saucepan. Add the beaten eggs and cook for about 4 minutes, stirring constantly with a wire whisk (do not beat). When thick and creamy, add the diced salmon, 1 tablespoon of cream, another tablespoon of butter, and salt and pepper. Cook and stir for 1 minute more (the finished eggs will look more like a thick custard than like scrambled eggs).

To serve the eggs

Place the slices of fried bread on a large ovenproof serving dish or on individual plates. Spoon an equal amount of eggs over each piece.

Fold the whipped cream into the *hollandaise* and spoon the sauce over the eggs. Place the dish or plates under the grill to glaze the sauce for a few seconds – watch to see that it browns lightly but does not burn. Serve immediately.

Suggestions

Any smoked fish – sturgeon, trout, herring, mackerel and so on – may be used instead of salmon.

The finely chopped zest of half a lemon can be blanched and added to the *hollandaise* with the whipped cream.

Wine

A very dry white wine, such as a Quincy.

Salmon Tarts with Beurre Blanc
Tartes de saumon, beurre blanc aux herbes

For 4 people

450g (1 lb)	salmon, to be filleted
250g (9 oz)	puff pastry (see p.242)
50g (1¾ oz)	melted butter

	For the sauce
2 tsps	butter
3	shallots, finely chopped
150ml *(¼ pint)*	dry white wine
8 tsps	wine vinegar
120g *(4 oz)*	butter, at room temperature, cut into small cubes
	salt, freshly ground pepper
3 tbsps	melted butter (for the tarts)
2 tsps	parsley, finely chopped
2 tsps	chives, finely chopped
2 tsps	chervil, finely chopped

Equipment

rolling pin · 2 baking sheets · small saucepan · wire whisk · pastry brush
To serve: 4 heated salad plates and a sauceboat

The salmon

Remove the bones and skin from the salmon. Use a sharp knife to slice it thinly, cutting at a slight angle as you would smoked salmon.

The puff pastry

Pre-heat the oven to 425°F/220°C/Reg. 7.

Roll out the puff pastry on a lightly floured table. Make a sheet about 2mm *(¹⁄₁₆ in)* thick and, with a sharp knife, cut it into 4 circles about 12cm *(5 in)* in diameter. (Cut around a plate. If 4 circles cannot be cut at once, pile up the trimmings and roll them out again.)

Lightly butter 2 baking sheets. Place the circles of pastry on one baking sheet, prick them with a fork, then lay the other baking sheet, buttered side down, on top. Allow to rest in a cool place for 20 minutes. Bake for 18 minutes; the second baking sheet will keep the pastry from rising too much. Remove the top baking sheet and bake for 2 minutes more.

The *beurre blanc*

Make the *beurre blanc* sauce as described in the recipe for Hot Fish Terrine (see p.71), using the ingredients listed here. When all the butter has been added, season the sauce, remove from the heat and keep warm.

To finish and serve the tarts

Pre-heat the grill.

Cover each pastry with salmon, placing the slices so that each one slightly overlaps the preceding one. Cover the pastry completely. Brush each tart with melted butter and place under the grill for about 2–4 minutes (just long enough to heat them through). Watch carefully to see that the salmon remains tender and juicy.

Place a tart on each plate. Gently reheat the sauce, whisking constantly. Place the freshly chopped herbs in a sauceboat and strain the sauce on to them. Stir the sauce, then serve the tarts with the sauce on the side.

Suggestion
Any firm-fleshed fish, such as sea bass or sea bream, may be used instead of salmon.

Wine
White burgundy, white Mâcon or white Beaujolais. If you use tarragon in the sauce, then choose a Provençal white or a Côtes du Rhône.

Endive Feuilletés with Mushrooms
Feuilletés d'endives

For 4 people

For the endives

8	very small or 4 medium endives
I tsp	butter
2	crisp white mushrooms, finely chopped
	salt, freshly ground pepper
150ml *(¼ pint)*	champagne or white wine
150ml *(¼ pint)*	double cream or *crème fraîche* (see p.290).

For the mushrooms

175g *(6 oz)*	mushrooms (7 medium mushrooms), chopped
I tsp	butter
2	shallots, finely chopped
	salt, freshly ground pepper
3 tbsps	double cream or *crème fraîche* (see p.290)

300g *(10½ oz)*	puff pastry (see p.242)
3	egg yolks (for the sauce)
30g *(1 oz)*	butter, cut into small cubes (for the sauce)
	salt, freshly ground pepper

Equipment
large saucepan, with lid · 2 small saucepans · rolling pin · baking sheet · wire whisk
To serve: serving plate and a sauceboat

The endives

Cut off the base and remove any discoloured leaves from the endives. Use a sharp knife to hollow out a cone in the centre of each one at the base end. Wipe the endives to remove any dirt, then cut off the leafy end, if necessary, so that the endives are no more than 8cm *(3 in)* long.

Melt the teaspoon of butter in a large saucepan, add the mushrooms, season lightly with salt and pepper, and cook slowly for 2 minutes. Stir in the champagne and cream, then add the endives. Season again with salt and pepper, cover the pan and simmer slowly for about 45 minutes or until the endives are completely tender. Remove the pan from the heat and reserve.

The mushroom garnish

Melt the teaspoon of butter in a small saucepan, add the shallots and cook slowly for 2–3 minutes or until soft, then add the mushrooms, salt and pepper. Cook for 3 minutes, then add the cream, bring to the boil, lower the heat and simmer for 8 minutes. Remove the pan from the heat and reserve.

The feuilletés

On a lightly floured table roll out the puff pastry into a rectangle about 10 × 32cm *(4 × 12 in)* after the edges have been trimmed. Use a large knife to cut it into 4 rectangles about 8 × 10cm *(3 × 4 in)*. With a pastry brush, brush off any excess flour, then place the pastries upside down on a lightly buttered baking sheet with plenty of space between them. Leave in a cool place for 30 minutes before baking.

Pre-heat the oven to 425°F/220°C/Reg. 7.

Just before baking, with the tip of a knife lightly cut a rectangle in each piece of pastry, about 1cm *(½ in)* from the edge (do not cut right through the pastry). This inner rectangle will form the top of the *feuilleté* when it is baked. Bake the *feuilletés* for 10 minutes, then lower the heat to 350°F/180°C/Reg. 4 and bake for 12 minutes more. Remove from the oven and allow to cool for 3–4 minutes.

To fill the *feuilletés*

Run the tip of a knife around the top of each *feuilleté*, lift it off and reserve it. If the insides are soft, scoop them out with a small spoon to make room for the endives.

Reheat the endives and the mushroom garnish.

Lift the endives out of their cooking liquid and slice them in half lengthwise. Season with salt and pepper. Place a spoonful of the mushroom garnish on one half of each endive, then place the other half on top, sandwiching each endive with some mushroom filling in the centre. Place the endives in the *feuilletés*.

To make the sauce and serve the *feuilletés*

Pre-heat the grill.

Place the egg yolks in a small saucepan away from the heat. Whisk gently, then strain the endive cooking liquid on to them, whisking constantly. Place the saucepan over a low heat and whisk until the mixture becomes foamy and thick (do not allow to boil). Remove from the heat and whisk in the butter bit by bit, then taste for salt and pepper.

Place the filled *feuilletés* on a serving plate and spoon some of the sauce into each one. Place the plate under the grill to glaze the sauce (watch to see that the pastry does not burn). Replace the tops and serve with the remaining sauce on the side.

Suggestions

The whites of 4 large or 8 small leeks, or small cos lettuces or escaroles may be used instead of Belgian endives.

If wild mushrooms such as chanterelles or ceps (boletus mushrooms) are used, they give the dish a marvellous flavour.

Wine

A young, cool red or a Médoc.

Skate en Croûte with Watercress Sauce
Raie en croûte au cresson

For 4 people

For the pastries

500g *(1 lb)*	skate (for substitutes, see Suggestions)
½	bunch watercress
150ml *(¼ pint)*	double cream or *crème fraîche* (see p.290)
	salt, freshly ground pepper
250g *(9 oz)*	puff pastry (see p.242)
1	egg yolk

For the beurre blanc

4 tsps	butter
4	shallots, finely chopped
350ml *(12 fl. oz)*	dry white wine
5 tbsps	wine vinegar
150g *(5 oz)*	butter, at room temperature, cut into cubes
	salt, freshly ground pepper

Equipment

filleting knife · mixing bowl · 2 bowls · baking sheet · rolling pin ·
9 cm *(3½-in)* round biscuit cutter or glass · 10cm *(4-in)* round biscuit
cutter or glass · pastry brush · small saucepan · wire whisk
To serve: large serving dish and a sauceboat

Preliminary preparations

With a filleting knife remove the skin from the skate. Cut the meat off the
bone, chop it coarsely and place it in a bowl.

Carefully wash and drain the watercress leaves. Chop half the leaves and
place them in the bowl with the fish. Cut the remaining leaves into thin
strips and reserve in another bowl.

Pre-heat the oven to 425°F/220°C/Reg. 7. Lightly oil or butter a baking
sheet.

Making the pastries

Add the cream to the skate and watercress, stir well and season
generously with salt and pepper.

Roll out the puff pastry to a thickness of about 4mm *(¼ in)*. Cut out 4
circles with the 9cm *(3½-in)* biscuit cutter, then pile up the leftover
pastry, roll it out again, and cut out 4 circles with the 10cm *(4-in)* biscuit
cutter.

In a bowl, beat the egg yolk with a pinch of salt, then, using a pastry
brush, paint a thin band of egg around the border of each small circle. (Be
careful not to let the egg drip over the edge of the circle.)

Place a large spoonful of the fish mixture in the centre of each small
circle, then cover each one with a large circle, pressing down around the
edges to be sure it is well sealed. Brush the top of each pastry with a little
beaten egg. Leave the pastries in a cool place for 10 minutes before
baking.

Place the pastries on the baking sheet with plenty of space between them
and bake in the oven for 18 minutes or until golden brown.

To make the sauce and serve the pastries

Make the *beurre blanc* as described in the recipe for Hot Fish Terrine (see
p.71), using the measurements given here. When all the butter has been
added, season the sauce with salt and pepper, strain into a sauceboat
and stir in the strips of watercress.

Serve the pastries as soon as they come from the oven, with the sauce on
the side.

Suggestions

Instead of skate, whiting, carp or pike may be filleted and used in making the pastries (be sure to remove all the tiny bones from pike).
The watercress may be replaced by an equal amount of spinach, the green of Swiss chard, or parsley.

Wine

A white Graves, or a young white Burgundy such as Rully.

Asparagus Feuilletés with Beurre Blanc

Feuilletés d'asperges

For 4 people

For the pastry

250g *(9 oz)*	puff pastry (see p.242)
1	egg
	salt
20	large or 32 small asparagus, weighing 1¼kg *(2¾ lb)*

For the sauce

2 tsps	butter
8	shallots, finely chopped
3 tbsps	wine vinegar
300ml *(½ pint)*	dry white wine
200g *(7 oz)*	butter, at room temperature, cut into small cubes
	salt, freshly ground pepper
2 tsps	chervil, finely chopped
2 tsps	parsley, finely chopped
2 tsps	chives, finely chopped

Equipment

rolling pin · baking sheet · mixing bowl · pastry brush · kitchen string · large saucepan · small saucepan · wire whisk
To serve: 4 heated plates and a sauceboat

The pastry

Lightly flour a table and roll out the pastry into a rectangle measuring about 32 × 15cm *(12 × 6 in)* after the edges have been trimmed. Cut the pastry into 4 rectangles about 8 × 15cm *(3 × 6 in)* after the edges have been trimmed and place them on a lightly buttered baking sheet with plenty of space between them.

In a small bowl, beat the egg with a pinch of salt and brush it over each rectangle, being careful not to allow the egg to drip over the edges (this will prevent the pastry from rising properly). With the tip of a pointed knife lightly cut a rectangle in each piece of pastry, about 1cm *(½ in)* from the edge. (Do not cut right through the pastry.) This central rectangle will form the top of the *feuilleté* when it is baked. Leave the pastry in a cool place for 20–30 minutes.

Pre-heat the oven to 425°F/220°C/Reg. 7.

Bake the *feuilletés* for 10 minutes, lower the oven to 400°F/200°C/Reg. 6 and bake for 10 minutes more.

The asparagus

Break off the tough parts of the asparagus, peel the lower ends of the stalks and cut them off 9–10cm *(3½–4 in)* down from the tips. Cut the stem ends in half lengthwise if the asparagus are large. Tie the tips into 3 or 4 bunches. Boil the stems and tips for 10 minutes in rapidly boiling salted water, drain, cover to keep warm, and reserve.

The sauce

Make the *beurre blanc* as described in the recipe for Hot Fish Terrine (see p.71), using the measurements given here. When all the butter has been added, taste for salt and pepper, strain the sauce into a sauceboat and whisk in the chopped herbs.

To serve the *feuilletés*

Use the tip of a pointed knife to cut carefully around the tops of the *feuilletés*. Lift them off and, if the insides are soft, hollow out the *feuilletés* with a small spoon. Place each pastry on a hot plate. Place the asparagus stems in the *feuilletés*, then arrange the tips on top so that they stick up above the edge. Moisten with a little sauce. Replace the tops and serve immediately, with the remaining sauce on the side.

Suggestion

Caviare, truffles or freshwater crayfish, cooked and shelled, may be used instead of herbs in the sauce.

Wine

It is fairly difficult to find a wine that harmonises with asparagus. Perfectionists prefer water, but you could try a Château Chalon or a sherry.

Feuilletés of Crawfish, Oysters and Scallops
Feuilletés de langouste

For 4 people

For the court bouillon *and crawfish*

2 litres *(3¼ pints)*	water
1	carrot, sliced
1	onion, sliced
	bouquet garni of thyme, bay leaf, parsley stalks and a leek leaf
20	whole peppercorns
1	generous tbsp coarse salt
1	live crawfish or lobster, weighing about 575g *(1¼ lb)*

For the sauce

2 tbsps	olive oil
2 tbsps	dry white wine
3 tbsps	cognac
1	medium carrot, finely diced
1	stalk celery, finely diced
1	small onion, finely diced
1	leek, white part only, finely diced
¼	small fennel bulb, finely diced
1	medium tomato, skinned, seeded and diced
750ml *(1¼ pints)*	whipping cream or thin *crème fraîche* (see p.290)

For the vegetables and pastry

1 tbsp	butter
200g *(7 oz)*	young spinach, stems removed (see Note)
100g *(4 oz)*	watercress
	salt, freshly ground pepper
250g *(9 oz)*	puff pastry (see p.242)

For the seafood filling

12	oysters
12	small scallops, weighing about 120g *(4 oz)*

Equipment

large saucepan (for crawfish) · high-sided frying pan or *sauteuse*, 24cm *(9½ in)* in diameter · skimmer or slotted spoon · 2 large saucepans · rolling pin · baking sheet
To serve: 4 heated plates and a sauceboat

The *court bouillon* and lobster
Place the water, carrot, onion, bouquet garni, peppercorns and salt in a large pan and boil for 5 minutes.

Plunge the tip of a large knife into the crawfish where the head meets the tail to kill it. Cut off the tail and drop it into the boiling *court bouillon*. (If using a lobster, break off the claws and add them as well.) Bring back to the boil and boil gently for 7 minutes, drain and reserve.

The sauce
Cut the crawfish head into pieces, removing the creamy parts and spongy grey gills. Heat the olive oil in a high-sided frying pan or *sauteuse*. Add the pieces of head and sauté over a moderate heat for about 3 minutes. Add the white wine and cognac, bring to a boil and light with a match. When the flame goes out, add the diced carrot, celery, onion, leek, fennel and tomato. Boil rapidly for 4 minutes to soften the vegetables and evaporate their water, then add the cream, lower the heat and simmer for 30–45 minutes, skimming from time to time. Strain the sauce into a clean saucepan. Press the vegetables and shells with a wooden spoon to extract all the juices. Cover the saucepan and reserve.

The spinach and watercress
Melt the butter in a large saucepan, add the spinach and watercress, a little salt and pepper, and allow to soften, stirring lightly with a wooden spoon. Simmer over a low heat for about 5 minutes, stirring frequently. Remove from the heat and reserve.

The pastry
Roll out and cut the pastry as described in the recipe for Endive Feuilletés with Mushrooms (see p.48). Pre-heat the oven to 425°F/220°C/ Reg. 7. Bake for 15–18 minutes and reserve.

The filling
Remove the shell from the poached crawfish tail (and claws). Cut the tail in half lengthwise. Remove the black intestine. Cut the meat into little slices about 3mm (⅛ in) thick.

Open the oysters, remove them from their shells and drain. Wash the scallops and cut them into slices about 5mm (¼ in) thick.

Gently heat the sauce, season with salt and pepper if necessary, and add the slices of crawfish, the oysters and scallops. Simmer very gently for 3 minutes.

To fill and serve the *feuilletés*
With the tip of a knife detach the tops of the *feuilletés* and, if necessary, carefully remove the soft parts from the inside. Gently reheat the spinach–watercress mixture if it has cooled, then place a spoonful in each *feuilleté*.

Lift the seafood out of the sauce with a slotted spoon and divide it between the 4 *feuilletés*. Pour some of the sauce over each pastry, put the top back in place, and serve immediately, with the rest of the sauce in a sauceboat.

Suggestions

A simpler version of this recipe can be made without the pastry by serving the seafood on a bed of spinach and watercress and pouring the sauce over and around it. The crawfish could be replaced by a lobster, freshwater crayfish or Dublin Bay prawns.

Note

It is not absolutely necessary to make a *court bouillon*. The crawfish can be simply cooked in boiling salted water.

If the spinach has thick, very large, dark green leaves, parboil it for 2 minutes in boiling water, drain, cool under running water and press dry before cooking as described.

Wine

Meursault, Puligny-Montrachet or Condrieu.

Mussels with Spinach and Curry
Moules d'Espagne au cari

For 4 people

900g *(2 lb)*	very large mussels (about 20 mussels; for substitute, see Suggestions)
175ml *(6 fl. oz)*	dry white wine
½ tsp	mild curry powder
350g *(12 oz)*	fresh spinach, cleaned and stems removed
	salt, freshly ground pepper

For the sauce

2 tsps	butter
3	shallots, finely chopped
250ml *(8 fl. oz)*	dry white wine
2 tbsps	wine vinegar
120g *(4 oz)*	plus 3 tbsps butter, at room temperature, cut into cubes
	salt, freshly ground pepper
	a generous ½ tsp mild curry powder

Equipment
large saucepan, with lid · medium saucepan · bowl · 2 small
saucepans · wire whisk · large roasting tin or gratin dish
To serve: 4 heated plates

Preliminary preparations
Wash and scrape the mussels clean and remove the beard from the edges
of the shells. Discard any mussel that is not tightly closed.

Place the wine and the curry powder in a large saucepan, bring to the boil
and simmer gently, uncovered, for 2 minutes. Remove from the heat,
cover the pan and reserve.

The spinach
Bring a pan of water to the boil, add the spinach, bring back to the boil
and cook, uncovered, for 1 minute. Drain, and cool under running water
for a few seconds. Drain well and spread the leaves out on a board ready
to use. If necessary, pat them dry with a teatowel.

The sauce
Make the *beurre blanc* as described in the recipe for Hot Fish Terrine (see
p.71), using the measurements given here. When all the butter has been
added, remove the pan from the heat and strain the sauce into another
small saucepan, pressing the shallots with a wooden spoon to extract all
the juices. Season with salt and pepper, add the curry powder, whisk to
make the sauce perfectly smooth, and keep warm.

To cook and serve the mussels
Pre-heat the oven to its maximum temperature.

Place the mussels in the saucepan with the white wine–curry mixture.
Cover the pan, place over a high heat and boil rapidly for about 5 minutes
or until all the mussels have opened, shaking the pan occasionally.
Remove the mussels from their shells and reserve. Reserve one shell from
each mussel as well and place them in a large roasting tin or gratin dish.

Place a cooked spinach leaf in each mussel shell, crumpling it to make it
fit, and place a mussel on top. When all the shells are filled, cover the
roasting tin with a sheet of aluminium foil and place it in the oven for
about 5 minutes, just long enough to warm the mussels.

Over a low heat, reheat the sauce to warm, whisking constantly. Arrange 5
mussels on each plate, spoon a little of the sauce into each one and serve
immediately.

Suggestions
Oysters may be used instead of mussels. In this case, open the oysters
with an oyster knife and poach them for 2 minutes in the wine–curry
infusion.

The green of Swiss chard leaves or watercress may be used instead of spinach.

Paprika may be used instead of curry powder, but in this case (bear this in mind whenever paprika is used) add a little sugar or chopped onion to both the sauce and the wine–paprika infusion.

Wine
A white wine, or possibly a rosé, from Provence, a white Côtes du Rhône or a Tavel rosé.

Mussel Soufflé
Soufflé aux moules

For 4 people

For the mussels
1.4kg *(3 lb)*	mussels
1 tbsp	butter
2	shallots, finely chopped
4	mushrooms, finely chopped
	bouquet garni of thyme, bay leaf, and parsley stalks
250ml *(8 fl. oz)*	dry white wine
½ tsp	mild curry powder (optional)
	salt, freshly ground pepper

For the beurre blanc
2 tsps	butter
2	shallots, finely chopped
250ml *(9 fl. oz)*	dry white wine
3 tbsps	wine vinegar
6 tbsps	butter, at room temperature, cut into cubes
	salt, freshly ground pepper

For the soufflés
4	egg yolks
1½ tbsps	softened butter
6	egg whites
	a pinch of salt

Equipment
4½-litre *(8-pint)* pan, with lid · clean cloth · 2 small saucepans · wire whisk · 4 individual soufflé dishes, 10cm *(4 in)* in diameter · mixing bowl · 2 large bowls · large roasting tin

The mussels and stock

Clean and cook the mussels as described in the recipe for Mussels with Tomatoes and Basil (see p.60), using the ingredients listed here (cook the mushrooms with the shallots). When the mussels have cooked for 4 minutes, remove 20 of them from the pan, remove them from their shells, cover and reserve.

Add the curry to the pan and boil the cooking liquid and the rest of the mussels for about 10 minutes or until the liquid has reduced to a scant 250ml (½ pint). Strain carefully and discard the mussels. Return the liquid to the boil and reduce for a further 5 minutes. Allow to cool.

The sauce

Make the *beurre blanc* as described in the recipe for Hot Fish Terrine (see p.71), using the measurements given here. When all the butter has been added, remove from the heat, season the sauce with salt and pepper, and reserve.

The soufflés

Pre-heat the oven to 425°F/220°C/Reg. 7. Butter the soufflé dishes.

Place the egg yolks in a mixing bowl, beat lightly and pour the hot cooking liquid from the mussels on to them, whisking vigorously. Pour the mixture into a saucepan and heat gently, still whisking, until it becomes thick, opaque and foamy (do not allow it to boil). Whisk in 1½ tablespoons of butter, transfer to a large bowl and allow to cool.

Place the egg whites in a large bowl with a pinch of salt and whisk until very stiff, then fold them into the egg-yolk mixture with a wooden spatula. When smooth, fold in the reserved mussels.

Pour this mixture into the soufflé dishes, distributing the mussels evenly among them. Fill them to within ½cm (¼ in) of the rim and wipe the top edge with your finger to help the soufflés to rise.

Place them in the roasting tin, pour in enough boiling water to come halfway up the sides of the dishes, and bake for 15 minutes or until a straw plunged into the centre of a soufflé comes out clean.

To serve the soufflés

Over a low heat, reheat the sauce, whisking constantly.

Remove the soufflés from the oven, hollow out the centre of each one with the tip of a knife and pour in some of the sauce. Serve immediately.

Suggestion

Clams may be used instead of mussels.

Wine

Gros Plant, Muscadet or white Mâcon.

Mussels with Tomatoes and Basil
Moules au basilic et à la tomate

For 4 people

For the tomato sauce

1 tbsp	butter
3	shallots, finely chopped
5	large tomatoes, peeled, seeded and chopped
1	small clove of garlic, crushed
	bouquet garni of thyme, bay leaf, and parsley stalks
	salt, freshly ground pepper

For the mussels

1kg *(2¼ lb)*	mussels
30g *(1 oz)*	butter
3	shallots, finely chopped
175ml *(6 fl. oz)*	dry white wine
1	small clove of garlic, crushed
	pepper
12	large or 24 small basil leaves, cut into thin strips
1 tbsp	parsley, chopped

Equipment
2 large saucepans, with lids
To serve: large serving bowl (optional)

The tomato sauce
Melt the butter in a large saucepan, add the shallots and cook, stirring, over a low heat for about 2 minutes or until soft and transparent. Add the tomatoes, garlic, *bouquet garni*, salt and pepper, simmer for 15 minutes, stirring frequently, and remove the pan from the heat. Remove the *bouquet garni* and discard. Cover the sauce and reserve.

The mussels
Wash the mussels and scrape them very clean with a knife; remove the stringy beard from the edges of the shells. Discard any mussels that are not tightly closed.

Heat the butter in a large saucepan, add the shallots and cook until soft and transparent. Add the white wine and boil for 2 minutes. Add the garlic, mussels and a little pepper, stir, raise the heat and cover the pan. Boil very rapidly for 1–2 minutes or until all the mussels have opened, shaking the pan occasionally.

To finish and serve the mussels

Add the tomato sauce to the pan with the mussels and continue cooking, covered, over a high heat for 4 minutes.

Serve the mussels either in the pan they were cooked in or in a large serving bowl. Just before serving, sprinkle with the strips of basil and the chopped parsley.

Suggestion

Clams may be used instead of mussels.

Wine

Perfection – a white Muscadet-sur-Lie. Otherwise, a Quincy or a white Provençal or Bellet.

Hot Oysters with Leek Sauce
Belons chaudes à la julienne de poireaux

For 4 people

2	medium leeks, white only
1 tbsp	butter
	salt, freshly ground pepper
2½ tbsps	water

For the sauce

2 tsps	butter
5	shallots, finely chopped
150ml *(¼ pint)*	dry white wine (or champagne)
3 tbsps	white wine vinegar
120g *(4 oz)*	butter, at room temperature, cut into cubes
	salt, freshly ground pepper

For the oysters

12–16	very large oysters in their shells
3 tbsps	white wine (or champagne)
	salt, freshly ground pepper

Equipment

wide shallow pan, with lid · 2 small saucepans · wire whisk · oyster knife · mixing bowl · clean cloth · baking sheet · skimmer or slotted spoon
To serve: 4 large plates

The leeks

Cut the leeks into pieces about 5cm *(2 in)* long. Cut in half lengthwise, then into julienne strips. Wash carefully under cold running water and drain.

Melt the tablespoon of butter in a wide shallow pan, add the leeks and spread them out in a single layer. Cook for 3 minutes to soften, but do not allow to brown. Season with salt and pepper, add the water and bring to a boil. Lower the heat, cover and simmer very slowly for 15 minutes or until all the liquid has evaporated and the leeks are tender. Reserve.

The sauce

Make the *beurre blanc* as described in the recipe for Hot Fish Terrine (see p.71), using the ingredients listed here. Remove the pan from the heat and reserve.

To cook and serve the oysters

Pre-heat the grill to a moderate heat.

Open the oysters over a mixing bowl in order to catch all their liquid. Place the oysters in a small saucepan, then strain their liquid on to them through a clean cloth.

Save the lower (concave) shell of each oyster. Rinse the shells, place them on a baking sheet and heat them gently under the grill while cooking the oysters.

Add 3 tablespoons of white wine to the oysters and heat them slowly until almost boiling; at the first bubble, remove the pan from the heat. Use a skimmer or slotted spoon to lift the oysters out of the liquid at once and place them on a towel to drain.

Boil the oyster liquid for about 3 minutes. Add 1 tablespoon of this liquid and the *beurre blanc* to the leeks. Stir gently over a low heat to reheat the leeks. Add a little salt and pepper if needed.

Remove the oyster shells from the grill and place 2 or 3 on each plate. Place an oyster in each shell. Lightly whisk the leek sauce, using a fork, lift a few strips of leek out of the sauce and place them on each oyster. Spoon a little sauce over each one and serve.

Wine

A dry white Loire wine, Muscadet, Gros Plant or a white Aligoté.

Frogs' Legs with Watercress

Grenouilles cressonière

For 4 people

For the frogs' legs

24	pairs of frogs' legs
500ml *(17 fl. oz)*	water
½	bay leaf
	a sprig of thyme (or a pinch of whole thyme leaves)

For the vegetables

4 tsps	butter
1	carrot, cut into fine julienne strips
	a pinch of sugar
4	bunches of watercress (2–3 large bunches)
	salt, freshly ground pepper

For the sauce

2 tsps	butter
6	shallots, finely chopped
375ml *(13 fl. oz)*	dry white wine
3 tbsp	white wine vinegar
120g *(4 oz)*	plus 2½ tbsps butter, at room temperature, cut into cubes
	salt, freshly ground pepper

Equipment

2 medium saucepans · skimmer or slotted spoon · frying pan · liquidiser or food processor · small saucepan · wire whisk · small ovenproof dish
To serve: 4 heated plates and a sauceboat, warm but not hot

The stock

Cut the frogs' legs off the backs with scissors, then cut the lower leg at the knee. Reserve the meaty thighs; place the backs and lower legs in a medium saucepan. Add 500ml *(17 fl. oz)* water, place over a low heat and bring slowly to the boil. Boil gently, uncovered, for 5 minutes, then skim off any foam. Add the bay leaf and thyme and cook for a further 5 minutes.

The vegetables

In a frying pan, melt 2 teaspoons of butter, add the julienne strips of carrot, salt, pepper and a pinch of sugar, and cook over a low heat for 3–5 minutes, stirring frequently (the carrots should just begin to colour).

Wash the watercress and remove the stalks. In a medium saucepan, melt 2 teaspoons of butter and add the watercress leaves. Stir, turning the leaves over until they have melted down, season with a little salt and pepper, and simmer for 4 minutes.

Purée the cooked watercress in a liquidiser or food processor, return the purée to the saucepan, taste for seasoning and reserve.

The sauce

Using the measurements given here, make the *beurre blanc* as described in the recipe for Hot Fish Terrine (see p.71). When all the butter has been added, season the sauce with salt and pepper and strain it into a sauceboat.

To cook and serve the frogs' legs

Pre-heat the oven to 425°F/220°C/Reg. 7.

While the shallots and wine are reducing for the sauce, arrange the reserved frogs' legs in an ovenproof dish just large enough to hold them in one layer. Season the legs with salt and pepper, strain the hot stock over them and cook in the oven for 5 minutes.

Reheat the carrots and the watercress purée.

When the frogs' legs have finished cooking, lift them carefully from the oven dish with a skimmer or slotted spoon and drain on a cloth.

Place some watercress purée in the centre of each plate and arrange the frogs' legs on top. Spoon a little sauce around the frogs' legs, sprinkle the carrots over the top and serve, with the rest of the sauce in a sauceboat.

Suggestions

An equal amount of lettuce or spinach leaves may be used instead of the watercress.

A little curry powder or freshly chopped herbs may be added to the sauce.

If you do not have time to make the stock, the frogs' legs may be simply sautéed in a frying pan with a little butter, salt and pepper for about 5 minutes.

Wine

A dry white wine from the Loire or a white Mâcon, a white Burgundy or white Beaujolais, or a Riesling.

Frogs' Leg 'Soup'
'Soupe' de grenouilles

For 4 people

120g (4 oz)	mangetout peas, strings and stems removed
1 tbsp	butter
1	medium tomato, peeled, seeded and diced
	salt, freshly ground pepper

<table>
<tr><td align="right">16</td><td>For the frogs' legs</td></tr>
</table>

For the frogs' legs

16	pairs of frogs' legs
2 tsps	butter
250ml *(9 fl. oz)*	water
1	clove of garlic, sliced
4cm *(1½-in)*	piece of fresh ginger, finely chopped

For the sauce

2 tsps	butter
2	shallots, finely chopped
200ml *(6 fl. oz)*	dry white wine
3 tbsps	white wine vinegar
120g *(4 oz)*	butter, at room temperature, cut into cubes
	salt, freshly ground pepper

To finish

1 tbsp	butter (for the frogs' legs)
	salt, freshly ground pepper
4	small poached or tinned artichoke hearts, finely sliced
	a pinch of cayenne pepper
6	small or 3 large basil leaves, cut into thin strips

Equipment

2 medium saucepans · small frying pan · bowl · small saucepan · wire whisk · large frying pan   *To serve:* 4 heated soup plates

Preliminary preparations

Cook the mangetout peas in a saucepan of lightly salted water for 6–8 minutes, cool under running water, drain and reserve.

Melt a tablespoon of butter in a small frying pan, add the tomato, season lightly with salt and pepper, and simmer for 10 minutes. Reserve.

The stock

Cut the backs off the frogs' legs and cut off the lower leg at the knee. Separate the thighs from each other and reserve.

Melt 2 teaspoons of butter in a saucepan, add the frogs' backs and lower legs and cook gently for about 3 minutes without browning. Add the water, bring to the boil and skim off any foam that appears. Add the garlic and ginger and boil slowly for about 40 minutes or until there is only 150ml *(¼ pint)* of liquid left. Strain the stock into a bowl and reserve.

The sauce

Make the *beurre blanc* as described in the recipe for Hot Fish Terrine (see p.71), using the measurements given here. Once all the butter has been added, season with salt and pepper and strain the sauce into the bowl with the stock. Whisk together and reserve.

The frogs' legs

Heat a tablespoon of butter in a large frying pan. Season the frogs' legs generously and add them to the hot butter. Brown over a moderate heat for about 5 minutes, shaking the pan often to roll the frogs' legs in the butter. Remove from the pan, and drain the thighs for a few seconds on kitchen paper. Cover and keep warm.

To finish and serve the soup

Place the mangetout peas, tomato and sliced artichoke bottoms in a saucepan. Add the mixture of stock and *beurre blanc*, taste for salt and pepper, add the cayenne pepper and heat for 1–2 minutes, stirring occasionally. The 'soup' should be very hot, but do not allow it to boil.

Ladle the liquid and vegetables into the soup plates, place the frogs' legs on top, sprinkle with the strips of basil and serve immediately.

Wine

A young Côtes du Rhône or a white wine from Provence, a Riesling or a dry white Loire wine such as Sancerre.

Ragoût of Frogs' Legs, Oysters and Dublin Bay Prawns
A Wicked Stew
Ragoût malin

For 4 people

2 tsps	butter
5	shallots, finely chopped
375ml *(13 fl. oz)*	red wine
6 tbsps	red wine vinegar
350ml *(12 fl. oz)*	whipping cream
12	pairs of frogs' legs, trimmed (see p.63; for substitute see Suggestions)
12	Dublin Bay prawns, shelled
12	oysters, shelled
	salt, freshly ground pepper
8	basil leaves, cut into thin strips

Equipment

saucepan
To serve: serving dish or 4 heated plates

66

The sauce

Melt the butter in a saucepan, add the shallots and simmer until soft and transparent. Add the wine and vinegar and boil rapidly until most of the liquid has evaporated and only 1 tablespoon remains. Stir in the cream and simmer gently for 10 minutes.

To make the stew and serve

Season the frogs' legs, Dublin Bay prawns and oysters with salt and pepper.

Add the frogs' legs to the sauce and simmer for 2 minutes. (If an absolutely smooth sauce is desired, place the frogs' legs in a clean saucepan and strain the sauce over them.) Add the Dublin Bay prawns, simmer for 1 minute, add the oysters and simmer for 2 minutes more.

Either serve on a serving dish or on individual plates; if using plates, arrange 3 Dublin Bay prawns, 3 oysters and 3 pairs of frog's legs on each one. Spoon the sauce over them, sprinkle with the basil and serve immediately.

Suggestions

This ragoût can be served in *feuilletés*.

The red wine vinegar and red wine may be replaced by equal amounts, respectively, of cider vinegar and hard cider, or by white wine and tarragon-flavoured vinegar.

About 175g *(6 oz)* of shelled scallops (4 large sea scallops) may be used instead of the frogs' legs.

Instead of basil, a julienne of small French beans, or a julienne of truffles or of carrots, sautéed in butter with a little salt and pepper, or some boiled asparagus tips, may be used.

Note

Instead of Dublin Bay prawns, 450g *(1 lb)* of large prawns or shelled, sliced lobster, poached separately and reheated in the sauce, may be used.

Wine

A dry white wine, Riesling or Burgundy, a Chablis or a Loire wine such as Pouilly-Fumé.

Feuilleté of Frogs' Legs with Chervil Butter Sauce
Feuilletés de grenouilles au beurre de cerfeuil

For 4 people

250g *(9 oz)*	puff pastry (see p.242)
20–24	pairs of frogs' legs
475ml *(16 fl. oz)*	water
1	large clove of garlic, crushed
2½cm *(1-in)*	piece of fresh ginger, finely chopped
	bouquet garni
	salt, freshly ground pepper

For the beurre blanc

2 tsps	butter
5	shallots, finely chopped
175ml *(6 fl. oz)*	dry white wine
3 tbsps	white wine vinegar
240g *(8 oz)*	less 2 tbsps butter, at room temperature, cut into cubes
	salt, freshly ground pepper
1	heaped tbsp whole chervil leaves (see Note)

For the garnish

2 tsps	butter
225g *(8 oz)*	young fresh spinach, stems removed
1	bunch of watercress

Equipment
rolling pin · baking sheet · 3 small saucepans · slotted spoon · wire whisk · small frying pan
To serve: serving dish or 4 plates, and a sauceboat

To roll and cut the pastry
Roll out the pastry ½cm *(¼ in)* thick, cut it into 4 rectangles, and make an incision to form a top as described for Endive Feuilletés with Mushrooms (see p.48). Place the pastry on a baking sheet and leave in a cool place for 30 minutes before baking.

The frogs' legs
Cut the frogs' legs from the backs. Cut the lower part of the leg from the thigh at the knee. Place the backs and lower legs in a small saucepan and reserve.

Using a small sharp knife, carefully de-bone the thighs, trying to keep the meat as whole as possible. Place the meat on a plate, season with salt and pepper, and reserve.

Place the bones from the thighs in the saucepan with the backs and lower legs; add just enough water to cover them – 250ml *(½ pint)* or a little more – bring to a boil, skim off any foam, and add the garlic, ginger, and *bouquet garni*. Lower the heat and simmer slowly for 15 minutes, then strain the liquid into a small saucepan and season lightly with salt and pepper. Bring to a boil, add the boned frogs' legs and simmer for 4 minutes. Lift them out with a slotted spoon and drain on kitchen paper.

The *beurre blanc*

Make the *beurre blanc* as described in the recipe for Hot Fish Terrine (see p.71), using the ingredients listed here. When all the butter has been added, season the sauce with salt and pepper and reserve.

Baking the *feuilletés*

Pre-heat the oven to 425°F/220°C/Reg. 7.

Place the *feuilletés* in the oven and bake for 11 minutes, lower the heat to 400°F/200°C/Reg. 6, and bake for 8–10 minutes more.

Remove the *feuilletés* from the oven. With the tip of a knife, lift off the top of each *feuilleté*; hollow out the middles with a small spoon. Leave the oven on at the same temperature.

To finish and serve the *feuilletés*

Melt 2 teaspoons of butter in a small frying pan, add the spinach leaves and watercress, stir until melted down, then simmer, uncovered, for 4 minutes. Season with salt and pepper, then place a little of this garnish inside each *feuilleté*. Divide the meat from the frogs' legs among the *feuilletés*, then put the tops back in place. Place the filled *feuilletés* back in the oven for a minute or two to warm through.

Gently reheat the *beurre blanc*, whisking constantly. Place the fresh chervil leaves in a sauceboat, strain the butter sauce over them and stir.

Remove the *feuilletés* from the oven, place them on a serving dish or plates, and serve, with the sauceboat of sauce on the side.

Suggestion

The frogs' legs can be replaced by freshwater crayfish, Dublin Bay prawns, oysters or fish.

Wine

Riesling or a white Loire wine.

Snails with Cream and Herbs
Fricassée d'escargots à la crème

For 4 people

2 × 125g *(4-oz)*	tins of snails (5 dozen snails; for substitutes, see Suggestion)
1½ tbsps	butter
225g *(8 oz)*	medium mushrooms, each cut into 8 pieces
8	shallots, finely chopped
3 tbsps	white wine vinegar
	salt, freshly ground pepper
	nutmeg
4 tbsps	dry white wine
350ml *(12 fl. oz)*	whipping cream
2 tsps	parsley, finely chopped
2 tsps	chervil, finely chopped
2 tsps	chives, finely chopped
2	leaves of basil, finely chopped
1	mint leaf, finely chopped

Equipment
large frying pan
To serve: 4 heated plates or *cocottes*

To cook and serve the snails
Wash and drain the snails thoroughly.

Melt the butter in a large frying pan. Add the mushrooms and cook for 5 minutes, stirring often, until the mushroom juices have evaporated and the mushrooms have begun to brown. Add the shallots and cook for 1–2 minutes. Add the vinegar, stir and boil until it has almost completely evaporated. Add the snails, season with salt, pepper and a little nutmeg, and add the wine. Boil until almost all the wine has evaporated. Stir in the cream, lower the heat and simmer for 5 minutes or until the sauce is thick and creamy. Stir in the fresh herbs and serve immediately on plates or in individual *cocottes*.

Suggestion
Cooked Dublin Bay prawns, freshwater crayfish, or even chicken livers may be prepared and served in the same way as the snails. (Brown the chicken livers in a little butter for about 1 minute before following the above recipe.)

Wine
Aligoté, a white Côtes du Rhône or a white wine from Provence. A young chilled red wine such as this year's Côtes-du-Jura.

Hot Fish Terrine
Terrine de poissons chaude

For 1 terrine, serving 4–6 people

For the terrine

2	crisp white mushrooms, finely chopped
2	shallots, finely chopped
200g *(7 oz)*	hake fillets (for substitute, see Note)
100g *(4 oz)*	pike or trout fillets (for substitute, see Note)
½ litre *(16 fl. oz)*	crème fraîche (see p.290) or double cream
1	egg, beaten
120g *(4 oz)*	plus 2 tbsps butter, softened
1	generous tsp chives, finely chopped
1	generous tsp chervil or parsley, finely chopped
1 tsp	salt
¾ tsp	freshly ground pepper
	a pinch of cayenne pepper

For the beurre blanc

4 tsps	butter
6	shallots, finely chopped
250ml *(8 fl. oz)*	dry white wine
3 tbsps	white wine vinegar
225g *(8 oz)*	butter, at room temperature, cut into cubes
	salt, freshly ground pepper

Equipment
large pan · rectangular terrine, 15 × 10cm *(6 × 4 in)* by 8cm *(3 in)* deep · small saucepan · food processor or heavy-duty liquidiser · 2 mixing bowls · large roasting tin · wire whisk
To serve: 6–8 heated plates and a warm sauceboat

Preliminary preparations
Pre-heat the oven to 400°F/200°C/Reg. 6.

Bring a large pan of water to the boil to fill the bain-marie. Butter the inside of the terrine lightly.

Making the terrine
Place the fish fillets and cream in a food processor or liquidiser and blend to a smooth purée. Transfer this mixture to a mixing bowl and stir in the shallots and mushrooms and the egg.

In another mixing bowl, beat the butter with a wooden spoon until creamy. Add several spoonfuls of the fish mixture and stir it in. Stir the rest of the fish mixture into the butter, little by little. Stir in the herbs, salt, pepper and cayenne pepper. Transfer the mixture to the buttered terrine and cover (if the terrine has no lid use aluminium foil).

Pour enough boiling water into a roasting tin to half fill it, place the terrine in the roasting tin and bake for 45 minutes, or until a trussing needle or a knife blade stuck into the centre of the terrine and held there for 5 seconds comes out hot (touch it to the inside of your wrist). Keep warm and serve hot with the following *beurre blanc*.

The sauce

Melt 2 teaspoons of butter in a small saucepan, add the shallots and simmer until soft and transparent. Add the white wine and the vinegar and cook at a gentle boil, uncovered, for about 10 minutes or until only 1 tablespoon of liquid is left. Over a moderate heat, add a piece of softened butter, then lift the pan off the heat and whisk it in. Continue to add butter in this way, setting the pan down on the heat, then lifting it off to maintain an even heat. Test the temperature of the sauce by touching it with the back of the fingers; the sauce should feel hot but should not burn. When all the butter has been added, taste for salt and pepper, then strain the sauce into a warm (not hot) sauceboat.

Place a slice of terrine on each plate, spoon a little sauce around it and serve immediately, with the rest of the sauce in a sauceboat.

Note

Other fish fillets of your choice may be used, but try to respect the proportions of 200g *(½ lb)* of saltwater fish to 100g *(¼ lb)* of freshwater fish.

Wine

A young white wine – Sancerre, Pouilly-Fuissé, white Beaujolais or Pouilly-Fumé.

Crayfish with Ceps
Ecrevisses aux cèpes

For 4 people

450g *(1 lb)*	firm, fresh young ceps (boletus mushrooms; for substitutes, see Suggestions)
600g *(1 lb 6 oz)*	live crayfish (for substitutes, see Note)
2 tsps	butter
8	shallots, finely chopped
250ml *(8 fl. oz)*	dry white wine
½ litre *(16 fl. oz)*	double cream or *crème fraîche* (see p.290)
	salt, freshly ground pepper
1 tbsp	butter (for the mushrooms)
1 tsp	each of chopped parsley, chervil and chives

Equipment

pastry brush · *sauteuse* or high-sided frying pan, 22–25cm *(9–10 in)* in diameter, with lid · skimmer or slotted spoon · frying pan
To serve: serving dish or 4 plates

Preliminary preparations

Trim the ceps carefully; cut off the sandy end of the stalks. Rather than cutting the stems straight off, cut around the tip to form a point – this way none of the edible part of the stem is wasted. If the ceps are clean, simply brush the tops. If they are very dirty, or if there are little cracks in the tops, scrape them clean with a paring knife – in any case, don't wash them.

Cut each mushroom in half. The flesh of both cap and stem should be white and firm. Discard any mushrooms that have holes through them, as they have been attacked by parasites.

Separate the caps from the stems and cut everything into slices about 3mm *(⅛ in)* thick and then into strips about 3mm *(⅛ in)* wide.

Place the crayfish in a colander, rinse under cold running water, then remove the central fin and intestine as described in the recipe for Lamb with Crayfish (see p.166). Reserve.

The sauce and the crayfish

In a *sauteuse* or high-sided frying pan, melt 2 teaspoons of butter, add the shallots and simmer for about 2 minutes or until soft and transparent. Add the white wine, bring to the boil and boil rapidly for 4–5 minutes or until about 2 tablespoons of liquid are left.

Stir in the cream and boil gently for 3 minutes. Season with salt and pepper and add the crayfish, pushing them down into the cream as much as possible. Cover the pan, bring to the boil and boil gently for 5 minutes or until the crayfish have turned completely red, stirring once or twice.

Lift the crayfish out of the sauce with a skimmer or slotted spoon and place them upside down on a cutting board. With a large sharp knife, cut each one in half lengthwise, place them on a serving dish or on individual plates with the cut side (inside) facing up. Cover with aluminium foil and keep warm.

The mushrooms

In a frying pan, melt a tablespoon of butter. When it is very hot, add the mushrooms and cook over a high heat for 4–5 minutes, stirring constantly, so that they brown lightly on all sides. Season with salt and pepper.

73

To serve the crayfish

Arrange the crayfish on hot plates and keep warm. Place the sauce over a brisk heat and boil rapidly until reduced to 300ml *(½ pint)*. Taste for seasoning, spoon the sauce over the crayfish, place the mushrooms on top, sprinkle with fresh herbs and serve immediately.

Suggestions

Other wild mushrooms, such as chanterelles or morels, or even very fresh young ordinary mushrooms, may be used instead of the ceps.

Note

The cooking times of both crayfish and ceps are vital to the success of this dish.

Instead of crayfish, Mediterranean prawns may be used. Buy 700g *(1½ lb)* of raw prawns with heads, if possible, peel them and poach them in the cream as described for the crayfish. As they are peeled, it is unnecessary to cut them in half.

Wine

A white Graves or a young red Saint-Emilion.

Fricassee of Crayfish with Asparagus
Fricassée d'écrevisses aux asperges

For 4 people

32	live crayfish (for substitutes see Note)
2 tbsps	olive oil
6	shallots, coarsely chopped
1	medium tomato, sliced
1	medium carrot, coarsely chopped
¼	head of fennel, coarsely chopped
1	stick of celery, coarsely chopped
2 tbsps	white wine
3 tbsps	cognac
400ml *(¾ pint)*	double cream or *crème fraîche* (see p. 290)
16	medium asparagus, weighing about 700g *(1½ lb)*
2 litres *(3½ pints)*	water
2 tsps	coarse salt
	salt, freshly ground pepper
1 tbsp	freshly chopped *fines herbes* (parsley, chives, chervil and so on) – optional

Equipment

high-sided frying pan or *sauteuse*, 28cm *(11 in)* in diameter, with lid ·
small saucepan · kitchen string · large saucepan · skimmer or slotted
spoon   *To serve:* 4 heated plates

The crayfish

Wash the crayfish thoroughly. Remove the central fin and intestine from
the tail of each one as described in Lamb with Crayfish (see p.166).

In a high-sided frying pan or *sauteuse* heat the olive oil. When it is very
hot add enough of the crayfish to cover the bottom of the pan in a single
layer. Cover the pan and cook over a brisk heat, shaking the pan often,
until all the crayfish are red – about 6–8 minutes. Remove them from the pan
and reserve in a colander. Cook the rest of the crayfish in the same way.

When they are cool enough to handle, detach the tails of the crayfish and
peel them. Reserve the heads in the colander and the tails on a plate.

Return the pan to a high heat and add the crayfish heads, shallots,
tomato, carrot, fennel and celery. Stir together and cook, uncovered, for 5
minutes. Add the wine and cognac and light with a match. When the
flame has died down, add the cream and lower the heat. Stir, pressing on
the crayfish heads to extract their juices, then simmer gently, uncovered,
for 20 minutes, skimming the sauce from time to time.

Strain into a small saucepan, pressing on the shells and vegetables to
extract all the liquid. There should be about 250–300ml *(½ pint)* of sauce.

The asparagus

Peel the asparagus, cut them off about 12cm *(5 in)* below the tip and tie
them into 3 bundles. Bring the water to the boil in a large pan, add the
asparagus, bring back to the boil, add the salt and boil for 7 minutes.

To finish and serve the fricassée

Season the crayfish sauce with salt and pepper to taste, bring almost to a
boil, add the crayfish tails and heat gently for 3 minutes. Do not boil.

Drain the asparagus, untie them and place 4 on each plate. With a
skimmer or slotted spoon, lift the crayfish tails out of the sauce and place
8 of them on each plate, on and around the asparagus. Spoon the sauce
over them, sprinkle with the chopped herbs and serve.

Note

Instead of crayfish, 32 raw (live, fresh or frozen) Mediterranean prawns
with heads, if possible, weighing about 575g *(1¼ lb)*, may be used. Cook
as described for the crayfish, but turn each one over halfway through the
cooking time. All the prawns may be sautéed at the same time. Use both
the heads and the shells from the tails for making the sauce.

Wine

A white Burgundy – Puligny-Montrachet or Meursault.

Scallops with Julienne Vegetables and Champagne Sauce

Coquilles Saint-Jacques, julienne de légumes, au champagne

For 4 people

12	large scallops in their shells (see Note, p.25)

For the stock

1½ tbsps	butter
375ml *(13 fl. oz)*	water
	salt, freshly ground pepper

For the vegetables

1	medium leek, white only
5cm *(2-in)*	piece of cucumber, seeded and cut into julienne strips
1	small carrot, cut into julienne strips
2	large mushrooms, cut into julienne strips (see Suggestions)

For the sauce

1½ tbsps	butter
8	shallots, finely chopped
350ml *(12 fl. oz)*	champagne or dry white wine
250ml *(9 fl. oz)*	double cream or *crème fraîche* (see p. 290)
	salt, freshly ground pepper
3 tbsps	butter, at room temperature, cut into small dice

Equipment

saucepan · 2 small saucepans · wire whisk · small frying pan or medium saucepan · skimmer or slotted spoon
To serve: 4 heated plates

The stock

Make the scallop stock described in the recipe for Salad of Scallops with Fried Celery Leaves (see p.24), using the measurements given here (there is neither wine nor dill in this recipe).

The vegetables

Cut the white part of the leek into pieces about 5cm *(2 in)* long; cut each piece in half lengthwise, then into julienne strips. Rinse under cold running water, drain and reserve.

Bring 1 litre *(1¾ pints)* of lightly salted water to a boil and add the carrots and leek. Boil for 1 minute, then add the cucumber and mushrooms and boil for 30 seconds more. Drain, cool under running water, drain well and reserve in a clean saucepan.

The sauce

Melt 1½ tablespoons of butter in a small saucepan, add the shallots and simmer for 2–3 minutes or more, until soft. Add the champagne or white wine and boil until it has almost completely evaporated. Add the cream and continue boiling rapidly for about 3 minutes or until it is thick and creamy, then remove the pan from the heat and whisk in the butter bit by bit. Season with salt and pepper, then strain the sauce into the saucepan with the cooked vegetables.

To cook the scallops and serve

Heat the stock in a saucepan just large enough to hold the scallops in a single layer. Simmer, covered, for 3–4 minutes, lift them out and drain well.

Reheat the vegetables and sauce if necessary (do not allow to boil). Place 3 scallops on each plate. Lift the vegetables out of the saucepan with a slotted spoon and place them on top of the scallops, then spoon the sauce over and around the scallops and serve.

Suggestions

A teaspoon each of lemon and lime zest, cut into julienne strips, may be cooked with the vegetables. Or – even more luxurious – a fine julienne of truffles may be substituted for the mushrooms; add the truffles to the sauce after whisking in the butter.

Wine

Champagne or white Coteaux Champenois, white Loire wine or white Burgundy.

Scallops with Green Peas
Coquilles Saint-Jacques aux petits pois

For 4 people

225g *(8 oz)*	shelled fresh young peas
60g *(2 oz)*	butter, at room temperature, cut into cubes

For the garnish

1 tbsp	butter
8	little onions, thinly sliced
4	lettuce leaves, cut into wide strips
	salt, freshly ground pepper
5 tbsps	water

For the scallops

1 tbsp	butter
2	shallots, finely chopped .
	salt, freshly ground pepper
450g *(1 lb)*	shelled sea scallops (or queen scallops)
175ml *(6 fl. oz)*	white wine

For the sauce

175ml *(6 fl. oz)*	whipping cream or liquid *crème fraîche* (see p.290)
	salt, freshly ground pepper

Equipment

liquidiser or food processor · bowl · large frying pan, with lid · oval or rectangular ovenproof dish, 30cm *(12 in)* long · skimmer or slotted spoon · wire whisk
To serve: 4 heated plates

The green butter

Use half the peas for making the green butter and save the rest for the garnish. Purée the peas for the green butter in a liquidiser or food processor. Add the butter, liquidise, place in a sieve and rub the mixture through with a wooden spoon. Place the butter in a bowl and reserve.

The garnish

Melt 1 tablespoon of butter in a large frying pan. Add the onions and cook until soft; do not allow to brown. Add the reserved peas, lettuce, salt and pepper, stir, and cover the pan. Simmer very slowly for 5–6 minutes, then add the water and simmer, covered, for 5 minutes or until all the water has been absorbed. Remove from the heat and reserve.

The scallops

Clean and trim the scallops and separate the white parts from the corals. Dry them carefully. Pre-heat the oven to 425°F/220°C/Reg. 7.

Melt a tablespoon of butter in an ovenproof dish, add the shallots and cook over a moderate heat until soft.

Season the scallops and corals generously with salt and pepper, place them in the ovenproof dish in a single layer, add the white wine, bring just to the boil, then place the dish in the oven and cook for 5 minutes (cook queen scallops for 3 minutes). Lift out the scallops and their corals with a skimmer or slotted spoon and place them in the pan with the onions, lettuce and peas.

The sauce

Boil the liquid in the ovenproof dish over a high heat for about 3 minutes or until there are about 2 tablespoons left. Add the cream and boil for 3 minutes or until the sauce is thick and creamy. Taste for salt and pepper, remove the dish from the heat and whisk in the green butter.

To finish and serve the scallops

Strain the sauce into the pan with the vegetables and scallops. Reheat over a moderate heat, shaking the pan to mix the vegetables and sauce together. When very hot (do not allow to boil), serve immediately.

Suggestion

The scallops can be replaced with a firm fish, either filleted or cut into cubes.

Wine

A white Burgundy such as Pouilly-Fuissé.

Smoked Fish Terrine with Whipped Cream Sauce

Terrine de poissons fumés

For 1 terrine, serving 4–6 people

For the jelly

20g (¾ oz)	powdered gelatine
200ml (7 fl. oz)	cold water

For the terrine

200g (7 oz)	smoked salmon, thinly sliced
200g (7 oz)	smoked sturgeon, thinly sliced
175ml (6 fl. oz)	crème fraîche (see p. 290) or double cream
1 tbsp	parsley leaves, coarsely chopped
1 tbsp	chervil, coarsely chopped
1 tbsp	chives, finely chopped
	salt, freshly ground pepper

For the sauce

¾ tsp	lemon zest, finely chopped
200ml (7 fl. oz)	double cream or crème fraîche, lightly whipped
	salt, freshly ground pepper
	a pinch of cayenne pepper
¼ tsp	lemon juice
1	large or 2 small tomatoes, peeled, seeded and diced
2 tbsps	whole chervil leaves
2 tbsps	whole parsley leaves
2 tbsps	chives, finely chopped
	slices of toast (for serving)

Equipment

medium pan · small bowl · large bowl · wire whisk · sieve · muslin cloth · saucepan · weight · rectangular terrine, 15 × 10cm *(6 × 4 in)* by 8cm *(3 in)* deep · liquidiser or food processor · small saucepan · 4 mixing bowls
To serve: sauceboat, serving dish and plates

Making the jelly

The day before, put the water and gelatine in a saucepan and bring slowly to simmering point, whisking all the time. Strain through a sieve lined with a cloth and reserve in a cool place. If you like you can use a well-flavoured fish stock, clarified, instead of water.

The terrine

Place the empty terrine in the refrigerator for at least 1 hour to chill it.

If the jelly has set, place it in a saucepan and heat, stirring, until it is just liquid again. Remove from the heat.

Reserve one-third of each fish. Purée the remaining salmon with 6 tablespoons of the cream in a liquidiser or food processor until smooth. Reserve in a bowl.

Purée the remaining sturgeon, using the rest of the cream. Reserve in another bowl.

Set the saucepan of jelly into a bowl filled with ice cubes and water and stir constantly until cool (but not cold) to the touch.

Pour 5 tablespoons of the jelly into the bowl with the salmon purée, add half the herbs and stir to combine. Season lightly with salt and pepper.

Add the remaining herbs and 5 tablespoons of the jelly to the sturgeon purée, mix well and season with salt and pepper.

Place the remaining jelly back over the ice and stir until cold and the consistency of olive oil. At this point it will be on the verge of setting. Remove the terrine from the refrigerator and pour the remaining jelly into it. Tip and turn the terrine so that the sides and bottom are coated with jelly – a pastry brush may be used to paint the sides with jelly if preferred. Refrigerate the terrine for about 5 minutes or until the jelly is set.

Pour half the salmon purée into the terrine, smooth the surface with the back of a spoon dipped in warm water, and lay half the sturgeon slices on top (they should cover the purée). Pour half the sturgeon purée on top of this, smooth the surface and top with half the salmon slices. Finish filling the terrine with the remaining fish purées and slices, in the same order as before, ending with slices of salmon.

Cover the terrine tightly with aluminium foil and refrigerate for 24 hours before serving.

To make the sauce and serve

Place the lemon zest in a saucepan, cover with cold water and bring to a boil; boil for 5 minutes and drain.

Season the whipped cream with salt, pepper, cayenne pepper and lemon juice. Delicately fold in the diced tomato pulp, herbs and lemon zest. The sauce should be fairly stiff; if it is not, whisk once or twice until it is the right consistency. Pour the sauce into a sauceboat and chill.

Just before serving, quickly dip the terrine into a bowl of hot water, run the blade of a knife around the inside of the mould and turn the terrine out on to a serving platter. Serve, with the sauce in the sauceboat and slices of hot toast on a plate.

Suggestion

You can use smoked trout or smoked eel in the making of this terrine. If using eel, add a little sorrel.

Wine

A vigorous wine – Pouilly-Fumé or Saint Véran – or a white wine such as Palette.

Steamed Scallops with Fennel and Pernod

Coquilles Saint-Jacques au fenouil et au Ricard

For 4 people

12	scallops
	salt, freshly ground pepper
1 tbsp	fresh dill, chopped
2 tbsps	Pernod or Ricard
1 tbsp	butter
2	medium heads of fennel, cut into 2cm (¾-in) julienne strips
	salt, freshly ground pepper
¾ tsp	curry powder
6½ tbsps	butter, at room temperature, cut into cubes

Equipment

steamer or large pan and steaming basket, with lid · saucepan · slotted spoon · wire whisk
To serve: heated serving dish

The scallops

Place the scallops on one half of a large sheet of aluminium foil. Sprinkle with salt, pepper, dill and the Pernod or Ricard. Fold the other half of the foil over the scallops and roll the edges together, pressing them to seal the scallops inside, *en papillote*.

Bring some water to a boil in the bottom of a steamer (or a large pan with a steaming basket set in it), place the *papillote* in the basket, cover the pan and steam for 9 minutes.

The fennel

While the scallops are steaming, melt 1 tablespoon of butter in a saucepan over a moderate heat. Add the fennel, season with salt, pepper and curry powder, stir, then add just enough water almost to cover and simmer for 3 minutes.

Lift the fennel out of the saucepan with a slotted spoon and place it on a serving dish. Keep it warm while making the sauce.

The sauce

Reduce the fennel cooking liquid until there are about 2 tablespoons left, then whisk in the butter, little by little, as described for the *beurre blanc* in Hot Fish Terrine (see p.71). When all the butter has been added, remove the sauce from the heat and taste for seasoning.

To serve the scallops

When the scallops are cooked, remove the *papillote* from the steamer and put it on to a plate. Open it carefully and place the scallops on the bed of fennel. Whisk the cooking juices from the scallops into the sauce, pour over the scallops and serve.

Suggestions

The scallops can be replaced by mussels, fillets of sea bass or turbot, or other firm-fleshed fish, or even by salmon.

The fennel can be replaced by celery, but in this case do not use curry powder or Pernod. Instead, add 2 tablespoons of white wine or cherry brandy to the *papillote*.

Wine

A white or rosé Provençal or Côtes du Rhône, a white Châteauneuf-du-Pape – Domaine de Beaucastel – or Pouilly-Fuissé.

Lobster Fricassee with Cucumbers and Mint

Fricassée de homard au concombre et à la menthe fraîche

For 4 people

For the lobster

2.75 litres *(5 pints)*	water
4 tsps	coarse salt
1	medium carrot, thinly sliced
1	small onion, thinly sliced
1	clove of garlic
1	medium tomato, cut into 8 wedges
	bouquet garni of thyme, bay leaf, and parsley stalks
12	whole peppercorns
1kg *(2¼-lb)*	live lobster

For the sauce

2 tbsps	olive oil
1	small carrot, diced
1	stick of celery, diced
½	medium onion, diced
¼	head of fennel, diced
1	medium tomato, coarsely chopped
5 tbsps	cognac
3 tbsps	white wine
275ml *(½ pint)*	whipping cream or *crème fraîche* (see p.290)

For the cucumbers

1 tbsp	butter
2 tbsps	shallots, finely chopped
2	medium cucumbers, weighing 450g *(1 lb)*, peeled, seeded and scooped into balls or cut into 1.5cm *(½-in)* cubes
	salt, freshly ground pepper
10	fresh mint leaves, cut into thin strips

Equipment

large pan with lid · kitchen scissors · hammer or cleaver · large high-sided frying pan or *sauteuse*, 28–32cm *(11–12 in)* in diameter · small high-sided frying pan or *sauteuse*, 24cm *(9½ in)* in diameter
To serve: heated serving dish or 4 heated plates

The lobster

In a large pan, bring the water and salt to a boil. Add the carrot, onion, garlic, tomato, *bouquet garni* and peppercorns, bring back to the boil and cook gently for 10 minutes.

83

Raise the heat and, when the liquid is boiling rapidly, drop the lobster into the pan. Cover the pan until the water comes back to the boil, then remove the lid and boil the lobster, uncovered, for 9 minutes.

Remove the lobster from the *court bouillon* and place it on kitchen paper to drain. Reserve 2 ladlefuls of the *court bouillon*, strained.

When the lobster has cooled enough to handle, separate the tail from the head. With a pair of scissors, cut the shell on the underside of the tail in half lengthwise and remove the meat. Crack each claw with a hammer or the blunt edge of a cleaver and remove the meat. Reserve the shelled lobster on a plate.

The sauce

With a cleaver or large knife, split the lobster head in half lengthwise. With a small spoon, scoop out and discard the greenish matter *(tomali)* along the top of each half, then chop the head into small pieces.

In a large high-sided frying pan or *sauteuse* heat the olive oil over a brisk heat. When it is nearly smoking, add the pieces of lobster head, stirring well to coat them. Add the carrot, celery, onion, fennel and tomato. Stir well, add the cognac and white wine, and light with a match. When the flame has died down, stir in the cream, bring to the boil and simmer, uncovered, for 20 minutes, skimming from time to time until the sauce is reduced by half and has thickened.

The cucumbers

While the sauce is cooking, melt the butter in a small high-sided frying pan or *sauteuse*, add the shallots and simmer until soft and transparent, stirring occasionally. Add the cucumber balls, stir to coat them with the butter and spread them out in a single layer.

Pour just enough of the reserved *court bouillon* over the cucumbers almost to cover them. Simmer, uncovered, for 12 minutes or until the liquid has almost evaporated.

To finish and serve the sauce

While the sauce and cucumbers are cooking, open the lobster tail along the back and carefully remove the blackish intestine, then cut the meat into round slices ½cm (¼ in) thick. Cut the meat from the claws into small slices.

Season the cucumbers with salt and pepper, stir, then strain the lobster sauce over them. Press on the vegetables and shells with a wooden spoon to extract any liquid and taste for seasoning. Be sure the sauce is hot (it should not boil), add the slices of lobster and heat over a very low heat, stirring occasionally, for 3 minutes.

Place the lobster on a serving dish, or divide it between 4 plates. Arrange the cucumber round the lobster, coat lightly with the sauce, sprinkle with the strips of mint and serve immediately.

Suggestions

A crawfish can be cooked in the same way – or perhaps Dublin Bay prawns or crayfish, which would need less cooking than a lobster.

The cucumber can be replaced by balls of celeriac and the mint with basil.

Wine

Montrachet or white Châteauneuf-du-Pape.

Fricassee of Asparagus, Scallops and Oysters

Fricassée aux asperges, coquilles Saint-Jacques, et huîtres

For 4 people

600g *(1 ¼ lb)*	asparagus (about 3 stalks per person)

For the sauce

2 tsps	butter
2	large shallots, finely chopped
3 tbsps	white wine vinegar
200ml *(7 fl. oz)*	dry white wine
200ml *(7 fl. oz)*	double cream or *crème fraîche* (see p. 290)
5 tbsps	butter, at room temperature, cut into cubes

For the shellfish

8	large scallops, each cut into 3 slices (or 24 queen scallops)
	salt, freshly ground pepper
	pinch cayenne pepper
8	large oysters, shelled

Equipment

large pan · 2 medium saucepans · wire whisk · skimmer or slotted spoon
To serve: 4 heated plates

The asparagus

Cut off each asparagus about 9–10cm *(3½–4 in)* from the tip. Peel them, if necessary, being careful not to damage the tips, then drop them into a large pan of boiling salted water. Bring back to the boil and boil for 10 minutes. Lift the asparagus out of the pan and drain on a cloth or towel.

The sauce

Melt 2 teaspoons of butter in a saucepan, add the shallots and cook for about 2 minutes or until soft and transparent. Add the vinegar and wine and boil rapidly for 10 minutes or until about 2 tablespoons of liquid are left. Add the cream and boil rapidly for 2 minutes or until thick and creamy, stirring occasionally.

To cook and serve the shellfish

Wash and trim the scallops, dry them and sprinkle them generously with salt and pepper, add a pinch of cayenne, then place them with the oysters in a saucepan. Strain the sauce on to them and heat for about 3 minutes. As soon as the sauce begins to simmer, but before it boils, the shellfish are cooked.

Divide the asparagus tips, scallops and oysters between the heated plates. If necessary, boil the sauce rapidly until a creamy consistency is obtained. Away from the heat, whisk in the butter little by little. Taste for seasoning, spoon the sauce over the asparagus tips and shellfish, and serve.

Wine

Pouilly-Fuissé.

Asparagus and Morels Meunière

Asperges et morilles meunière

For 4 people

150g *(5 oz)*	approx. fresh morels or 40g *(1½ oz)* dried morels
2 tbsps	wine vinegar
16	large asparagus, weighing about 900g *(2 lb)*
4 tbsps	butter
	salt, freshly ground pepper
6	shallots, finely chopped
4 tsps	lemon juice
1 tbsp	chives, finely chopped
1 tbsp	parsley, finely chopped
1 tbsp	chervil, finely chopped

Equipment

mixing bowl · kitchen string · large saucepan · large frying pan (preferably non-stick) · skimmer or slotted spoon
To serve: large heated serving dish

Preliminary preparations

If using fresh morels, cut off the earthy end and cut any large ones in half lengthwise. Place the morels in a large bowl of cold water, add the vinegar and soak for 3–4 minutes. Drain, rinse thoroughly two or three times in cold water and allow to drain completely on paper towels before cooking.

Dried morels should be soaked as described on their packet (generally about 30 minutes in warm water). If necessary, cut off the base of the stems and drain the morels on a towel.

Break off 5–8cm *(2–3 in)* from the bottom of each asparagus. Peel the asparagus if necessary, being careful not to damage the tips. Tie them in 2 or 3 bunches, grading them according to thickness.

To cook and serve the asparagus and morels

Drop the asparagus into a large pan of boiling salted water. When the water comes back to the boil, cook them for 7 minutes, then remove the thin asparagus and continue cooking the thicker ones for 3–4 minutes more. Lift them carefully out of the water, untie them and drain them on a towel. Cut each asparagus in half crosswise.

Heat a tablespoon of butter in a large (preferably non-stick) frying pan. Add the asparagus and cook over a moderate heat for about 4 minutes, shaking the pan to brown them lightly on all sides. Season with salt and pepper, remove them with a skimmer or slotted spoon and keep them hot on the serving dish while cooking the morels.

Add another tablespoon of butter to the frying pan; when hot, add the morels, salt and pepper. Cook over a moderate heat, covered, for 6–10 minutes or until tender, shaking the pan occasionally. Remove the morels from the pan with the slotted spoon and place them on the platter with the asparagus.

Melt the remaining 2 tablespoons of butter in the same pan, add the shallots, salt and pepper, and cook for 2–3 minutes or until tender and transparent, but not brown.

Sprinkle the asparagus and mushrooms with the lemon juice, the butter and shallots, and finally with the chopped herbs, and serve immediately.

Suggestions

Try fresh chanterelles or any other fresh wild mushroom instead of morels – even ordinary mushrooms may be used.

The herbs may be added to the butter and cooked shallots in the pan. Stir them round once or twice, then sprinkle them over the asparagus and mushrooms.

Wine

Château Chalon or Château Grillet.

Chicken Liver Mousse with Bacon and Cream Sauce

Gâteaux de foies de volaille à la crème de bacon

For 4 people

For the mousse

250g *(9 oz)*	chicken livers
4	shallots, finely chopped
3	eggs
475ml *(16 fl. oz)*	double cream or *crème fraîche* (see p. 290)
4	generous tbsps parsley, chopped
I tsp	salt
	a pinch of freshly ground pepper

For the sauce

150g *(5 oz)*	smoked streaky bacon, finely diced
I	shallot, finely chopped
2 tbsps	red wine vinegar
250ml *(9 fl. oz)*	whipping cream
	freshly ground pepper
I tsp	butter (for the parsley)
2	sprigs of flat parsley, stalks removed
I	generous tsp Dijon mustard

For the tomato garnish

I tsp	butter
I	shallot, finely chopped
2	medium tomatoes, peeled, seeded and cut into dice
	salt, freshly ground pepper

Equipment

roasting tin · 4 ramekins, 8cm *(3 in)* across · food processor or heavy-duty liquidiser · large frying pan · small frying pan · slotted spoon
To serve: 4 heated plates and a sauceboat

Preliminary preparations

Pre-heat the oven to 425°F/220°C/Reg. 7.

Pour water into a roasting tin to a depth of 1½cm *(½ in)* and place the tin in the oven. Lightly butter each ramekin.

The mousse

Trim the chicken livers, removing strings and greenish parts, which are bitter.

Purée the chicken livers, shallots, eggs, cream and chopped parsley in a food processor or liquidiser until smooth. Season with salt and pepper and pour the mixture into the ramekins. Place in the roasting tin, put into the oven and immediately lower the heat to 350°F/180°C/Reg. 4. Bake for 10 minutes, reset the oven to 425°F/220°C/Reg. 7 and bake for 30 minutes.

The sauce

Heat the chopped bacon and shallots in a frying pan over a moderate heat until the bacon fat runs out, stirring frequently. Cook until the shallots are soft and transparent. Add the vinegar, stirring constantly, and simmer until it has completely evaporated, then stir in the whipping cream and plenty of pepper (no salt is needed because of the bacon). Lower the heat and simmer the sauce for 10 minutes, cover, and keep hot over a very low heat.

Melt a teaspoon of butter in a small frying pan, add the parsley leaves and simmer slowly for 2 minutes. Remove the parsley leaves and reserve.

The tomato garnish

In the same small frying pan, melt another teaspoon of butter and add the shallots. Simmer until soft and transparent, then add the tomato. Season with a little salt and pepper, then simmer for 4–5 minutes, stirring occasionally.

To finish the mousse and serve the sauce

Just before the mousse is done, taste the sauce for seasoning. Stir in the mustard and strain the sauce into a sauceboat, stirring so that all the liquid goes through. Stir in the cooked parsley.

See if the mousses are cooked by inserting the blade of a knife into one; if it comes out clean, the mousse is done – if not, cook for 5–10 minutes longer and test again. Remove the ramekins from the roasting tin and turn out each one on to a plate (if necessary, run the blade of a knife around the inside of the ramekin). Garnish each plate with a little tomato, pour a little of the sauce over each mousse and serve immediately, with the remaining sauce in a sauceboat.

Suggestions

Individual soufflé dishes of the same capacity may be used instead of ramekins, or a large soufflé dish or earthenware baking dish may be used instead of individual dishes. Cooking times will be longer; be sure to test before serving.

Calf's liver may be used instead of chicken livers.

The mousse can also be served cold, with a cold tomato sauce flavoured with finely chopped fresh herbs, and a green salad. It can also be spread on little rounds of hot toast and served with drinks.

Wine

A young Graves, chilled – perhaps Givry.

Stuffed Turnips
Navets farcis

For 4 people

4	large turnips, weighing 700g *(1½ lb)* as round and regular as possible
450g *(1 lb)*	duck breast or legs or 350g *(¾ lb)* boneless breast meat
1	shallot, finely chopped
2 tsps	parsley, finely chopped
2 tsps	chives, finely chopped
2 tsps	chervil, finely chopped
	salt, freshly ground pepper
	a pinch of thyme
750ml *(1¼ pints)*	dry cider (1 large bottle)
1 tbsp	butter
175ml *(6 fl. oz)*	double cream or *crème fraîche* (see p. 290)

Equipment
melon baller · large pan · slotted spoon · liquidiser or *mouli-légumes* · 2 mixing bowls · large frying pan · wire whisk · large oven dish
To serve: 4 heated plates

The turnips
Peel, wash and dry the turnips. Slice a little off the bases so that they will stand upright. Use a melon baller to hollow out each turnip, forming a round cup with walls and a bottom a little more than 3mm *(⅛ in)* thick. Reserve the flesh.

Bring a large pan of lightly salted water to a boil, drop in the turnips and cook for 3 minutes. Remove with a slotted spoon and drain on a cloth or on paper towels. Drop the turnip flesh into the same water, cook for 10 minutes, drain, purée in a liquidiser or *mouli-légumes* and reserve in a mixing bowl.

The stuffing
Bone the duck and remove all the skin and fat. Chop the meat coarsely and place it in a bowl with the shallot, herbs, salt, pepper and a pinch of thyme (the stuffing can take a lot of salt and pepper). Mix well, then form the stuffing into 4 little balls and reserve.

To cook and stuff the turnips
Heat the cider in a large pan and boil for 20 minutes or until reduced by half. Reserve.

Heat 2 teaspoons of butter in a large frying pan. Add the hollowed-out turnips and fry them over a moderate heat, browning them on all sides for 5 minutes. Remove and drain on a cloth.

Heat the reduced cider until boiling, add the turnips and boil gently for 10–12 minutes to finish cooking. Lift the turnips out and drain on a cloth. Measure the remaining cider – there should be 100ml *(4 fl. oz)* left; if not, boil to reduce to this amount – remove from the heat and reserve.

Add 1 teaspoon of butter to the pan used to brown the turnips and brown the 4 balls of stuffing in it, turning them frequently until they are brown on all sides (about 5 minutes). Drain the stuffing on a cloth, then carefully stuff each turnip with one of the balls of stuffing.

To finish and make the sauce and serve the turnips
Pre-heat the oven to 425°F/220°C/Reg. 7.

Whisk the cider and cream into the reserved turnip purée. Pour this sauce into an oven dish, place the stuffed turnips in the dish and heat to just below boiling point. Place in the oven and bake for 9 minutes.

Carefully lift out each turnip and place it on a plate. Whisk the sauce, add salt and pepper if needed, and spoon it over and round the turnips. Serve immediately.

Suggestions
A less refined version of this dish can be made using sausage meat or chicken livers instead of duck – or you could even use cold roast duck or other meat to which you could add some chopped mushrooms and a little cream.

Wine
A dry or sweet farm-made cider, well chilled, is better than wine with these turnips.

Fish
and
Shellfish

Salad of Sea Bream with Spinach, Sweetcorn and Tomatoes

Filets de dorade sur lit d'épinards, maïs et tomates

For 4 people

1	sea bream, weighing 1¼kg *(2¾ lb)* (see Suggestions)
450g *(1 lb)*	fresh spinach, stems and ribs removed
2	medium tomatoes, peeled, seeded and diced
100g *(4-oz)*	tin sweetcorn, drained
1 tsp	melted butter
150ml *(¼ pint)*	dry white wine
6 tbsps	olive oil
2 tbsps	sherry vinegar
	salt, freshly ground pepper

Equipment

filleting knife · pastry brush · oval or rectangular oven dish, 33–35cm *(13–14 in)* long · spatula   *To serve:* 4 plates

Preliminary preparations

Ask the fishmonger to scale and fillet the fish, but to leave the skin on. If he removes each side of the fish in one piece, ask him to cut each one in half lengthwise so that there will be 4 fillets.

Pre-heat the oven to 425°F/220°C/Reg. 7.

Cut the spinach leaves into thin strips with a large knife and reserve in a salad bowl with the tomatoes and sweetcorn.

The fish

Brush the oven dish with the melted butter. Season the fish fillets with salt and pepper, place them skin-side up in the oven dish, add the white wine and bake for 7 minutes.

To finish and serve the salad

While the fish is cooking, dress the spinach, sweetcorn and tomatoes with 5 tablespoons of olive oil and the sherry vinegar. Season generously, toss the salad and place some on each plate.

When the fillets are done, remove them with a spatula from the oven dish and place them on a clean cloth to drain. Remove the skin with a filleting knife and place each fillet on a bed of spinach. Pour a tiny amount of olive oil over each fillet (use only 1 tablespoon in all) and serve immediately.

Suggestions

Almost any fish can be used in making this recipe.

Watercress or a mixture of salads may be used instead of spinach, if desired. A little fennel, cut into small dice, may also be added to the salad with the sweetcorn and tomatoes.

The zest of half a lemon, blanched for 2 minutes then finely chopped, or a tablespoon of finely chopped fresh herbs may be added to the salad dressing.

Wine

A white Provençal or Côtes du Rhône, or a Loire wine – Quincy or Sancerre.

Brill with Endive Sauce
Barbue aux endives

For 4 people

For the endives

450g *(1 lb)*	Belgian endives
1 tbsp	butter
	salt, freshly ground pepper
	juice of half a lemon
	a large pinch of sugar

For the fish

1 tbsp	butter
5	shallots, finely chopped
100g *(4 oz)*	firm white mushrooms, finely chopped
	salt, freshly ground pepper
4	fillets of brill, weighing about 700g *(1½ lb)* altogether (from a 1.4kg *(3-lb)* fish)
6 tbsps	dry white wine
250ml *(9 fl. oz)*	double cream or *crème fraîche* (see p. 290)
2 tsps	Dijon mustard
2 tsps	softened butter

Equipment

medium saucepan, with lid · oval or rectangular oven dish, 33–35cm *(13–14 in)* long · spatula
To serve: heated serving dish and a sauceboat

The endives

Cut off the base of each endive, wipe clean (do not wash) and cut in half lengthwise. Cut out the central section near the base, separate the leaves and cut them into julienne strips.

Melt the butter in a saucepan, add the strips of endive and season with salt and pepper. Stir in the lemon juice and sugar, cover and simmer, stirring occasionally, for 10 minutes. Reserve.

The fish

Pre-heat the oven to 400°F/200°C/Reg. 6.

Melt the butter in an oven dish, add the shallots and mushrooms, season with salt and pepper, stir, then remove from the heat.

Season the brill fillets, lay them in the dish on top of the vegetables, skin-side down, add the white wine, place the dish back over a moderate heat and bring the wine to a boil. Cover the dish with aluminium foil and bake the fish for 5 minutes, remove the foil and bake for 5 minutes more.

To make the sauce and serve the fish

Remove the fish from the oven dish with a spatula and place the fillets on a serving dish. Cover with aluminium foil and keep warm.

Place the oven dish over a high heat and boil the cooking liquid until the dish is almost dry. If the fish gives out liquid during this time, add it to the oven dish.

Whisk the cream into the reduced liquid, bring to the boil and boil rapidly over a high heat for 4 minutes or until thick and creamy. Taste for seasoning, then strain the sauce into the saucepan with the endives, pressing on the shallots and mushrooms.

Heat the endives and the sauce over a moderate heat, stirring constantly. When the sauce is hot, but not boiling, remove from the heat and whisk in the mustard, then the butter, a teaspoon at a time. Taste for seasoning and add salt and pepper if necessary.

Coat the fish lightly with a little of the sauce and serve immediately, with the remaining sauce in a sauceboat.

Suggestions

Virtually any fish can be used to make this recipe: turbot, sole or any other flatfish, as well as whiting, sea bass, salmon, etc.

The zest of a lemon or half an orange, cut into julienne strips and parboiled, may be used instead of mustard.

Beer may be used instead of white wine. In this case, serve beer with the fish as well.

Wine

A white Condrieu or Coteaux du Layon.

Sea Bass with Courgettes

Bar aux courgettes

For 4 people

For the fish

1.4kg *(3 lb)*	sea bass
1 tbsp	butter
3	shallots, finely chopped
3	medium, firm white mushrooms, coarsely chopped
	salt, freshly ground pepper
175ml *(6 fl. oz)*	dry white wine
3 tbsps	water
2 tsps	thyme leaves
250ml *(9 fl. oz)*	whipping cream

For the courgettes

2 tbsps	olive oil
450g *(1 lb)*	courgettes, cut into julienne strips (do not peel)
	salt, freshly ground pepper
	a handful of thyme flowers
1 tbsp	butter (to finish the sauce)

Equipment

oval or rectangular cast-iron oven dish, 33–35cm *(13–14 in)* long ·
spatula · sieve · saucepan · frying pan · wire whisk
To serve: serving dish

The fish and the sauce

Ask the fishmonger to scale the fish, dividing it into 4 fillets, but leave the skin on the fillets.

Melt the butter in the oven dish, add the shallots and mushrooms, season with salt and pepper and simmer for 5 minutes, stirring occasionally.

Pre-heat the oven to 425°F/220°C/Reg. 7.

Season the fish fillets with salt and pepper, then place them skin-side up on the bed of vegetables; add the wine, water and a little thyme. Cover with aluminium foil and bake in the oven for 6–10 minutes.

Remove the fish from the oven dish with a spatula, drain on a clean cloth, lift off the skin with a knife and place the fillets on a serving dish. Keep warm.

Place the oven dish over a high heat, stir in the cream and boil rapidly for 6–8 minutes or until thick and creamy. Strain into a saucepan, pressing on the shallots and mushrooms with the back of a wooden spoon.

The courgettes

While the cream is reducing, heat the olive oil in a frying pan until very hot and add the strips of courgette, salt and pepper. Sauté, stirring constantly, for 3–4 minutes, then sprinkle with thyme and sauté for 1–2 minutes more. The courgettes should just begin to brown.

To finish and serve the fish

Heat the sauce, if necessary, then whisk in a tablespoon of butter. Taste for salt and pepper, spoon the sauce over the fish, sprinkle the strips of courgette on top and serve immediately.

Suggestions

Any fish fillets may be prepared in this way.

As an alternative, 450g (1 lb) of green or red peppers, mushrooms, carrots or spinach may be cut into julienne strips and prepared as described for the courgettes.

Wine

A white Châteauneuf-du-Pape – Domaine de Beaucastel, champagne or a dry Graves.

Salmon with Caviare
Saumon au caviar

For 4 people

700g (1½ lb)	fresh salmon tail, in one piece
	zest of 1 small lemon, finely chopped
	salt, freshly ground pepper
1 tbsp	butter
5	shallots, finely chopped
3	medium, firm white mushrooms, finely chopped
150ml (¼ pint)	dry white wine
100ml (4 fl. oz)	water
250ml (9 fl. oz)	whipping cream or thin *crème fraîche* (see p.290)
3 tbsps (40g (1¾ oz))	caviare (see Suggestion)

Equipment

filleting knife · small saucepan · oval or rectangular oven dish 33–35cm (13–14 in) long · spatula · wire whisk
To serve: Serving dish or 4 heated plates

Preliminary preparations

Using a filleting knife, cut the salmon from the bone into 2 fillets, but leave the skin and scales on. Remove any small bones left in the flesh.

Pre-heat the oven to 425°F/220°C/Reg. 7.

Place the chopped lemon zest in a small saucepan, cover with cold water and bring to the boil. Boil for 1 minute, drain, cool under running water and drain again. Return the zest to the dry saucepan and reserve.

The salmon

Season the salmon fillets with salt and pepper.

Melt the butter over a low heat in an oven dish. Add the shallots and soften for about 6 minutes or until tender, add the mushrooms and cook gently for another 3 minutes.

Place the fillets skin-side down on top of the shallots and mushrooms, add the wine and water and cook in the oven for 8 minutes.

To make the sauce and serve the salmon

Remove the fish from the oven dish with a spatula and place it on a clean cloth for a few seconds to drain. Carefully remove the skin with a filleting knife, then either place the fillets on a serving dish or cut each one in half and place a piece on each plate. Keep warm while making the sauce.

Place the oven dish over a high heat and boil the cooking liquid until the dish is nearly dry. Whisk in the cream, mixing in any juices caramelised on the bottom of the dish and boil rapidly for 2–3 minutes or until thick and creamy. Taste for seasoning, then strain into the saucepan containing the lemon peel, pressing the vegetables. Make sure the sauce is very hot, but do not allow to boil.

Pour the sauce lightly over the salmon fillets, sprinkle some of the caviare over each one and serve immediately.

Suggestions

Broccoli or steamed potatoes, dressed with a little butter, are excellent with this dish. Or the salmon fillets can be served on a layer of buttered spinach.

The caviare may be replaced by lumpfish or salmon roe, or by a few finely diced vegetables (carrots, turnips, celery, green beans, for example) cooked for about 3 minutes in boiling salted water.

Wine

A good white Burgundy – Bâtard-Montrachet or Aloxe-Corton.

Sea Bass with Red Butter Sauce
Bar au beurre rouge au Bouzy

For 4 people

For the beurre rouge

1 tbsp	butter
2	shallots, finely chopped
	salt, freshly ground pepper
½	bottle red wine (if possible use Bouzy)
1 tbsp	water
150g *(5 oz)*	butter, at room temperature, cut into cubes

For the fish

20g *(1 oz)*	butter
1	shallot, finely chopped
	salt, freshly ground pepper
700g *(1½ lb)*	fillets of sea bass from a 1.4kg *(3-lb)* fish
6 tbsps	red wine

Equipment
saucepan · oval or rectangular oven dish, 33–35cm *(13–14 in)* long ·
wire whisk · spatula
To serve: 4 heated plates or a heated serving dish

The reduction for the sauce
Melt 1 tablespoon of butter in a saucepan, add the shallots and simmer
gently, stirring occasionally, for 2–3 minutes or until soft and transparent.

Sprinkle the shallots with salt and pepper, add the red wine and cook,
uncovered, at a moderate boil for 30–45 minutes or until all but about a
tablespoon of wine has evaporated.

The fish
Pre-heat the oven to 425°F/220°C/Reg. 7.

Melt the butter in the oven dish over a moderate heat, add the shallot,
season lightly and simmer, stirring occasionally, until soft and transparent.

Season the fish fillets with salt and pepper, place them on the bed of
shallots, skin-side down, add the wine, cover with aluminium foil and
bake for 10 minutes, or until just cooked through.

To finish and serve the fish
Add 1 tablespoon of cold water to the saucepan with the shallots, then
whisk in the butter as described in the recipe for Hot Fish Terrine (see
p.71). Taste for salt and pepper.

Carefully lift the fish fillets out of the oven dish with a spatula and drain for a few seconds. Place them on the plates or serving dish, spoon the sauce over them and serve.

Suggestions

Any fish with firm white flesh may be used for this recipe; sole is especially good.

White wine may be used instead of red wine. In this case, a few chopped herbs, or a little curry or paprika may be added with the wine to the sauce reduction.

The reduction may also be made with 3 tablespoons of Ricard, Pernod or ouzo, for example, instead of wine.

The bass may be served with a julienne of vegetables, cooked separately (see p.98) and added to the sauce at the end, or with a julienne of spinach (see p.112).

Wine

Obviously if you have used Bouzy for the sauce you should serve Bouzy; with a white wine sauce serve white wine.

Salmon with Leek Sauce
Saumon aux poireaux

	For 4 people
700g *(1½ lb)*	fresh salmon tail
	For the leeks
1½ tbsps	butter
3	medium leeks, weighing 450g *(1 lb)*, white part only, cut into julienne strips (see Suggestions)
	salt, freshly ground pepper
100ml *(4 fl. oz)*	water
	For the fish
	salt, freshly ground pepper
250ml *(9 fl. oz)*	dry white wine
	For the sauce
2	shallots, finely chopped
175ml *(6 fl. oz)*	dry white wine
3 tbsps	white wine vinegar
225g *(½ lb)*	butter, at room temperature, cut into cubes
	salt, freshly ground pepper

Equipment

medium deep frying pan or *sauteuse*, with lid · oven dish · spatula ·
filleting knife · bowl · small saucepan · wire whisk
To serve: 4 heated plates

Preliminary preparations

Ask the fishmonger to scale and cut the salmon into 2 deep fillets, leaving
the skin on the fillets.

Pre-heat the oven to 425°F/220°C/Reg. 7.

The leeks

Melt the butter over a moderate heat in a deep frying pan or *sauteuse*.
Add the leeks, season lightly and cook gently for 3 minutes without
allowing to brown. Add the water, cover and simmer for 20 minutes more;
the water should have evaporated completely. Reserve.

The salmon

Lightly butter an oven dish and sprinkle it with salt and pepper. Place the
salmon fillets in the dish skin-side down, season with salt and pepper,
add the white wine and cook in the oven for 7–12 minutes, until just
done.

Using a spatula, lift the salmon fillets carefully out of the oven dish and
place them skin-side up on a clean cloth to drain for a few seconds.
Remove the skin with a filleting knife, then place the fillets on a plate,
cover with aluminium foil and keep warm while making the sauce.

Strain the salmon cooking liquid into a bowl and reserve.

The sauce

Make a *beurre blanc* as described in the recipe for Hot Fish Terrine (see
p.71), using the measurements listed here. When all the butter has been
added, strain the sauce, taste for seasoning and whisk in the reserved
salmon cooking liquid.

To serve the salmon

Place the leeks over a low heat until just warmed through, then pour the
sauce over them, stirring constantly. Remove from the heat, taste for
seasoning and stir gently (the pan should be on the heat just long
enough to warm the sauce).

Cut each salmon fillet in half and place a piece on each of the plates.
Cover lightly with the sauce and serve immediately.

Suggestions

The leeks can be replaced by broccoli, a julienne of fennel, concasséed tomatoes, or by a julienne of green or red peppers. Broccoli, fennel or peppers should be prepared exactly as described for the leeks. Tomatoes should be prepared as for Turbot Fillets with Tomato (see p.113).

Instead of making a *beurre blanc* and mixing it with the leeks, the leek sauce can be made as follows. Cook the leeks with the butter as described, then, instead of adding water, add 275ml *(½ pint)* of whipping cream, cover and simmer for 20 minutes. At the end of this time, the cream should have reduced to a creamy consistency. If it has not, remove the lid and boil gently until a creamy consistency is obtained. Taste for seasoning, spoon the sauce over the fish and serve.

Wine

A white Burgundy, such as Meursault. If you are using fennel instead of leeks, a white Côtes du Rhône would be preferable.

Fillets of Turbot with Carrots and Parsley
Suprême de turbot à la carotte et au persil

For 4 people

For the carrot and parsley colourings

8	medium carrots, peeled and sliced
850ml *(1½ pints)*	water
2	bunches of parsley, stalks removed

For the garnish

1 tbsp	butter
4	medium carrots, cut into julienne strips
	salt, freshly ground pepper
1	bunch of flat parsley, stalks removed

For the fish

4	fillets of turbot, weighing about 700g *(1½ lb)* (from a 1.4kg *(3-lb)* fish) (see Suggestions and Note)
	salt, freshly ground pepper
1 tbsp	butter
7	shallots, finely chopped
4	medium, firm white mushrooms, chopped
250ml *(9 fl. oz)*	dry white wine
350ml *(12 fl. oz)*	whipping cream
2 tsps	softened butter

Equipment

food processor or liquidiser · 2 saucepans · 2 clean cloths · fine
sieve · 2 small bowls · large frying pan · oval or rectangular oven dish
40cm *(16 in)* long · spatula · small saucepan · wire whisk
To serve: heated serving dish and a sauceboat

The carrot and parsley colourings

Place the sliced carrots in a food processor or liquidiser with 250ml
(8 fl. oz) of the water and grind to a pulp. Add another 250ml *(8 fl. oz)* of
water and blend.

Line a saucepan with a clean cloth and pour the contents of the
processor into it. Twist the ends of the cloth together as hard as possible
to squeeze out all the liquid. Discard the solids in the cloth.

Bring the carrot juice to a boil; a thick foam will rise to the surface. Boil
gently for 45 seconds, then strain the juice through a very fine sieve. With
a spoon, scoop everything out of the sieve and place it in a small bowl;
this is the carrot colouring. If you haven't a fine enough sieve, use a cloth.

Rinse out the cloth used for the carrots and line the rinsed saucepan with
it. Make the parsley colouring as described for the carrot colouring (use
only 250ml *(8 fl. oz)* water in total) and put it into a separate bowl.

The vegetable garnish

Melt a tablespoon of butter in a large frying pan and add the julienne of
carrots. Season, stir and cook over a moderate heat, stirring occasionally.
The carrots should become shiny and very lightly browned. Reserve.

Bring a saucepan of water to the boil and add the parsley leaves. Boil for
1 minute, drain, cool under running water and drain again. Place the
parsley leaves in a small saucepan and reserve.

The fish

Pre-heat the oven to 425°F/220°C/Reg. 7. Season the fish on both sides
with salt and pepper.

Melt a tablespoon of butter in an oven dish, add the shallots and simmer
until soft and transparent. Add the mushrooms, salt and pepper, stir
together and simmer, stirring occasionally, for 2 minutes more. Place the
fillets of turbot on top of the vegetables, add the white wine, bring to the
boil, cover with aluminium foil and bake for 6 minutes or until just done.

When the fish is done, lift the fillets out of the dish with a spatula, drain
on a clean cloth, place them on a serving dish, cover with foil and keep
warm while making the sauce.

To make the sauce and serve

Place the oven dish over a high heat and boil the cooking liquid rapidly,
until it has almost completely evaporated. Stir in the cream and boil
rapidly for a further 4 minutes or until thick and creamy.

Strain the sauce into a saucepan, pressing on the vegetables to extract all their liquids. Taste for seasoning.

Add 2 tablespoons of the sauce to the parsley leaves and reheat them over a low heat. Add salt and pepper if necessary. Reheat the carrots.

Whisk the carrot and parsley colourings into the sauce – it will be speckled with orange and green flecks. Heat gently for about 2 minutes, whisking occasionally until the sauce is hot (do not boil). Away from the heat, whisk in the butter, a teaspoon at a time, then pour into a sauceboat.

Place little mounds of glazed carrots and fresh parsley around the fish, alternating them, and serve immediately, with the sauce in a sauceboat.

Suggestions
Sea bass may be used instead of turbot, and the parsley may be replaced by an equal quantity of watercress leaves.

Note
An equal weight of fillets of sole or halibut, or other fish with firm white flesh, may also be used.

Wine
A white Burgundy – Meursault would be perfect. Or for lovers of a really full sweet wine, a white wine from the Bordeaux region – Loupiac, Barsac or Sainte-Croix-du-Mont.

Turbot with Five Vegetables
Turbot aux cinq légumes

For 4 people

For the vegetables

100g (¼ lb)	very thin French beans, cut into 5cm (2-in) pieces
1 tbsp	butter
2	medium carrots, cut into julienne strips
325ml (11 fl. oz)	water
1 tsp	curry powder
1	small courgette, unpeeled, cut into julienne strips
	a piece of cucumber, 10cm (4 in) in length, peeled, seeded and cut into julienne strips
100g (4 oz)	large, firm white mushrooms, cut into julienne strips, stalks chopped
	salt, freshly ground pepper

For the fish

1 tbsp	butter
5	shallots, finely chopped
2	fillets of turbot, weighing about 700g *(1½ lb)* altogether
325ml *(11 fl. oz)*	white wine
300ml *(½ pint)*	whipping cream
	salt, freshly ground pepper

Equipment

medium saucepan · *sauteuse* or deep frying pan, 24cm *(9½ in)* in diameter · oval or rectangular oven dish, 33–35cm *(13–14 in)* long · spatula · clean cloth · wire whisk · slotted spoon
To serve: heated serving dish

The vegetables

Cook the French beans in well-salted water for 6 minutes, drain, cool under running water, drain again and reserve.

In a *sauteuse* or deep frying pan, melt the butter, add the carrots, stir for a few seconds and add the water and curry powder. Stir again and boil, uncovered, for 7 minutes. Add the courgette and cucumber and cook for 1 minute longer, add the julienne of mushrooms and cook for 1 minute more. Add the beans, season with salt and pepper, stir all the vegetables together, then remove the pan from the heat. Reserve.

The fish

Pre-heat the oven to 425°F/220°C/Reg. 7.

Melt the butter in the oven dish over a moderate heat, add the shallots and simmer until soft and transparent. Add the chopped mushroom stalks, salt and pepper and cook, stirring occasionally, for 1 minute.

Season the turbot fillets, lay them on top of the vegetables, add the white wine, bring the liquid to the boil, cover with aluminium foil and bake for 6–10 minutes or until just cooked.

When the fish is cooked, lift the fillets out of the oven dish with a spatula and drain on a clean cloth. Place on a serving dish, cover with aluminium foil and keep hot.

To make the sauce and serve the fish

Place the oven dish over a high heat, boil rapidly until the liquid is reduced to about 2 tablespoons, then whisk in the cream. Bring back to the boil and boil for 2–3 minutes or until beginning to thicken and turn velvety.

Heat the vegetables over a low heat, then strain the sauce over them, pressing on the shallots and mushrooms with a wooden spoon. Stir and taste the sauce for seasoning. Lift the vegetables out of the sauce with a slotted spoon, arrange them around the fish, then pour some of the sauce lightly over the top and serve immediately.

Suggestions
Almost any fish may be used in making this dish, particularly John Dory or brill, but if using fish other than flatfish (such as salmon, sea bass, etc.), allow a little longer for it to cook.

Wine
A white Côtes du Rhône or a white Burgundy such as Puligny-Montrachet or Pouilly-Fuissé. Or champagne.

Turbot with Wild Mushrooms
Turbot aux cinq champignons

For 4 people

For the mushrooms

350g *(12 oz)*	wild mushrooms (ideally, use equal amounts of chanterelles, morels, mousserons-millers, horn-of-plenty and ceps (boletus mushrooms); see Suggestion and Note)
2 tsps	butter
	salt, freshly ground pepper

For the fish

4	fillets of turbot, weighing about 700g *(1½ lb)* (from a 1.4kg *(3-lb)* fish)
2 tsps	butter
2	shallots, finely chopped
2	large mushrooms, chopped
175ml *(6 fl. oz)*	dry white wine
350ml *(12 fl. oz)*	whipping cream
	salt, freshly ground pepper

Equipment
frying pan · oval or rectangular oven dish, 33–35cm *(13–14 in)* long · spatula · wire whisk
To serve: heated serving dish

The mushrooms

Cut off the sandy base of each mushroom stem and carefully wash, drain and dry the mushrooms. Slice any large ceps but leave other mushrooms whole.

In a frying pan, melt the butter over a moderate heat. When it is very hot, add the mushrooms, stir and sprinkle with salt and pepper. Sauté lightly for 2–3 minutes, until slightly browned, stirring frequently. Lower the heat and cook very slowly, uncovered, for 8 minutes more, stirring occasionally. Reserve.

The fish

Pre-heat the oven to 425°F/220°C/Reg. 7. Sprinkle the fish fillets with salt and pepper.

Melt the butter in the oven dish, add the chopped shallots and mushrooms, salt and pepper, and simmer for 3 minutes, stirring occasionally; do not allow to brown.

Place the fish on the bed of vegetables, add the wine, bring to the boil, cover with aluminium foil and bake for 6 minutes or until just cooked.

To make the sauce and serve the fish

When the fish is done, lift it out of the oven dish with a spatula, drain it on a clean cloth for a few seconds, place it on a serving dish, cover it with aluminium foil and keep it warm.

Place the oven dish over a high heat and boil the cooking liquid until the dish is nearly dry. Add the cream and reduce for about 3 minutes or until thick and creamy.

Place the wild mushrooms over a low heat to warm through. When hot, strain the sauce over them, stir together and taste for salt and pepper.

Remove the turbot from the oven, arrange the mushrooms round and over the fillets, coat lightly with the sauce and serve immediately.

Suggestion

Dried wild mushrooms may be used instead of fresh ones. In this case, use a small handful of each kind of dried mushroom. Allow to soak for about 20 minutes in warm water (or follow the directions on the packet) before cleaning and using them as you would fresh ones.

Note

Any kind of wild mushrooms may be used – and if only one kind is available, either fresh or dried, use it. Using ordinary mushrooms would completely change the character of the dish.

Note

A white Burgundy; choose a good wine for this dish.

Brill with Dry Cider and Asparagus

Barbue au cidre sec et aux pointes d'asperges

For 4 people

20	medium sticks of asparagus, weighing about 900g *(2 lb)*
1½ litres *(2½ pints)*	water
1½ tsps	coarse salt
4	fillets of brill, weighing about 700g *(1½ lb)* (from a 1.4kg *(3-lb)* fish)
2 tsps	butter
3	shallots, finely chopped
2	firm white mushrooms, finely chopped
175ml *(6 fl. oz)*	dry cider
350ml *(12 fl. oz)*	whipping cream or thin *crème fraîche* (see p.290)
	salt, freshly ground pepper

Equipment

saucepan · skimmer or slotted spoon · oval oven dish, about 40cm *(16 in)* long · spatula
To serve: heated serving dish

The asparagus

Cut off the tough, stringy ends of the asparagus; the remaining asparagus should be about 10cm *(4 in)* long. Peel them if necessary, rinse under running water and drain.

Bring the water and coarse salt to a boil in a saucepan, throw in the asparagus and boil for 5 minutes or until tender. Lift the asparagus out of the pan with a skimmer or a slotted spoon to avoid damaging the tips, drain on a cloth and reserve.

The fish

Pre-heat the oven to 425°F/220°C/Reg. 7. Season the fish fillets on both sides.

Melt the butter in an oven dish, add the shallots and simmer, stirring frequently, until soft and transparent. Stir in the mushrooms, lay the fish on the bed of vegetables, add the cider, bring to the boil, cover with aluminium foil and bake for 8 minutes or until the fillets are just cooked.

To make the sauce and serve the fish

When the fish fillets are cooked, lift them out of the oven dish with a spatula and drain on a cloth. Place on a serving dish, cover with aluminium foil and keep warm.

Place the oven dish over a high heat and boil rapidly until there are about 2 tablespoons of liquid left. Stir in the cream, add salt and pepper, and boil for 4 minutes more or until thick and creamy, whisking from time to time.

Strain the sauce into a saucepan, pressing on the vegetables, taste for seasoning, add the asparagus and heat for about 2 minutes, without boiling, to warm the asparagus.

Arrange the asparagus on top of the fish, spoon the sauce delicately over it and serve immediately.

Suggestion
Any firm white fish can be used for this dish.

Wine
Dry cider instead of wine, or a dry white Loire wine such as Sancerre.

Turbot with Curry Sauce and Spinach
Turbot aux épinards et au cari

For 4 people

2 tsps	butter (for the spinach)
700g *(1½ lb)*	fresh young spinach, well washed (see Note and Suggestions)
1 tbsp	butter (for the fish)
6	shallots, finely chopped
3	medium, firm white mushrooms, finely chopped salt, freshly ground pepper
1 tsp	mild curry powder
2	fillets of turbot, weighing about 700g *(1½ lb)* together (from a 1.4kg *(3-lb)* fish)
100ml *(4 fl. oz)*	dry white wine
375ml *(13 fl. oz)*	whipping cream
2 tsps	softened butter (for the sauce)

Equipment
large pan · oval or rectangular oven dish, 33–35cm *(13–14 in)* long · spatula · small saucepan · wire whisk
To serve: heated serving dish and a sauceboat

The spinach

Melt the butter in a large pan. Add the well-drained spinach, stirring until it has melted, season with salt and pepper and cook over a low heat, uncovered, for 4 minutes, stirring occasionally.

The fish

Pre-heat the oven to 425°F/220°C/Reg. 7.

Melt the butter for the fish in an oven dish and add the shallots. Stir for a few seconds, add the mushrooms and season with salt, pepper and curry powder. Stir, then simmer for 3 minutes.

Season the fillets of turbot, place them on the bed of vegetables and add the wine. Bring the liquid to the boil, cover with aluminium foil and bake for 6 minutes or until just cooked.

When the fillets are done, lift them out of the oven dish with a spatula and place on a cloth for a few seconds to drain.

Place the spinach on a serving dish, arrange the fillets on top, cover with foil and keep warm in the oven with the door ajar while making the sauce.

To make the sauce and serve the fish

Place the oven dish over a high heat and boil the cooking liquid rapidly until the dish is nearly dry. Add the cream and boil for 3–4 minutes or until thick and creamy.

Strain the sauce into a small saucepan, taste for seasoning and bring back to the boil. Remove from the heat and whisk in the butter, a teaspoon at a time.

Remove the fish from the oven, spoon a little of the sauce over it and serve immediately, with the rest of the sauce in a sauceboat.

Suggestions

Instead of the spinach, 4 bunches of watercress, or the outside leaves of lettuce, may be used in making this recipe (prepare exactly as described for the spinach); or cucumber balls, blanched for 5 minutes in salted water, may be added to the sauce instead of the spinach.

Note

Older spinach, with large, very dark green leaves, should be parboiled in unsalted water for 2 minutes, drained, cooled under cold running water and squeezed dry before preparing as described.

Wine

A white Côtes du Rhône or Provençal wine – Palette or Condrieu.

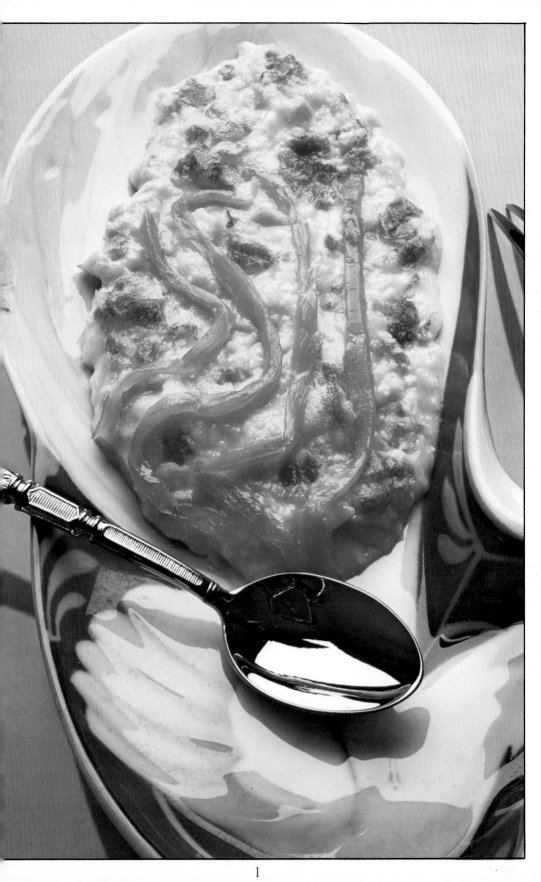

Turbot Fillets with Tomato
Suprême de turbot à la tomate

For 4 people

For the tomatoes

I tbsp	butter
6	shallots, finely chopped
900g *(2 lb)*	tomatoes, peeled, seeded and coarsely chopped
	salt, freshly ground pepper

For the fish

I tbsp	butter
6	shallots, finely chopped
3	medium, firm white mushrooms, finely chopped
4	fillets of turbot, weighing about 700g *(1½ lb)*, (from a 1.4kg *(3-lb)* fish)
325ml *(11 fl. oz)*	dry white wine
350ml *(12 fl. oz)*	whipping cream
	salt, freshly ground pepper

Equipment

medium saucepan · *mouli-légumes* · oval or rectangular oven dish, 33–35cm *(13–14 in)* long · spatula · wire whisk · small saucepan
To serve: heated serving dish

The tomatoes

Melt the butter in a medium saucepan. Add the shallots, stir, and simmer for 2–3 minutes or until soft and transparent. Add the tomatoes, salt and pepper and cook over a low heat, uncovered, for 25 minutes, stirring occasionally.

Purée half the tomato mixture in a *mouli-légumes*. Reserve separate from the rest of the tomatoes (which are still in pieces).

The fish

Pre-heat the oven to 425°F/220°C/Reg. 7. Season the fillets of turbot with salt and pepper.

Melt the butter in an oven dish, add the shallots and cook gently until soft, then add the mushrooms, season, stir and spread the mixture over the bottom of the dish. Lay the fillets on top, add the wine, cover the dish with aluminium foil and bake for 7 minutes or until just cooked.

To make the sauce and serve the fish

When the fillets are done, remove them from the oven dish with a spatula and place on a cloth to drain for a few seconds. Place them on a serving dish, cover with foil and keep warm in the oven with the door ajar while making the sauce.

Place the oven dish over a moderate heat and boil the cooking liquid until it has almost completely evaporated. Add the cream, then boil rapidly for 2–3 minutes or until thick and creamy, whisking the sauce lightly. Strain it into a small saucepan, pressing on the shallots and mushrooms with a wooden spoon. Add the tomato purée, stir together gently, taste for salt and pepper, and heat without allowing to boil.

Reheat the pieces of tomato. Remove the fish from the oven, pour the sauce over and around it and place some of the tomato on each fillet. Serve immediately.

Suggestions

A mixture of chopped fresh herbs (parsley, chervil, chives, tarragon) or freshly chopped basil may be added to the tomatoes. The dish can be made with all kinds of fish.

Wine

Château Grillet, Hermitage Blanc or Savennières.

Chicken Turbot with Grapes and Tea
Turbotin aux raisins et au thé

For 4 people

20	large or 40 small sweet white grapes
1 tbsp	butter (for the fish)
5	shallots, finely chopped
2	medium, firm white mushrooms, finely chopped
	salt, freshly ground pepper
4	fillets of young turbot, weighing about 700g *(1½ lb)* (from a 1.4kg *(3-lb)* fish)
150ml *(5 fl. oz)*	dry white wine
350ml *(12 fl. oz)*	whipping cream
3 level tsps	Ceylon tea
3 tsps	softened butter

Equipment

toothpick or small, pointed knife · oval or rectangular oven dish, 33–35cm *(13–14 in)* long · spatula · small saucepan · wire whisk
To serve: heated serving dish and a sauceboat

Preliminary preparations:
Pre-heat the oven to 425°F/220°C/Reg. 7.

Remove the seeds from each grape, using a toothpick or a small, pointed knife (see Note). Carefully skin each grape and reserve.

The fish
Melt the butter in an oven dish, add the shallots and cook for 1 minute over a moderate heat, stirring constantly. Add the mushrooms, season with salt and pepper, and cook for 1 minute more. Season the turbot fillets, place them on top of the vegetables, add the wine, bring the liquid to the boil, cover the dish with aluminium foil and bake for 6 minutes or until just cooked.

When the fillets are done, lift them out of the oven dish with a spatula and place them on a serving dish. Keep them hot in the oven with the door ajar while making the sauce.

To make the sauce and serve the fish
Place the oven dish over a moderate heat and reduce the cooking liquid for 2 minutes or until there are about 3 tablespoons left, then add the cream. Raise the heat and boil rapidly for 4–5 minutes or until the cream has thickened slightly, then stir in the tea. Lower the heat and allow to infuse for 1 minute, simmering gently, then strain the sauce into a small saucepan. Away from the heat, whisk in the butter a teaspoon at a time, then add the grapes. Taste for seasoning and heat the sauce for 1 minute over a low heat, stirring very gently.

Remove the fish from the oven and pour off any liquid it has given out. Spoon a little of the sauce over the fish and serve immediately, with the rest of the sauce in a sauceboat.

Suggestions
The flavour of the sauce can be varied by using different kinds of tea; you can even experiment with perfumed tea (Earl Grey, Jasmine and so on).

Other fish may be used instead of turbot, but it is preferable to use those with firm white flesh.

Note
Removing the seeds from the whole grapes is quite painstaking. To make it easier, the grapes may be peeled, then slit down one side, or cut in half, to remove the seeds.

Wine
Aloxe–Corton, Sauternes, champagne.

Monkfish with Leek, Coriander and Saffron Sauce

Lotte aux blancs de poireaux, sauce au coriandre frais et safran

For 4 people

1kg *(2¼ lb)*	monkfish, filleted and cut into 4 pieces (see Suggestions)
4	large leeks, white only, cut into 5cm *(2-in)* pieces
2	sprigs of fresh coriander, leaves only
	a pinch of saffron
	salt, freshly ground pepper
3 tsps	butter
2	shallots, finely chopped
2	firm white mushrooms, finely chopped
150ml *(¼ pint)*	dry white wine
350ml *(12 fl. oz)*	double cream or *crème fraîche* (see p. 290)

Equipment

large pan · medium saucepan · oval or rectangular oven dish, 33–35cm *(13–14 in)* long · spatula · skimmer or slotted spoon
To serve: 4 heated plates or a heated serving dish

Preliminary preparations

If the pieces of fish are very thick, flatten them slightly with the flat side of a cleaver.

Pre-heat the oven to 425°F/220°C/Reg. 7.

The leeks

Bring a large pan of water to the boil, add salt and simmer the leeks uncovered for 10 minutes, then drain. Place them in a saucepan with the coriander and saffron and reserve.

The fish

Season the fish with salt and pepper. Melt the butter in an oven dish, add the shallots and simmer for about 3–4 minutes or until soft and transparent. Stir in the mushrooms, place the pieces of fish on top and add the white wine. Bring to the boil, cover with aluminium foil, then bake for 6 minutes or until just cooked.

Remove the fish from the oven dish with a spatula and drain for a few seconds. Place on heated plates or in a deepish serving dish and keep hot while making the sauce.

116

To make the sauce and serve the fish

Reduce the liquid in the oven dish until there are only about 3 tablespoons. Whisk in the cream and boil rapidly for 2–3 minutes or until creamy.

Place the leeks over a moderate heat and strain the sauce over them, pressing on the shallots and mushrooms with a wooden spoon. Bring the sauce to the boil, stir and simmer for 3–4 minutes; season generously.

With a skimmer or slotted spoon, lift the leeks out of the saucepan and place round the fish, pour over the pale-golden sauce with its coriander and saffron, and serve.

Suggestions

Any fish with firm white flesh can be used instead of monkfish.

Instead of using leeks, cucumbers (peeled, seeded, cut into finger-sized pieces and boiled for 5 minutes) may be used, and mint and curry may be used to flavour the sauce instead of coriander and saffron.

Wine

A white Côtes du Rhône such as Condrieu, or a white Provençal wine.

Turbot with Broad Beans and Cabbage
Turbot aux fèves et au chou

For 4 people

1	fillet of turbot, weighing 800g *(1¾ lb)*
900g *(2 lb)*	fresh broad beans
8	cabbage leaves (preferably from a young green cabbage)
50g *(2 oz)*	softened butter
	salt, freshly ground pepper
2 tbsps	butter
3	shallots, finely chopped
2	medium mushrooms, finely chopped
150ml *(¼ pint)*	dry white wine
325ml *(11 fl. oz)*	whipping cream

Equipment

food processor or liquidiser · oval or rectangular oven dish, 33–35cm
(13–14 in) long · large pan · spatula · medium saucepan · wire
whisk · skimmer or slotted spoon
To serve: heated serving dish or 4 heated plates

Preliminary preparations

Ask the fishmonger to prepare the fillet for you, but to leave the skin on –
it adds a good flavour.

Shell the broad beans and remove the skin that surrounds each bean. Set
aside a quarter of the beans for the sauce. Reserve the rest for the
garnish.

Cut out the central rib from each cabbage leaf, then wash and drain them.
Set aside 2 leaves for the sauce. Take the remaining 6 leaves, pile them on
top of each other and cut them lengthwise into thin strips. Reserve for the
garnish.
Pre-heat the oven to 425°F/220°C/Reg. 7.

The vegetable butter

Place the beans and cabbage leaves to be used in the sauce in a food
processor or liquidiser and blend until the vegetables are finely puréed.
Add the softened butter, blend to mix well, then use a wooden spoon to
rub the vegetable butter through a sieve and into a bowl.

The fish

Season the turbot with salt and pepper.

Melt 2 teaspoons of butter in an oven dish, add the shallots and simmer
until soft and transparent. Add the mushrooms, season with salt and
pepper, stir, and cook for 1 minute longer. Place the fish on top of the
shallots and mushrooms, skin-side up, add the white wine and bring the
liquid to the boil. Cover with aluminium foil, and bake for 7 minutes or
until just cooked.

The vegetables for the garnish

Bring a large pan of salted water to a boil and add the broad beans. Boil
for 3 minutes, add the strips of cabbage and boil for 2 minutes more.
Drain, cool under running water and drain again.

To make the sauce and serve the fish

When the fish is done, remove it from the oven dish with a spatula and
place it on a cloth to drain. With a knife, remove the skin, place the fish on
a serving dish or divide it between 4 heated plates and keep warm.

Place the oven dish over a high heat and reduce the cooking liquids until
the dish is almost dry. Add the cream, stir, and boil gently for 2 minutes,
then strain into a saucepan.

Over a low heat, whisk the vegetable butter into the sauce, little by little, taste for seasoning and add the cooked beans and strips of cabbage. Stir until the vegetables are hot, but do not allow to boil. The vegetable butter gives a pretty, pale-green tint to the sauce.

With a skimmer or slotted spoon, lift the vegetables out of the sauce and arrange them around the fish. Spoon the sauce over the fish and serve immediately.

Suggestion
The turbot can be replaced by virtually any fish with firm white flesh, particularly bass, hake or skate. If using skate, cook it in a *court bouillon* before proceeding with the recipe. Instead of broad beans and cabbage, you could try peas and lettuce, peas and mint, asparagus tips and mangetout peas, or asparagus tips and a julienne of carrots.

Wine
Pink champagne, Pouilly-Fumé, white Coteaux Champenois.

Roast Lobster with Fennel
Homard à la coque

For 2 people

1	lobster, weighing about 1kg *(2¼ lb)*
2 tbsps	olive oil

For the sauce

2 tsps	butter
4	shallots, finely chopped
100ml *(4 fl. oz)*	dry white wine
1½ tbsps	white wine vinegar
150g *(5 oz)*	butter, at room temperature, cut into cubes
	salt, freshly ground pepper
1 tbsp	mixed chopped parsley, chives and chervil

For the fennel

1 tbsp	butter
450g *(1 lb)*	fennel, thinly sliced
	salt, freshly ground pepper
1 tbsp	water
2 tbsps	double cream
¼ tsp	mild curry powder

Equipment
cleaver or hammer · large rectangular oven dish, 35cm *(14 in)* long ·
scissors · aluminium foil · 2 saucepans · wire whisk · deep frying pan
or *sauteuse*, with cover
To serve: 2 heated plates

The lobster
Place the oven dish on the middle shelf and pre-heat the oven to
475°F/240°C/Reg. 9.

With the blunt edge of a cleaver or a hammer, crack the lobster claws.
Place the lobster in the hot oven dish, pour the oil over it and roast for
15 minutes. The lobster is done when it has turned red.

When the lobster is cool enough to handle, remove the meat from the
claws and detach the tail from the head with a twisting motion. With a
pair of scissors, cut the shell on the underside of the tail in half
lengthwise and remove the meat. With the tip of a knife, scrape out any
blackish matter near the top of the tail, then cut the tail meat into slices
about ½cm *(¼ in)* thick. Place the lobster meat on a plate, cover with
aluminium foil and keep warm.

The sauce
Make the *beurre blanc* as described in the recipe for Hot Fish Terrine (see
p.71), using the measurements given here and whisking all the time until
it is thick and creamy. When all the butter has been added, taste for
seasoning and reserve.

The fennel
In a deep frying pan or *sauteuse*, melt the butter, add the fennel, salt,
pepper, water, cream and curry powder, stir together, cover and simmer
for 7 minutes.

To serve the lobster
Gently reheat the sauce to warm, whisking constantly, then stir in the
chopped herbs.

Place a bed of fennel on each plate, arrange the pieces of lobster and the
claws on top, spoon the sauce lightly over the lobster and serve
immediately.

Suggestion
Instead of fennel, the lobster could be placed on a bed of spinach and
watercress, lightly cooked in a little butter for 5 minutes (see recipe on
p.128).
Wine
A fine white Burgundy – Chevalier-Bâtard, Montrachet or a good, rather
powerful Meursault.

Lobster Fricassee with Fresh Peas

Fricassée de homard aux petits pois frais

For 4 people

For the court bouillon

5½ litres *(10 pints)*	water
4 tsps	coarse salt
1	large carrot, sliced
1	small onion, sliced
1	medium tomato, cut into 8 pieces
1	stick of celery, sliced
	leaves of 1 small leek, sliced
	a slice of lemon
1	bay leaf
3	parsley stalks
	a sprig of thyme
15	whole peppercorns
2	cloves of garlic
2	live lobsters, weighing about 900g *(2 lb)* each

For the sauce

2 tbsps	olive oil
1	medium carrot, diced
5	shallots, finely chopped
	white of 1 small leek, sliced
1	tomato, diced
1	stick of celery, diced
¼	fennel bulb, diced
3 tbsps	dry white wine
5 tbsps	cognac
375ml *(13 fl. oz)*	whipping cream

For the peas

1 tbsp	butter
2	shallots, finely chopped
575g *(1¼ lb)*	small young garden peas, shelled
	salt, freshly ground pepper

Equipment

large pan, with lid · cleaver or hammer · 2 bowls · scissors · large *sauteuse* or deep frying pan · medium *sauteuse* or deep frying pan · wire whisk
To serve: 4 heated soup plates

121

The lobster

Put the water and coarse salt in a large pan and bring to the boil. Add all the ingredients for the *court bouillon*, except the lobsters, and simmer, uncovered, for 25 minutes.

Bring the *court bouillon* to a rapid boil and drop the lobsters into it. Cover the pan until the liquid comes back to the boil, then boil rapidly, uncovered, for 8–9 minutes. (Do not cook longer as the lobsters will be cooked again with the peas.) Lift the lobsters out of the *court bouillon* and drain, head down, in a colander until cool enough to handle.

Break off the claws and crack the shells with a hammer or the blunt edge of a cleaver. Remove the meat, cut it into ½cm *(¼-in)* cubes and place in a bowl.

With a twisting motion, separate the tails from the heads. Reserve the heads. Cut the underside of each tail in half lengthwise with a pair of scissors and remove the meat. Cut the tail in half lengthwise, remove the grainy, blackish intestine, then cut each half tail into 1cm *(½-in)* slices. Place the tail meat in the bowl with the claw meat, cover and reserve. Cut each head in half and remove the greenish part *(tomali)* with a teaspoon; discard it.

Strain 275ml *(½ pint)* of the *court bouillon* and reserve in a bowl.

The lobster sauce

Chop up all the shells, including the head, with a cleaver.

In a large *sauteuse* or deep frying pan, heat the olive oil until almost smoking, add the pieces of lobster shell and cook for 3 minutes, stirring frequently. Add the carrot, shallots, leek, tomato, fennel and celery and cook for about 4 minutes or until the water they give out has evaporated. Add the white wine and cognac, heat through, light with a match and boil over a high heat until the flame goes out.

Stir in the cream, lower the heat and simmer very gently, uncovered, for 20 minutes, skimming when necessary and stirring occasionally. Strain the sauce into a bowl, pressing on the lobster shells with a small ladle or wooden spoon to extract all the juices. There should be about 275ml *(½ pint)* of strained sauce. Reserve.

The peas

In a medium *sauteuse* or deep frying pan, melt a tablespoon of butter. Add the shallots and simmer, stirring occasionally, until soft and transparent. Add the peas, sprinkle with salt and pepper, stir gently for 2 minutes, then add the reserved *court bouillon*. Simmer for 5–6 minutes or until there are only about 5 tablespoons of liquid left, then remove from the heat. Add the lobster to the peas and reserve.

To finish the sauce and serve the lobster

Place the lobster sauce over a moderate heat and simmer for 6–7 minutes, whisking occasionally. Season with salt and pepper, then add the sauce to the lobster and peas. Simmer gently for 1–2 minutes or until the lobster is hot, then divide among the soup plates and serve immediately.

Suggestions

The lobster can be replaced by crawfish or Dublin Bay prawns and the peas by broad beans.

Wine

A fine white Burgundy – Montrachet – or a white Côtes du Rhône, or a dry Graves – Château Carbonnieux.

Crawfish Fricassee with Morels and Asparagus

Fricassée de langouste aux morilles et asperges

For 4 people

175g *(6 oz)* approx.	fresh morels or other wild mushrooms (see Note)
2 tbsps	vinegar
600g *(1¼ lb)*	very thin asparagus
1	live crawfish, weighing 1.4kg *(3 lb)* (for substitutes, see Suggestion)

For the court bouillon

4 litres *(7 pints)*	water
4 tsps	coarse salt
1	bay leaf
	a sprig of thyme
3	parsley stalks
15	whole peppercorns
2	cloves of garlic, crushed
1	large carrot, sliced
1	onion, sliced
1	stick of celery, sliced
1	tomato, cut into 8 pieces
	green leaves of 1 small leek, sliced
	a slice of lemon

For the crawfish sauce

2 tbsps	olive oil
1	medium carrot, diced
5	shallots, finely chopped
	white of 1 small leek, sliced
1	tomato, diced
1	stick of celery, sliced
¼	fennel bulb
5 tbsps	cognac
2 tbsps	dry white wine
375ml *(13 fl. oz)*	whipping cream
	salt, freshly ground pepper
1 tbsp	butter (for the morels)

Equipment

pastry brush · large bowl · kitchen string · large pan · scissors · bowl · large pan or *sauteuse*, 29cm *(11½ in)* in diameter · medium *sauteuse* or deep frying pan, 24cm *(9½ in)* in diameter · non-stick frying pan · skimmer or slotted spoon · large saucepan
To serve: 4 heated soup plates

Preliminary preparations

Cut off the sandy end of the stems and remove any damaged parts of the morels, then cut them in half lengthwise. With a pastry brush, brush the morels gently to remove as much dirt as possible from the crevices, drop them into a large bowl of water laced with 2 tablespoons of vinegar and allow to soak for 5–6 minutes. Drain, then wash the mushrooms very carefully in a large bowl of water, changing the water 2 or 3 times. Drain and pat dry in a cloth.

Break off the woody ends of the asparagus, then cut into 10cm *(4-in)* lengths. Wash and tie them together with kitchen string in 3 or 4 equal bundles and reserve.

The crawfish

The crawfish may simply be cooked in salted water (3¾ litres *(6½ pints)* of water and 4 teaspoons of coarse salt), but it is preferable to make a *court bouillon* as follows. Place the water and coarse salt in a large pan, add the bay leaf, thyme, parsley and peppercorns and bring to a boil. Add all the other ingredients for the *court bouillon* and simmer for 15 minutes.

Bring to a rapid boil and drop in the crawfish. Cover the pan until the liquid comes back to the boil, then boil, uncovered, for 13 minutes. Lift the crawfish out of the liquid and drain, head down, in a colander until cool enough to handle.

Remove the claws, then with a twisting motion separate the tail from the head. Using a pair of scissors, cut the underside of the tail shell in half lengthwise and remove the meat. Cut the tail in half lengthwise and remove the blackish intestine that runs along the top, then cut the meat into pieces about 1cm (½ in) thick and reserve in a bowl. Remove the meat from the claws and add it to the tail meat.

With a large knife, cut the head in half lengthwise. Remove any meat, place it in the bowl with the tail and claws and sprinkle with salt and pepper. Cover and reserve.

The crawfish sauce
Using a large knife, chop the tail shells, head and legs into several pieces.

In a large pan or *sauteuse*, heat the olive oil until almost smoking, add all the pieces of shell, and sauté for 6–7 minutes, stirring often.

Add the carrot, shallots, leek, tomato, celery and fennel and cook over a moderate to high heat for 3–5 minutes or until the water that the vegetables have given out has evaporated completely. Add the cognac and white wine, heat, light with a match and boil rapidly for about 4 minutes or until almost all the liquid has evaporated. Stir in the cream, lower the heat and simmer for 20 minutes, skimming frequently.

Strain the finished sauce into a smaller *sauteuse* or deep frying pan, pressing on the vegetables and pieces of shell to extract as much liquid as possible; there should be about 300ml (½ pint) of strained sauce. Season with salt and pepper and reserve.

The morels
Melt a tablespoon of butter in a non-stick frying pan, add the morels and sprinkle with salt and pepper. Sauté over a moderate heat for 5–10 minutes or until tender, stirring often to brown them lightly on all sides. Remove from the heat and reserve.

The asparagus
Bring a large saucepan of salted water to a boil, drop in the bundles of asparagus and boil for 5–7 minutes or until tender. Lift the bundles of asparagus out of the water with a skimmer or slotted spoon, untie them and drain for a few seconds on a cloth.

To serve the crawfish
Heat the sauce until almost boiling, then add the pieces of crawfish and morels. Simmer for about 1 minute to heat them through, then divide the crawfish, mushrooms and sauce among the 4 plates. Decorate each with the asparagus and serve immediately.

Suggestion
Lobster, crayfish or Dublin Bay prawns may be used and prepared as described for the crawfish. Use a lobster of the same weight, be sure not to overcook, and cut the meat from the claws and tail into 1cm (½-in) slices.

Note
Tinned or dried morels may be used instead of fresh ones. Tinned morels should be rinsed and drained on a cloth before cooking. Dried morels should be soaked as described on their packet (generally for about 30 minutes in warm water) and drained on a cloth. Tinned and dried morels cook much more quickly than fresh ones – as soon as they begin to brown, in about 2–3 minutes, they are done.

Wine
Condrieu, or white Burgundy such as a Chassagne-Montrachet or a Puligny-Montrachet, or a dry Graves.

Salmon, Bass and Turbot with White Wine Sauce
Assiettes de poissons, sauce vin blanc

For 4 people

225g (½ lb)	fresh salmon
450g (1 lb)	sea bass or John Dory
450g (1 lb)	turbot

For the vegetables

2 tbsps	butter
5	medium carrots, cut into julienne strips
	salt, freshly ground pepper
½ tsp	mild curry powder
6 tbsps	water
450g (1 lb)	fresh spinach, stems removed

For the fish

1 tbsp	butter
5	shallots, finely chopped
4	white button mushrooms, finely chopped
	salt, freshly ground pepper
325ml (11 fl. oz)	dry white wine
325ml (11 fl. oz)	whipping cream

Equipment

2 medium saucepans, with lids · oval or rectangular oven dish, 38–40cm
(15–16 in) long · spatula · wire whisk · sieve
To serve: 4 heated soup plates

Preliminary preparations

Ask the fishmonger to fillet the fish for you and to divide each sort into 4
pieces. Ask him to scale the sea bass, but to leave the skin on the fillets.

Pre-heat the oven to 425°F/220°C/Reg. 7.

The vegetables

In a saucepan, melt 1 tablespoon of butter and add the julienne of carrot.
Season with salt, pepper and the curry powder and simmer over a low
heat for 1 minute. Add the water and simmer, uncovered, for 7 minutes
more or until the carrots are tender and the water has evaporated.
Reserve.

In another saucepan, melt 1 tablespoon of butter, add the spinach and
season with salt and pepper. Stir and toss the spinach until it has wilted,
lower the heat and simmer for 3 minutes, uncovered, stirring occasionally. Reserve.

The fish

Melt the butter for the fish in the oven dish over a low heat. Add the
shallots and simmer for 1 minute to soften; do not allow to brown.

Season the fish fillets with salt and pepper. Add the chopped mushrooms
to the shallots, stir gently and cook for 2 minutes, then place the fish on
top of the vegetables (place the sea bass skin-side up), add the white
wine, bring to the boil, cover with aluminium foil and bake for 7 minutes,
or until almost cooked.

Just before the fish has finished cooking, reheat the spinach if necessary.
Remove the fish from the dish with a spatula and place the fillets on a
cloth for a few seconds to drain. With a knife, remove the skin from the
bass fillets.

Place a bed of spinach on each plate, arrange the different kinds of fish on
top and keep warm in the oven with the door ajar while making the sauce.

To make the sauce and serve the fish

Place the oven dish over a moderate heat and reduce the cooking liquid
to 2 tablespoons. Whisk in the cream and boil for about 4 minutes or
until thick and creamy, then strain the sauce, pressing on the vegetables.
Reheat the carrots if necessary.

Remove the soup plates from the oven, coat the fish lightly with the
sauce, arrange the carrots around them and serve immediately.

Suggestions

The spinach may be replaced by watercress leaves, lettuce leaves or the green of Swiss chard, all prepared in the same way.

A little mustard or horseradish may be added to the sauce; the mustard or horseradish should be identifiable but not overpowering.

Wine

A white Burgundy such as Puligny-Montrachet, or a dry white Graves – Carbonnieux blanc – or champagne.

Roast Lobster with Vanilla Butter Sauce
Homard à la vanille

For 4 people

2	live lobsters, weighing about 1kg *(2¼ lb)* each
2 tbsps	olive oil

For the sauce

2 tsps	butter
5	shallots, finely chopped
250ml *(9 fl. oz)*	dry white wine
3 tbsps	white wine vinegar
150g *(5 oz)*	butter, at room temperature, cut into cubes
	salt, freshly ground pepper
1	vanilla pod, split in half lengthwise

For the garnish

1 tbsp	butter
700g *(1½ lb)*	fresh young spinach, stems removed
2	large bunches watercress, leaves only
	salt, freshly ground pepper

Equipment

cleaver or hammer · oven dish · scissors · 2 saucepans · wire whisk · large pan
To serve: 4 heated plates

The lobster

Place the oven dish on the middle shelf and pre-heat the oven to 475°F/240°C/Reg. 9.

With the blunt edge of a cleaver or a hammer, crack the lobster claws. Place the lobsters in the hot oven dish, pour a tablespoon of olive oil over each one and roast for 15 minutes or until red.

When the lobsters are cool enough to handle, remove the meat from the claws and detach the tails from the heads with a twisting motion. With a pair of scissors, cut the shell on the underside of each tail in half lengthwise and remove the meat. With the tip of a knife, scrape out any blackish matter near the top of the tails, then cut the tail meat into slices about ½cm (¼ in) thick. Place the slices of lobster and the claws on a plate, cover with aluminium foil and keep warm.

The sauce

Make the *beurre blanc* as described in the recipe for Hot Fish Terrine (see p.71), using the measurements given here and whisking until thick and creamy. When all the butter has been added, taste for seasoning, then with the tip of a knife scrape some of the pulp from inside the vanilla pod into it. Stir the sauce, then strain it into a clean saucepan, rubbing on the shallots with a wooden spoon to make sure all the sauce and vanilla goes through. Reserve.

The garnish

Melt a tablespoon of butter in a large pan and add the spinach and watercress. Stir until the vegetables have wilted down, then simmer, uncovered, for 5 minutes, stirring occasionally; season.

To serve the lobsters

Reheat the sauce to warm over a low heat, whisking constantly.

Place a bed of spinach and watercress on each plate, arrange the pieces of lobster on top, spoon the sauce over the lobster, and serve immediately.

Note

Only young, pale-green spinach should be prepared as described. If the spinach you use has large, thick, dark-green leaves, boil it in rapidly boiling unsalted water for 2 minutes once the water comes back to the boil. Drain the spinach, cool it under running water and squeeze out all the water with your hands. To prepare the garnish, first melt down the watercress in a pan with the butter as described, then add the parboiled spinach and cook for a further 5 minutes.

Suggestion

Large Mediterranean prawns or crawfish can also be prepared in this way.

Wine

A white Châteauneuf-du-Pape, or a fine white Burgundy such as Musigny. Or perhaps a late picked Gewürztraminer.

Crawfish and Dublin Bay Prawn Fricassee with Young Cabbage and Truffles

Fricassée de langoustes, langoustines, truffes et chou nouveau

For 4 people

For the court bouillon

4 litres *(7 pints)*	water
4 tsps	coarse salt
2	carrots, sliced
1	medium onion, sliced
1½	bay leaves
2	sprigs of thyme
3	sprigs of parsley
10	whole peppercorns
1	live crawfish or lobster, weighing 1¼kg *(2¾ lb)*
12	large Dublin Bay prawns, weighing 1.4kg *(3 lb)* or 16 live crayfish (for substitutes, see Note)

For the sauce

2 tbsps	olive oil
1	medium carrot, diced
¼	fennel bulb, diced
1	small onion, diced
1	stick of celery, diced
	white of 1 medium leek, diced
2	small tomatoes, peeled, seeded and diced
8 tsps	cognac
8 tsps	dry white wine
325ml *(11 fl. oz)*	double cream or *crème fraîche* (see p. 290)
3	leaves from a young cabbage (or from the heart of an ordinary loose-leaf cabbage)
1	tinned truffle, weighing about 30g *(1¼ oz)*, drained and cut into julienne strips
	salt, freshly ground pepper

Equipment

large pan · cleaver or hammer · skimmer or slotted spoon · scissors · bowl · large wide saucepan or *sauteuse* · saucepan or small *sauteuse* · medium pan
To serve: 4 heated plates

The crawfish

Bring the water and coarse salt to a boil, add all the ingredients for the *court bouillon* except the shellfish and simmer for 20 minutes.

Kill the crawfish by plunging the tip of a large knife into the slit where the head meets the tail. Cut the head from the tail. If using a lobster, break off the claws with a quick wrenching movement and crack them with the blunt edge of a cleaver or a hammer. Reserve the head for the sauce.

Drop the crawfish tail (and the claws if using a lobster) into the boiling *court bouillon*. Bring back to the boil and simmer for 5 minutes, add the Dublin Bay prawns or crayfish and cook for 8 minutes more.

With a skimmer or slotted spoon, lift the shellfish out of the *court bouillon* and drain in a colander until cool enough to handle. Cut open the underside of the crawfish tail shell with a pair of scissors and remove the meat. Remove the blackish intestine, then cut the tail into slices about ½cm (¼ in) thick. Remove the meat from the claws. Separate the tails from the heads of the Dublin Bay prawns or crayfish and peel them. Place all the shellfish in a bowl, cover and reserve.

The sauce

Cut the crawfish head into small pieces with a large knife.

Heat the olive oil in a large pan or *sauteuse* until it is nearly smoking, then add the pieces of head. Stir over a high heat for 3–4 minutes, add the carrot, fennel, onion, celery, leek and tomatoes, stir to mix well, add the cognac, then heat and light. When the flame dies down, add the white wine and boil rapidly for 1–2 minutes or until the bottom of the pan is nearly dry.

Add the cream, stirring and scraping the bottom of the pan to dissolve all the juices, and simmer, uncovered, for 16 minutes. Strain the sauce into a saucepan or smaller *sauteuse*, rubbing and pressing on the crawfish and vegetables with a wooden spoon to extract all the liquid. Reserve.

The cabbage

Wash and drain the cabbage leaves, then cut them lengthwise into strips about ½cm (¼ in) wide.

Bring a pan of salted water to the boil, add the cabbage and blanch for 2 minutes from the time the water comes back to the boil. Drain and cool under running water, drain again and reserve.

To finish and serve the fricassee

Heat the sauce over a moderate heat until simmering and add the reserved meat from the shellfish and the strips of cabbage. Stir gently and taste for seasoning.

When hot, add the julienne of truffle, heat for a few seconds more, then serve immediately on individual plates.

Suggestion

The cabbage may be replaced by a julienne of carrots, leeks or Belgian endives, prepared in the same way. Use 1½ medium carrots, the white of 2 medium leeks or 1 large endive.

Note

If Dublin Bay prawns or crawfish are unavailable, 2 lobsters, each weighing 900g *(2 lb)*, may be used instead of the combination of shellfish above. As they are slightly smaller than the crawfish used in this recipe, reduce the total cooking time to 10 minutes.

Wine

Bâtard-Montrachet, white Châteauneuf-du-Pape or pink champagne.

Grand Mixed Poached Fish with Aïoli
Aïoli garni

For 6 people

600g *(1¼ lb)*	best quality salt cod, cut into 6 pieces
6	very large mussels (about 225g *(½ lb)* if using smaller mussels)
6	eggs

For the court bouillon

4 litres *(7 pints)*	water
4 tsps	coarse salt
20	whole peppercorns
2	medium onions, sliced
6	shallots, sliced
1	fennel bulb, sliced
2	tomatoes, quartered
3	cloves of garlic, cut in half
3	carrots, sliced
1	green pepper, seeded and sliced
	bouquet garni (4 parsley stalks, 1½ bay leaves, 2 sprigs of thyme)
2	cloves

For the aïoli

8	cloves of garlic
2	egg yolks
	juice of 1 lemon
¼ tsp	salt
475ml *(¾ pint)*	olive oil

For the vegetables

6	medium carrots
6	artichoke bottoms, cooked or tinned
350g *(12 oz)*	broccoli (thick stems removed)
225g *(8 oz)*	French beans
450g *(1 lb)*	new potatoes, washed but not peeled
3	small turnips, each cut into 4 pieces

For the fresh fish and shellfish (see Suggestion and Note)

2 tbsps	melted butter
	salt, freshly ground pepper
700g *(1½ lb)*	sea bream fillets
700g *(1½ lb)*	sea bass fillets
700g *(1½ lb)*	turbot, filleted, or 350g *(¾ lb)* flatfish fillets
6	large sea scallops or 18 queen scallops
6	Dublin Bay prawns (for substitute see Note)
30	tinned snails, drained

Equipment

steaming basket or colander · large bowl or basin · small saucepan · large pan · 2 bowls · small square of muslin · wire whisk · 2 large saucepans · large steaming basket and pan, or steamer · skimmer or slotted spoon · pastry brush · large bowl · 3 large oven dishes, each about 35cm *(14 in)* long · 2 saucepans, 1 with lid · 1 small saucepan · spatula
To serve: large, heated serving dish or 6 heated plates, and a sauceboat

Preliminary preparations

The day before making the meal, soak the salt cod in a steaming basket or colander set in a large bowl or basin of water. To allow it to de-salt properly, it is important that the cod does not touch the bottom of the bowl. Soak it for 24 hours, changing the water at least 3 times.

The day of the meal, clean the mussels by scraping the shells clean with a knife, and remove the beards that protrude from the shells. Rinse the mussels under running water and reserve in the refrigerator.

Boil the eggs for 10 minutes, drain and cool under running water. Peel them, cover and reserve.

The *court bouillon*

Place the water in a large pan, add the coarse salt and peppercorns and bring to the boil. Add all the other ingredients for the *court bouillon*, return to the boil and simmer, uncovered, for 1 hour or until the liquid has reduced by a quarter. Strain into a bowl and reserve.

The aïoli

Peel the garlic, cut the cloves in half lengthwise and remove the central green sprouts. Chop the garlic as finely as possible and place it on a little piece of muslin. Gather the corners of the cloth together to form a ball. Hold the ball of garlic under cold running water, then squeeze it completely; this will eliminate the acrid taste of the raw garlic.

When it has been squeezed as dry as possible, empty the garlic into a bowl. Stir in the egg yolks, lemon juice and salt. Begin slowly whisking in the olive oil, a little at a time; make sure each spoonful of oil is incorporated before adding the next. When the sauce begins to thicken, the oil may be added more quickly. When it becomes too thick, add a little lemon juice. The finished sauce should be golden-yellow and should have the consistency of a thick mayonnaise. Taste for salt and pepper, place in a sauceboat, cover tightly with plastic film and reserve in a cool place, but *not* in the refrigerator.

The vegetables

Bring 2 saucepans of salted water to the boil.

Peel the carrots, cut them into quarters lengthwise, cut out the light-coloured central core, then cut each quarter into pieces about 4cm *(1½ in)* long. Place the artichoke bottoms in a large steaming basket or the top of a steamer (make a little pile) and reserve.

When the water boils in one of the pans, add the broccoli and boil for 7 minutes. Lift the broccoli out of the water with a skimmer or slotted spoon, drain, cool under running water, drain, then place in a pile next to the artichoke bottoms in the steamer.

Boil the French beans for 4 minutes in the pan that the broccoli cooked in. Lift out of the water, drain, cool under running water and place in a third pile in the steaming basket.

In the same pan, boil the potatoes until tender. Drain and place in the steaming basket.

In the second pan of boiling salted water, boil the carrots for 4 minutes, add the turnips and boil for 4 minutes more. Remove the pan from the heat (keep the vegetables in their cooking liquid) and reserve.

The fish

Pre-heat the oven to 425°F/220°C/Reg. 7. Brush 3 oven dishes with the melted butter. Sprinkle 2 of the dishes with salt and pepper.

Drain the pieces of salt cod and pat them dry on a cloth, then place them in the unseasoned oven dish. All the pieces should lie flat.

In one of the seasoned oven dishes, place the fillets of sea bream and sea bass; do not allow the fillets to overlap. In the other seasoned dish, place the fillets of turbot and the scallops. Add a scant 250ml (½ pint) of the strained court bouillon to each of the dishes and bake for 10 minutes.

The shellfish
Place the mussels in a saucepan with 125ml (¼ pint) of the court bouillon, cover the pan and bring to a rapid boil over a high heat. Cook the mussels for 3–5 minutes or until they have all opened, shaking the pan occasionally.

Bring 1.1 litres (2 pints) of the court bouillon to the boil, add the Dublin Bay prawns, bring back to the boil and cook, covered, for 3 minutes. Drain.

Place the drained snails in a small saucepan with 125ml (¼ pint) of court bouillon, bring almost to the boil and simmer for 1 minute.

To heat the vegetables and serve the Grand Fish Dinner
Reheat the carrots and turnips in the liquid they cooked in.

Bring a little water to the boil in a large pan or the bottom of a steamer, place the steaming basket with the vegetables in place, cover and steam for 1–2 minutes or until very hot.

Cut the hard-boiled eggs in half.

Arrange the different vegetables in little piles around the edge of a large serving dish or on individual plates. Inside the circle of vegetables, arrange the mussels and Dublin Bay prawns. Lift the fish out of their cooking liquid with a spatula or skimmer and place them round the centre; place the drained scallops and the hard-boiled eggs in the very middle, sprinkle the drained snails over the top and serve immediately, with the aïoli in a sauceboat on the side.

Suggestion
A simpler version of this recipe can be made with salt cod and shellfish only – in which case, double the weight of salt cod.

Note
Before serving, divide each fish into 3 pieces so that everyone has a taste of each kind of fish.

Instead of Dublin Bay prawns, large prawns may be used.

The mussels and Dublin Bay prawns or prawns may be cooked in advance and heated up in the steamer with the vegetables.

Wine
A white wine from Cassis or a Palette.

MEAT
AND
OFFAL

Rib of Beef with Red Wine Sauce
Côte de boeuf beaujolaise

For 4 people

For the beef

2	ribs of beef, weighing 1kg *(2¼ lb)* each, including the bone (for substitute, see Suggestions)
	salt, freshly ground pepper
1 tbsp	oil of arachide (refined peanut oil)
1 tbsp	butter

For the sauce

1 tbsp	butter
4	shallots, finely chopped
1	stick of celery, finely chopped
15	peppercorns, coarsely crushed
5 tbsps	red wine vinegar
150ml *(5 fl. oz)*	red wine (preferably Beaujolais)
200g *(7 oz)*	plus 1 tbsp butter, cut into cubes
	salt, freshly ground pepper
4 tbsps	mixed chopped parsley, chervil and chives

Equipment
large heavy frying pan · wire whisk · large non-stick frying pan
To serve: heated serving dish and a sauceboat

The beef
Season the steak on both sides with salt and pepper.

Heat the oil until very hot in a heavy frying pan, add the butter and, when it has melted, place the steak in the pan. Brown over a moderate to high heat for 7 minutes, then lower the heat and cook for 1 minute more. Turn the meat over and cook over a low heat for 14 minutes. Place on a plate, cover with aluminium foil and allow to rest for 10–15 minutes.

The sauce
Pour away the fat in the frying pan and pat the bottom dry with a paper towel. Place the pan over a moderate heat, melt a tablespoon of butter, add the shallots, celery and peppercorns and cook for about 1 minute, stirring constantly, to soften the vegetables. Add the vinegar, stir, scraping the bottom of the pan to dissolve the caramelised meat juices, and boil rapidly until the pan is almost dry. Add the wine, stir, and boil for about 5–6 minutes or until only 4 tablespoons of liquid remain.

Remove the pan from the heat and begin adding the butter cubes as described for the *beurre blanc* in the recipe for Hot Fish Terrine (see p.71). When all the butter has been added, taste for salt and pepper, stir in the chopped herbs and pour into a sauceboat.

To serve the steaks

Place each steak in a non-stick frying pan and reheat it for 2 minutes on each side over a moderate to high heat.

Lay the meat on a cutting board and cut it into slices, parallel to the bone, ½–1½cm (¼–½ in) thick. Sprinkle with salt and pepper, arrange the slices of meat on a serving dish and serve with the sauce on the side.

Suggestions

Home-made pasta (see p.225) makes an excellent accompaniment to this dish.

Other cuts of beef, such as *entrecôte* steaks, or fillet steaks, or even veal chops, may be used instead of ribs. Cooking times for the meat will be shorter than those given here, but the sauce is made in exactly the same way.

If you like, you can add to the sauce a *brunoise* of vegetables of your choice. (A *brunoise* means vegetables cut into tiny dice.)

Wine

Serve the same wine as you use for making the sauce – Saint-Amour, or Fleurie, for example.

Fillet of Beef à la Ficelle with Béarnaise Sauce
Filet de boeuf à la ficelle

For 6 people

1kg *(2¼ lb)*	fillet of beef in 1 piece, well trimmed
2 tsps	coarse salt
2¾ litres *(5 pints)*	water
4 tsps	coarse salt
	bouquet garni (including the green leaves of 1 leek)
18	small carrots
6	small leeks (use the white plus about 2½cm *(1 in)* of green)
1	green cabbage, weighing 700g *(1½ lb)*, cut into 6 pieces, each tied to hold its shape
6	small turnips
1	large onion, stuck with 2 cloves
3	sticks of celery, cut in half

For the sauce

225g *(½ lb)*	plus 1½ tbsps butter
2	shallots, finely chopped
15	peppercorns, coarsely ground or crushed
4 tsps	fresh tarragon, chopped
6 tbsps	dry white wine
6 tbsps	white wine vinegar
3	egg yolks
	salt

Equipment
earthenware or glass dish · large pan · 3 small saucepans · wire whisk skimmer or slotted spoon
To serve: heated serving dish and a sauceboat

Preliminary preparations
Place the meat in an earthenware or glass dish, rub it all over with 2 teaspoons of coarse salt and place it in the refrigerator for 2 hours.

The meat
Remove the meat from the refrigerator, wipe off any traces of salt and reserve while preparing the vegetable stock.

Bring the water to the boil in a large pan, add the coarse salt, *bouquet garni* and all the vegetables. Bring back to the boil, lower the heat and simmer for 20 minutes.

Pre-heat the oven to 275°F/140°C/Reg. 1. Bring the liquid to a rapid boil, add the fillet of beef and cook at a steady simmer for 10–15 minutes. Remove the meat and vegetables from the liquid, drain, place on a serving dish and cover with the aluminium foil. Place in the oven for 15 minutes while preparing the sauce.

The *béarnaise* sauce
Melt 225g *(½ lb)* of butter in a saucepan and clarify it by skimming off the foam that surfaces when the butter comes to a boil. Remove from the heat and reserve.

Melt 1½ tablespoons of butter in another saucepan and add the shallots, peppercorns, half the tarragon, the wine and the vinegar. Boil for 9–10 minutes or until the liquid is reduced by half, remove from the heat and allow to cool for 3–4 minutes (if it is too hot the egg yolks will curdle).

Place the egg yolks in a small heavy saucepan and strain the cooled liquid on to them, pressing on the shallots to extract all their juices. Place the saucepan over a low heat and whisk constantly until the mixture foams and starts to thicken (allow 3–4 minutes). Remove the pan from the heat and add the melted butter little by little, whisking in each addition completely before adding the next. The finished sauce should be smooth and velvety. Add a little salt, whisk in the remaining tarragon and pour the sauce into a sauceboat; the sauce is served warm, not hot.

To serve the beef

Remove the serving dish from the oven, serve the meat either whole or in slices, surrounded by the vegetables, with the sauce on the side.

Suggestions

The meat can be served without the sauce, accompanied simply by pickled gherkins *(cornichons)*, different mustards and a small bowl of coarse salt.

Note

In France, beef cooked this way is called *à la ficelle* ('on a string') because traditionally the meat would be tied with a string, suspended in the boiling liquid to cook and pulled out with the same string. Only the finest and most tender cut of beef can be cooked this way; it is always served quite rare.

Wine

A claret – Mercurey or Côtes-de-Buzet.

Veal Cutlets with Tarragon and Star Anise
Côtes de veau à l'estragon et à la badiane

For 4 people

For the infusion

2	sprigs of fresh tarragon (or 1 tsp dried)
10	whole star anise (see Note)
350ml *(12 fl. oz)*	water

For the cutlets

2 tbsps	oil of arachide (refined peanut oil)
	salt, freshly ground pepper
4	veal cutlets, weighing about 200g *(7 oz)* each
350ml *(12 fl. oz)*	whipping cream or *crème fraîche* (see p.290)
8	whole star anise (for serving)
8	whole tarragon leaves (for serving)

Equipment

small mixing bowl · small saucepan · very large frying pan · wire whisk
To serve: 4 heated plates

The infusion

Place the tarragon in a small mixing bowl with the star anise. Bring the water to a boil, pour it over the herbs, cover the bowl and leave to infuse for 10 minutes.

The veal cutlets

In a very large frying pan (or 2 smaller ones), heat the oil until very hot. Season the cutlets with salt and pepper and cook them for 5 minutes on each side over a moderate heat. Place on a plate, cover with aluminium foil and keep warm.

Pour off any fat in the pan and pat the pan dry with kitchen paper. Pour the herb infusion and herbs and spices into the pan and place it back over a moderate heat, stirring to detach any meat juices stuck to the bottom of the pan. Simmer the liquid for about 10 minutes. Add any juices the cutlets have given out, as well as the cream, and boil for 7 minutes more or until the sauce is thick and creamy.

To serve the cutlets

Place a cutlet on each plate. Decorate each one with 2 whole star anise and two leaves of tarragon and season lightly.

Whisk the sauce and strain it over the cutlets. Serve with a vegetable purée, home-made pasta or its variations (see p.225) or Archestrate Potatoes (see p.222).

Suggestions

Pork chops may be used instead of veal, and a little lemon juice may be added before serving.

Note

Star anise – so called because it looks like a star – is sometimes called Chinese anise. It can be found in delicatessens and in Chinese groceries.

Veal Cutlets with Limes and Ginger

Côtes de veau au gingembre et au citron vert

For 4 people

	zest of 1 lime, finely chopped
8cm *(3-in)*	piece of fresh ginger, peeled and finely chopped
5 tbsps	water
1 tbsp	sugar

4	veal cutlets, weighing about 200g *(7 oz)* each
	salt, freshly ground pepper
2 tbsps	oil of arachide (refined peanut oil)
1	medium tomato, chopped
325ml *(11 fl. oz)*	*crème fraîche* (see p.290) or double cream

Equipment
small saucepan · very large frying pan · slotted spoon
To serve: 4 heated plates

The lime and ginger
Place the lime zest in a sieve and rinse under cold running water, then put it into a small saucepan and add enough cold water to cover. Boil over a high heat for 2 minutes, drain, cool under running water, drain again and reserve.

Place the ginger in the same saucepan, add the water and sugar, bring to the boil, lower the heat and simmer until all the water has evaporated. Add the lime zest and reserve.

The veal cutlets and sauce
Season the cutlets with salt and pepper. Heat the oil in a very large frying pan (or 2 smaller ones), add the cutlets and brown over a moderate heat for 5 minutes on each side. Remove the cutlets from the pan with a slotted spoon, place on a plate, cover with aluminium foil and keep warm.

Pour off any fat in the pan and pat the pan dry with kitchen paper. Place the pan back over a low heat and add the tomato, scraping the bottom of the pan with a wooden spoon to dissolve any meat juices. Boil to evaporate almost all the liquid given out by the tomato, then add the cream and any juices the cutlets have given out. Boil for 4 minutes or until the sauce is thick and creamy.

To finish the sauce and serve the cutlets
Taste the sauce, season with a little salt and pepper, then strain it into the saucepan with the lime zest and ginger and reheat it.

Place the cutlets on the plates, spoon the sauce over them and serve immediately.

Suggestions
A julienne of mixed red and green peppers may be used instead of the lime zest and ginger. Blanch the peppers for 1 minute, drain, cool under running water, drain again and add to the sauce before serving. Or cook and purée the green pepper and serve it with the strips of blanched red pepper on top.

Note
Pork chops may be used instead of veal cutlets. Cook them for about 7–8 minutes on each side.

Wine
A young red Burgundy, a red Coteaux Champenois or a young Chinon.

Veal Viala
Quasi de veau Viala

For 4 people

2	medium onions
800g *(1¾ lb)*	chump end of loin of veal or outside top of leg
	salt, freshly ground pepper
2 tbsps	oil of arachide (refined peanut oil)
2	large tomatoes, skinned and cut into wedges
6 tbsps	white wine
	bouquet garni
5 tbsps	water
5 tbsps	*crème fraîche* (see p.290) or double cream (optional, see Suggestions)

Equipment
small casserole, with lid · skimmer or slotted spoon
To serve: heated serving dish and a sauceboat

To cook the veal
Cut each onion in half and cut each half into 5 wedges. Reserve.

Season the veal generously. Heat the oil in a small casserole; when very hot, add the veal and brown over a high heat for 3–4 minutes, turning frequently. Lower the heat, add the onions and cook for 8–10 minutes to brown them lightly, turning the meat once or twice. Add the tomatoes and white wine, scraping the bottom of the pan with a wooden spoon to detach any caramelised meat juices. Add the *bouquet garni*, water, salt and pepper and bring to a boil. Cover and simmer for 20 minutes, then turn the veal over and cook for 25 minutes more.

To make the sauce and serve the veal
Remove the meat from the pan. Discard the *bouquet garni*, add the cream (if using it) and boil the cooking liquid rapidly, uncovered, while carving the veal.

Cut the veal into relatively thin slices and place them on a hot serving dish. Season the veal lightly, then, using a skimmer or slotted spoon, lift the onions and tomatoes out of the pan and place them on top of the slices of veal. Pour the sauce into a sauceboat and serve.

Suggestions
The veal can be served with home-made pasta (see p. 225) or a mixture of green peas, glazed carrots and turnips, or broccoli with butter.

Wine
A claret – Graves.

Medallions of Veal with Capers and Horseradish
Noisettes de veau aux câpres et au raifort

For 4 people

½	medium, fresh horseradish root (for substitutes, see Suggestions)
175ml *(6 fl. oz)*	water
1 tbsp	sugar
8	medallions of veal, 1½–2cm *(½–¾ in)* thick, cut from the thin end of the loin
	salt, freshly ground pepper
1 tbsp	oil of arachide (refined peanut oil)
2 tsps	butter
5	shallots, chopped
1	medium tomato, cut into wedges
3 tbsps	madeira
175ml *(6 fl. oz)*	water
150ml *(¼ pint)*	*crème fraîche* (see p.290) or double cream
2 tsps	butter
2½ tbsps	capers, washed and drained
	salt, freshly ground pepper
	freshly chopped parsley, chervil or chives (optional)

Equipment
food processor, liquidiser or grater · 2 small saucepans · very large frying pan · wire whisk · small frying pan
To serve: heated serving dish

The horseradish

Peel the horseradish and either chop it finely in a food processor or liquidiser, or grate it on a grater. (There should be 100g *(4 oz)* tightly packed, grated horseradish.) Rinse the grated horseradish in cold water, drain well, then place it in a small saucepan with the water and sugar.

Simmer, uncovered, over a very low heat for 1 hour, then allow this horseradish preserve to cool for 2 hours.

The veal

Pre-heat the oven to 425°F/220°C/Reg. 7.

Season the veal with salt and pepper. Heat the oil in a very large frying pan (or 2 smaller ones) and brown the veal rapidly on both sides. Lower the heat and cook for 7 minutes more, then add the butter, turn the veal over, put the shallots and tomatoes in the pan between the medallions and cook another 6 minutes.

Place the veal on a serving dish, cover with aluminium foil and keep warm in the oven while making the sauce.

To make the sauce and serve the veal

Mix the tomatoes and onions together well, add the madeira to the pan in which the veal was cooked and cook for 2 minutes over a moderate heat, stirring frequently, then add the water and boil for 2 minutes more. Add the cream and whatever juices the veal has given out during this time. Season with salt and pepper, whisk, and boil gently for a final 2 minutes. Strain the sauce into a clean saucepan, pressing on the vegetables to extract the juices. Keep the sauce warm over a low heat.

Heat 2 teaspoons of butter in a small frying pan and quickly sauté the capers over a moderate heat to colour them lightly, then add them to the sauce. Add the horseradish, season with salt and pepper and stir gently.

Remove the serving dish from the oven, spoon the sauce over the veal, sprinkle with freshly chopped herbs and serve with home-made pasta (see p.225).

Suggestions

Instead of the fresh horseradish, 3 tablespoons of bottled horseradish may be used.

Fresh ginger may be grated and cooked instead of the fresh horseradish, or the peel of a lemon, cut into julienne strips and blanched for 2 minutes, may be added to the sauce instead of either horseradish or ginger.

Wine

Côtes du Rhône, red Hermitage or Médoc.

Veal Cutlets
with Red Pepper Sauce
Côtes de veau à la crème de poivrons rouges

For 4 people

2	very large red peppers (see Suggestions)
4	veal cutlets, weighing about 200g *(7 oz)* each (about 1cm *(¾ in)* thick)
	salt, freshly ground pepper
3 tbsps	oil of arachide (refined peanut oil)
150ml *(¼ pint)*	dry white wine
350ml *(12 fl. oz)*	*crème fraîche* (see p.290) or whipping cream
2 tbsps	mixed chopped parsley, chives and chervil

Equipment
oven dish · liquidiser · very large frying pan
To serve: 4 heated plates

The peppers
Cut each pepper in half lengthwise, remove the seeds and stems.

Pre-heat the oven to 425°F/220°C/Reg. 7.

Place the peppers in an oven dish, skin-side up, and bake for 20 minutes or until the skin has dried out and coloured, then peel off the skin. Cut one of the pepper halves into lengthwise strips about 3mm *(⅛ in)* thick. Reserve.

Purée the rest of the peppers in a liquidiser and reserve.

Lower the oven to 250°F/130°C/Reg. ½.

The cutlets and their sauce
Season each cutlet lightly with salt and pepper.

Over a moderate heat, heat the oil in a very large frying pan (or 2 small ones) until very hot. Add the cutlets and brown one side for about 5 minutes, turn them and brown the other side for 3 minutes. Both sides should be a good golden brown. Place on a plate, cover with aluminium foil and keep warm in the oven.

Pour off any fat in the frying pan and add the white wine. Scrape the bottom of the pan and boil the wine for about 2 minutes, add the pepper purée, simmer for 2 minutes more, then add the cream and any juices given out by the cutlets. Cook the sauce for 4–5 minutes or until thick and creamy, taste for salt and pepper, then add the strips of pepper, stir, and simmer for 1 minute.

To serve the cutlets
Place the cutlets on individual plates, spoon the pepper sauce over them, sprinkle with the herbs and serve.

Suggestions
Either red or green peppers may be used in this recipe.

The cutlets and their sauce are excellent with home-made pasta (see p.225), a vegetable purée or sautéed wild mushrooms.

Pork chops, lamb chops or chicken can be prepared in the same way.

Wine
A red wine – perhaps a lightly chilled Côte Rôtie.

Veal Cutlets with Cucumber and Tea
Côtes de veau au thé et concombre

For 4 people

1	medium cucumber, weighing about 280g *(10 oz)*
2 tbsps	butter
	salt, freshly ground pepper
2 tsps	tea leaves (preferably Ceylon)
175ml *(6 fl. oz)*	boiling water
2 tbsps	oil of arachide (refined peanut oil)
4	veal cutlets, weighing about 200g *(7 oz)* each
	salt, freshly ground pepper
350ml *(12 fl. oz)*	double cream or *crème fraîche* (see p. 290)
1 tsp	tea leaves

Equipment
vegetable peeler · medium frying pan · very large frying pan · slotted spoon · small teapot · large dish · wire whisk
To serve: 4 heated plates

The cucumber and the tea
Peel the cucumber and cut it lengthwise into quarters. Remove the seeds with a spoon and cut each half into symmetrical rectangles 1 × 1½ × 8cm *(½ × ½ × 3 in)*. Cut these diagonally across into lozenge-shaped slices 1.5cm *(½ in)* thick.

Heat the butter in a medium frying pan, add the cucumber, salt and pepper. Sauté over a moderate heat to brown lightly (about 5 minutes) and drain on paper towels. Reserve.

Place 2 teaspoons of tea in a teapot, add the boiling water, cover and steep for 8 minutes.

The veal cutlets and the sauce

Heat the oil in a very large frying pan. Season the cutlets with salt and pepper and brown over a moderate heat for 5 minutes on one side and 3 minutes on the other. Place on a dish, cover with aluminium foil and place in a 250°F/130°C/Reg. ½ oven while making the sauce.

Pour all the fat from the pan, return the pan to a moderate heat and strain the tea into the pan. Stir to detach all the juices stuck to the bottom of the pan and boil rapidly for 5 minutes or until there are about 1½ tablespoons of syrupy liquid left. Add the cream and any juices the cutlets have given out, whisk lightly and boil for 5 minutes more or until velvety.

To finish the sauce and serve the cutlets

Place the cucumbers over a low heat to warm up.

Add 1 teaspoon of new tea leaves to the cream sauce, remove from the heat and leave to infuse for 1 minute. Strain the tea sauce into the pan with the cucumbers and season with salt and pepper.

Place the cutlets on plates, spoon the cucumbers and sauce over them and serve.

Suggestions

The cutlets can be served with home-made pasta (see p.225) or spinach.

One tablespoon of lemon or orange juice, or the parboiled zest of either half a lemon or one-quarter of an orange may be added to the sauce before serving.

This dish can also be made with either veal sweetbreads or chicken.

Note

Everything can be done ahead of time. Keep the meat on the dish covered with aluminium foil and the cucumbers in the sauce. Five minutes before serving, uncover the meat and reheat in a pre-heated oven 350°F/180°C/ Reg. 4, reheat the cucumbers and sauce, and serve.

Wine

Try drinking tea. Otherwise, choose a young, refreshing red wine or a white Côtes du Rhône – Hermitage or Condrieu.

Navarin of Lamb with Vegetables

Navarin aux petits légumes

For 4 people

For the lamb

1 kg *(2¼ lb)*	boneless lamb shoulder or neck, fat removed, cut into 8 pieces
	salt, freshly ground pepper
3 tbsps	oil of arachide (refined peanut oil)
1 tbsp	butter
2	large tomatoes, peeled, seeded and chopped
2	cloves of garlic, crushed
	bouquet garni containing thyme, parsley stalks and a bay leaf
375ml *(13 fl. oz)*	chicken stock
1 tsp	tomato paste

For the vegetables

2	medium carrots, cut into sticks 4cm *(1½ in)* long and 1.5cm *(½ in)* thick
2	medium turnips, prepared like the carrots
20	button onions, peeled
200g *(7 oz)*	mangetout peas, strings removed
450g *(1 lb)*	broad beans, shelled
350g *(12 oz)*	fresh peas, shelled
	salt, freshly ground pepper
2 tbsps	whole chervil or parsley leaves

Equipment

large *sauteuse* or deep frying pan, 25cm *(10 in)* in diameter, with cover · skimmer or slotted spoon · bowl
To serve: large heated serving dish

The lamb

Season the lamb with salt and pepper. Heat the oil in a high-sided frying pan or *sauteuse*. When very hot, add the meat and brown over a moderate heat for 3 minutes, turning frequently. Add the butter and continue browning for 3 minutes more, then remove the meat with a skimmer or slotted spoon and drain on paper towels. Pour all the fat from the pan and pat the pan dry with a paper towel.

Place the meat back in the pan with the tomatoes, garlic, *bouquet garni*, stock and tomato paste. Season lightly with salt and pepper, bring to the boil, cover the pan, lower the heat and simmer for 40 minutes.

To cook the vegetables and serve the lamb

Remove the pieces of lamb from the pan and strain the cooking liquid into a bowl. Carefully spoon off any fat that surfaces. Pour the liquid into a clean pan, add the meat, carrots, turnips and onions, cover and simmer for 10 minutes. Add the mangetout peas, broad beans and peas, and cook, covered, for 10 minutes more.

Add salt and pepper to taste, transfer the navarin to a serving dish, sprinkle with the chervil or parsley leaves and serve.

Suggestions

Chicken or veal may be used instead of lamb.

Wine

A Bordeaux – perhaps Pouillac.

Lamb with Garlic Sauce
Emincé d'agneau à la crème d'ail

For 4 people

For the stock

1 kg *(2¼ lb)*	loin of lamb, all bones and fat removed (keep the bones for the stock)
1	small onion, thinly sliced
1	large carrot, chopped
1	large stick of celery, chopped
	bouquet garni of thyme, bay leaf, parsley stalks and a leek leaf
2	medium tomatoes, chopped
475ml *(16 fl. oz)*	chicken stock

For the garlic and sauce

2	whole heads of garlic (about 20 large cloves, separated but unpeeled)
	milk (to cover garlic)
1 tbsp	butter
	salt, freshly ground pepper
1 tsp	sugar
150ml *(5 fl. oz)*	double cream or *crème fraîche* (see p.290)

For the lamb

4	sprigs of fresh thyme, rubbed off their stalks
	salt, freshly ground pepper
2 tsps	butter

For the vegetables

100g *(4 oz)*	thin French beans, cut into 5cm *(2-in)* pieces (cut thick green beans in half lengthwise)
3 tsps	butter
2	medium carrots, cut into julienne strips
10cm *(4-in)*	piece of cucumber, peeled and cut into julienne strips
1	medium or 2 small courgettes, unpeeled, cut into julienne strips
4	large mushrooms, cut into julienne strips
	salt, freshly ground pepper
1 tsp	sugar

Equipment

large cast-iron casserole · 2 medium saucepans · small saucepan · small roasting tin · medium roasting tin · large frying pan
To serve: 4 heated plates and a sauceboat

The stock

Pre-heat the oven to 425°F/220°C/Reg. 7.

Place the lamb bones in a large cast-iron casserole and cook, without adding any fat, for 15 minutes over a low heat; turn the bones over a few times to brown them lightly. Transfer the casserole to the oven and cook for 15 minutes more. Leave the oven on when you remove the casserole.

Add the onion, carrot, celery and *bouquet garni*. Cook over a low heat for about 5 minutes, stirring frequently, to brown the vegetables lightly. Add the tomatoes and cook for 5 minutes or until most of their moisture has evaporated. Add the chicken stock, stirring to detach the juices stuck to the bottom of the pan, bring to the boil, lower the heat and simmer, uncovered, for 40 minutes, skimming off any foam that surfaces.

Strain the stock into a clean saucepan, pressing on the vegetables to extract any juices, and reserve.

The garlic

Place the unpeeled cloves of garlic in a saucepan, add enough milk to cover, and bring to a boil. Blanch for 1 minute, then drain.

Heat the butter in a roasting tin and add the garlic. Season generously with salt and pepper, add the sugar, then cook over a moderate heat for 2 minutes, stirring constantly.

Place in the oven and cook for 15 minutes, turning the garlic over every 5 minutes. Remove from the oven and leave the oven on.

Wrap 8 whole cloves of garlic in aluminium foil and reserve. Peel the remaining cloves and chop finely.

The sauce

Place the chopped garlic in the pan with the lamb stock and add the cream. Bring to the boil, stirring constantly, lower the heat and cook, uncovered, for 20–30 minutes or until the liquid has reduced to about 400ml (14 fl. oz).

Strain the reduced sauce into a clean saucepan, rubbing as much of the garlic through the sieve as possible. Taste the sauce for salt and pepper and keep warm over a very low heat while cooking the meat and vegetables.

The lamb

Place the 2 boned fillets of lamb in a lightly buttered roasting tin, season with thyme, salt and pepper, rubbing them into the meat. Top with 2 teaspoons of butter and roast for 16 minutes.

The vegetables

Cook the beans in lightly salted water for 4 minutes, drain and reserve.

In a large frying pan, melt 1½ teaspoons of butter. Add the julienne of carrots and cook over a moderate heat for 3 minutes, shaking the pan several times. Add another 1½ teaspoons of butter. When melted, add the juliennes of cucumber, courgettes and mushrooms. Season with a little salt and pepper and the sugar. Cook over a moderate heat for 7 minutes longer, stirring frequently, then stir in the French beans and remove the pan from the heat.

To serve the lamb

When the meat is done, place it on a chopping board. Place the 8 reserved garlic cloves in the oven to warm. Gently reheat the vegetables if necessary.

Cut the lamb into very thin slices; it should be rare and very pink inside. Season lightly with salt and pepper.

Spoon a little of the sauce on to each plate, place the slices of lamb in the middle, and garnish the edges with the vegetables. Spoon a little more sauce over the lamb.

Place 2 cloves of garlic on each plate and serve immediately, with any remaining sauce in a sauceboat.

Suggestions

If you serve this dish in early summer, you can make it with new season's garlic or, instead of garlic, you can use button onions or shallots and replace the lamb with pork, duck or chicken.

Note

The vegetables can be cooked up to an hour ahead of time and reheated quickly just before serving.

Wine

Saint-Emilion, Pomerol or red Châteauneuf-du-Pape.

Lamb Papadinas

Epaule d'agneau Papadinas

For 4–5 people

1	shoulder of lamb with bone, weighing 1.8kg *(4 lb)*, trimmed of fat
	salt, freshly ground pepper
2 tbsps	oil of arachide (refined peanut oil)
1 tsp	butter
3	large onions, thickly sliced
1 tbsp	sugar
1 tbsp	thyme flowers or leaves
1	whole bay leaf
½ litre *(17 fl. oz)*	water

Equipment

large casserole
To serve: large heated serving dish

To cook and serve the lamb

Pre-heat the oven to 400°F/200°C/Reg. 6.

Season the lamb generously with salt and pepper, rubbing it into the meat.

Heat the oil in a large casserole until almost smoking, add the lamb and brown on both sides over a moderate heat for 6–8 minutes. Lift the lamb out of the casserole and reserve.

Pour off all the fat, add the teaspoon of butter, onions, sugar and a little salt and pepper, and cook over a low heat for about 8 minutes or until the onions start to caramelise and brown; do not allow them to burn.

Put the lamb back into the casserole, add the thyme, bay leaf, water and a little salt and pepper. Bring to the boil, cover and place in the oven for 1 hour and 20 minutes.

To serve, remove the meat from the casserole and slice. Place the slices on a serving dish, taste the cooking liquid for seasoning (there should be about 300ml (½ pint) of liquid) spoon everything over the meat and serve.

Suggestion
This method of cooking could also be used for chicken, pork or veal.

Wine
Arbois-Pupillin or a young claret – a Saint Emilion.

Lamb Curry
Cari d'agneau

For 4 people

900g (2 lb)	boneless shoulder of lamb, cut into 4cm (1½-in) cubes
1½ tsps	mild Madras curry powder
	salt, freshly ground pepper
2 tbsps	olive oil
325ml (11 fl. oz)	water
1 tbsp	olive oil
1	large onion, coarsely chopped
1	clove of garlic, quartered
2	medium tomatoes, skinned, seeded and chopped
	bouquet garni of thyme and a bay leaf
2 tbsps	mild Madras curry powder
	a pinch of cayenne pepper
250ml (9 fl. oz)	plain yoghurt
½ tsp	salt

For the garnish

2 tbsps	butter
½	banana, diced
2	medium tomatoes, peeled and diced
½	apple, peeled, cored and diced
1	small onion, finely chopped
	salt, freshly ground pepper

Equipment
large frying pan · skimmer or slotted spoon · 2 large saucepans ·
small frying pan
To serve: heated serving dish

The meat
Sprinkle the pieces of lamb with 1½ teaspoons curry powder, salt and pepper, rolling the meat in the spices to coat them thoroughly.

Heat 2 tablespoons of olive oil in a large frying pan, add half the lamb and brown over a high heat on all sides (allow about 5 minutes). Drain the lamb while browning the remaining meat (add another tablespoon of oil if necessary). Remove from the pan and drain.

Pour all the fat from the pan, place it back over a moderate heat and add the water, stirring to detach any juices stuck to the bottom of the pan. Boil for 1 minute and reserve.

The curry
Heat 1 tablespoon of olive oil in a large saucepan, add the onion, garlic, tomatoes and *bouquet garni.* Sauté over a moderate heat for 5 minutes. Stir in 2 tablespoons of curry powder, the cayenne, yoghurt and the reserved pan juices. Add the meat, the salt, and a little more water if necessary (the liquid should not quite cover the meat) and simmer, uncovered, for 1 hour and 15 minutes.

The garnish
When the curry is almost done, heat the butter in a small frying pan. When very hot, add the banana, tomatoes, apple and onion and sauté over a moderate heat for 5 minutes, turning the fruit gently to brown it lightly and evenly. Season with salt and pepper and reserve.

To finish and serve the curry
Lift the pieces of meat out of the curry with a skimmer or slotted spoon and reserve. Boil the sauce for about 3 minutes (there should be about 450ml *(¾ pint)* of sauce left after reducing) and strain into a clean saucepan. Press the vegetables with a wooden spoon to extract all their juices, then add the meat and the garnish to the sauce. Heat gently for 3–4 minutes, taste for seasoning and serve with rice, pasta or (best of all) boiled cracked wheat (bulgur).

Suggestions
Chicken or pork may be used instead of lamb.

For a spicier curry, omit the fruit. For a more unusual taste, add a little cinnamon, cumin or star anise along with the curry powder.

Wine
A Côte Rôtie is the perfect wine to drink with this dish.

Goujonnettes of Lamb with Béarnaise Sauce
Goujonnettes d'agneau

For 4 people

450g *(1 lb)*	lean boneless lamb, from the leg
	salt, freshly ground pepper

For the béarnaise *sauce*

120g *(4 oz)*	butter (see Suggestions)
3	shallots, finely chopped
30	mint leaves, chopped
10	peppercorns, coarsely ground or crushed
3 tbsps	sherry vinegar
3 tbsps	dry white wine
1½	egg yolks
	salt

For deep frying

	oil
1	egg
	salt, freshly ground pepper
50g *(2 oz)*	freshly made fine breadcrumbs

Equipment
small saucepan · medium saucepan · wire whisk · skimmer or slotted spoon · large saucepan or deep fryer · deep-frying thermometer
To serve: heated serving dish and a sauceboat

Preliminary preparations
Cut the lamb into thin strips about 8 × 1½ × 1½cm *(3 × ½ × ½ in)*. Season with salt and pepper and reserve

Melt the butter in a small saucepan over a low heat. When it bubbles and a whitish foam appears, use a small spoon to remove all the impurities that float to the surface. Remove from the heat and reserve.

The sauce
Make a *béarnaise* as described in the recipe for Fillet of Beef à la Ficelle with Béarnaise Sauce (see p.140), using the ingredients and measurements given here.

To fry the lamb and serve
Heat the oil to 375°F/190°C in a large saucepan or deep fryer.

Beat an egg in a soup plate or shallow dish with salt, pepper and 2 tablespoons of water. Place the breadcrumbs in another soup plate.

Dip each piece of lamb first into the egg, then into the breadcrumbs, patting off any excess breadcrumbs. Place the prepared lamb on a plate.

When the oil is hot, drop in the pieces of lamb and fry for 1 minute. Lift them out with a skimmer or slotted spoon and drain for a few seconds on paper towels. Place on a serving dish and serve with the sauce on the side.

Suggestions

Butter at room temperature, cut into cubes, can be used instead of the clarified butter. In this case, add the butter as described for the *beurre blanc* in the recipe for Hot Fish Terrine (see p.71). The finished sauce can be reheated over a low heat if you are careful to whisk it constantly and to stop when it is warm, not hot.

Caramelised Pork with Cabbage

Jarret de porc caramélisé aux choux verts

For 4–6 people

1	foreleg of pork, weighing approximately 2kg *(4½ lb)*
	salt
60g *(2½ oz)*	granulated sugar
2 tbsps	olive oil
1½ tbsps	butter
2	medium carrots, chopped
1	large onion, chopped
3	cloves of garlic, chopped
2	sticks of celery, chopped
2	leeks, white part only, chopped
	bouquet garni of parsley stalks, bay leaf and thyme
3	tomatoes, chopped
375ml *(13 fl. oz)*	chicken stock
2	pointed or early green cabbages, weighing about 700g *(1½ lb)* each
	freshly ground pepper

Equipment

large rectangular roasting tin, 35cm *(14 in)* long · large saucepan · bowl
To serve: large heated serving dish

The pork

Two hours before cooking the pork, prepare it as follows. With a sharp knife, make several diagonal slits, about 2½ cm *(1 in)* deep, on the top and bottom of the leg. Pour salt generously over all the surfaces of the leg and rub it into the meat. (The leg should be caked in salt.) Set it aside on a large dish.

After 2 hours, rinse off all the salt under running water and pat the meat dry with a cloth.

Pre-heat the oven to 450°F/230°C/Reg. 8.

Rub the sugar all over the foreleg to coat it completely. Place 1 tablespoon of olive oil in a large roasting tin, add the pork and roast for 30 minutes, basting occasionally and turning the pork 2 to 3 times to brown it evenly on all sides. Take the pork out of the tin and rinse the tin to remove any burnt matter stuck to the bottom. Lower the oven to 375°F/190°C/Reg. 5.

Place the cleaned roasting tin on top of the stove, add the remaining tablespoon of olive oil and the butter, heat until very hot, then add the carrots, onion, garlic, celery, leeks, *bouquet garni* and tomatoes. Sauté the vegetables over a moderate heat for 6–7 minutes to soften, then place the pork on top of them and return the tin to the oven. After 15 minutes, turn the pork over; 7 minutes later add the stock and continue roasting for 1 hour, basting 2–3 times with the cooking liquid.

The cabbage

Slice each cabbage in half lengthwise, cut out the central core and cut the leaves into strips about ½cm *(¼ in)* wide. In a large saucepan of rapidly boiling salted water, boil the strips for 3 minutes from the time the water returns to the boil, drain, cool under running water and drain again.

To finish and serve the pork

Remove the pork from the oven, transfer it to a plate and strain the cooking liquid into a bowl. Press the vegetables with a wooden spoon to extract all their juices, then discard the vegetables.

Rinse the roasting tin and place the strips of cabbage in it. Salt and pepper the cabbage, add the strained cooking liquid, place the leg of pork on top and roast for a further 30 minutes.

Place the pork on a cutting board and carve it. Place the cabbage and cooking juices on a large serving dish, sprinkle with a little pepper, lay the slices of pork on top and serve.

Suggestions

The cabbage could be replaced by Swiss chard.

Wine

Saint-Emilion, Lirac or a red Corsican wine.

160

Boned Roast Shoulder of Lamb with Herbs

Epaule d'agneau en saucisson

For 5–6 people

1	shoulder of lamb, weighing about 1.5kg, *(3¼ lb)*, boned by the butcher (keep the bones)
1	large clove of garlic
2 tsps	butter
5	shallots, finely chopped
3 tbsps	cognac
175g *(6 oz)*	fresh pork back fat or beef suet
175ml *(6 fl. oz)*	double cream or *crème fraîche* (see p. 290)
½ tsp	*quatre épices* (see Note)
1 tsp	ground black pepper
5	large mint leaves, cut into thin strips
2 tbsps	chives, finely chopped
2 tbsps	chervil or parsley, finely chopped
1 tsp	salt
1 tbsp	oil of arachide (refined peanut oil)
325ml *(11 fl. oz)*	water

Equipment
small frying pan · large mixing bowl · small mixing bowl · mincer · trussing needle · kitchen string · oval or rectangular oven dish, 35cm *(14 in)* long
To serve: large heated serving dish and a sauceboat

Preliminary preparations
Lay the shoulder, skin-side down, on a board and use a knife to cut off about one-third of the lean meat, taking it as evenly as possible from the sides and centre of the shoulder. Reserve this meat for the stuffing.

Cut the clove of garlic lengthwise into slivers – about as thick as matchsticks. Lard the entire shoulder with the garlic by making small incisions in the meat with the tip of a pointed knife and sliding slivers of garlic into them.

The stuffing
Melt the butter in a small frying pan, add the shallots and cook for 1 minute or until soft. Add the cognac, boil for 5 seconds and transfer to a bowl to cool.

Cut half the reserved lamb into 1cm *(½-in)* cubes and place in a large mixing bowl. Mince the pork fat and remaining lamb in a mincer, using a coarse blade, and add to the cubes of meat. Using a wooden spoon, beat in the cream, spices, herbs, salt, and reserved shallots and cognac.

161

Season the shoulder with salt and pepper, and spread the stuffing over the surface of the meat. Fold the shoulder in half lengthwise and sew the edges together with a trussing needle and kitchen string to enclose the stuffing completely. If necessary, push the stuffing well into the part that has been sewn together as you go along, in order to use as much of the stuffing as possible (it may not all fit, depending on the shape of the shoulder).

To cook

Pre-heat the oven to 425°F/220°C/Reg. 7.

Heat the oil in the oven dish over a moderate heat. Place the stuffed shoulder and its bones in the dish and brown, turning frequently, for about 5 minutes. Pour off any fat, arrange the bones so that you can place the shoulder on top of them and roast for 20 minutes.

Pour off any fat, add the warm water and roast for 25 minutes more, basting frequently.

To serve the lamb

Place the meat on a serving dish, cover loosely with aluminium foil and keep hot in the turned-off oven for 10 minutes to let the roast rest.

Meanwhile, strain the liquid from the oven dish into a measuring jug. There should be about a generous 200ml *(7 fl. oz)* left; if there is more, boil the liquid to reduce it to that amount. Taste for salt and pepper.

Serve the roast on a serving dish, with its gravy in a sauceboat, with ratatouille, white haricot beans or lentils.

Note

Quatre épices: a blend of spices containing pepper, powdered cloves, ginger and nutmeg, mainly used with pork products.

Wine

A young, refreshing red wine, such as Savoie or Saint-Emilion, or a red Bandol.

Pork Apicius
Sauté de porc Apicius

For 4 people

For the dried fruits

100g *(4 oz)*	raisins
1 tbsp	honey
½ tsp	cumin seeds
1 tsp	dill seed
5	mint leaves, cut into thin strips
15	peppercorns, coarsely ground or crushed
100ml *(4 fl. oz)*	red wine
100g *(4 oz)*	dried apricots

For the pork

800g *(1¾ lb)*	shoulder of pork, cut into 5cm *(2-in)* cubes and boned
	salt, freshly ground pepper
5 tbsps	olive oil
150ml *(¼ pint)*	wine vinegar
6	shallots, sliced
1	large carrot, diced
3	sticks of celery, diced
2	medium tomatoes, coarsely chopped
	bouquet garni of thyme, parsley stalks and a bay leaf
250ml *(9 fl. oz)*	chicken stock

Equipment

2 mixing bowls · *sauteuse* or deep frying pan, 23–25cm *(9–10 in)* in diameter, with lid · skimmer or slotted spoon · large saucepan
To serve: large heated serving dish

Preliminary preparations

The day before cooking the pork, place the raisins in a bowl with the honey, cumin, dill, mint, crushed peppercorns and red wine. Stir to dissolve the honey, cover the bowl with aluminium foil and leave overnight.

Place the dried apricots in another bowl, cover with warm water and leave to soak overnight.

The pork

Generously season the meat with salt and pepper. Heat the olive oil in a *sauteuse* or deep frying pan. Brown the pork on all sides over a moderate heat for about 10 minutes, lift it out of the pan with a skimmer or slotted spoon and drain.

Pour all the fat from the pan and place the pan back over a moderate heat. Add the vinegar, stirring to detach the juices stuck to the bottom of the pan, and boil for 2–3 minutes or until almost all the vinegar has evaporated and it is the consistency of a thick glaze. Add the shallots, carrot, celery, tomatoes and *bouquet garni*, stir over a moderate heat to soften the vegetables, then add the chicken stock and pork. Bring to the boil, lower the heat and simmer, uncovered, for 15 minutes. Then cover the pan and simmer for 1 hour and 10 minutes longer, skimming the surface from time to time.

To finish and serve the pork

Lift the pork out of the pan and reserve. Strain the cooking liquid into a large, clean saucepan, pressing the vegetables with a wooden spoon to extract all their juices.

Drain the apricots and add them, as well as the raisins and their marinade, to the strained sauce. Put the pork back in the sauce and simmer slowly, uncovered, for 25 minutes.

Skim off any fat that surfaces, taste for salt and pepper and serve very hot.

Suggestions

Pork cooked this way is excellent with a carrot or celeriac purée.

Wine

A red Côtes du Rhône or a red Provençal – at any rate a young, refreshing red wine, something simple: perhaps a Coteaux d'Auvergne or a red Saint-Pourçain.

Pork Sautéed Chinese Style
Sauté de porc à la chinoise

For 4 people

For the pork

800g *(1¾ lb)*	boneless shoulder of pork, cut into 3cm *(1½-in)* cubes
	salt, freshly ground pepper
50g *(2 oz)*	granulated sugar
2 tbsps	oil of arachide (refined peanut oil)
3 tbsps	wine vinegar
½ tbsp	tomato purée
300ml *(½ pint)*	chicken or beef stock

For the vegetables

1	carrot, cut into julienne strips
50g *(2 oz)*	green cabbage, cut into julienne strips
3 tbsps	olive oil
100g *(4 oz)*	bean sprouts, trimmed, washed and dried
	salt, freshly ground pepper

Equipment

large frying pan · large saucepan · small frying pan
To serve: large heated serving dish

The pork

Season the pieces of pork generously with salt and pepper, then roll them in the sugar.

Heat the oil of arachide in a large frying pan until very hot, add the pork (in a single layer) and brown over a moderately high heat. The sugar should caramelise but not burn (lower the heat if necessary).

When the pork has browned all over, add the vinegar, stirring in any meat juices and sugar stuck to the bottom of the pan. Lower the heat and boil gently for 2 minutes, then add the tomato and stock. Bring to the boil, stirring constantly, lower the heat and simmer for 50 minutes, uncovered, turning the pieces of pork once or twice.

The vegetables

Bring a large pan of salted water to a boil and add the carrots. Boil for 2 minutes, then add the cabbage and cook for 1 minute longer. Drain, cool under running water and drain again.

Heat 3 tablespoons of olive oil in a small frying pan until very hot, add the bean sprouts, salt and pepper, and sauté for 3 minutes. Drain the bean sprouts thoroughly.

To serve the pork

Taste the pork for salt and pepper.

Wipe the oil from the small frying pan and place the pan over a moderate heat.

Place the pork and its sauce on a large serving dish, then rapidly sauté all the vegetables in the hot pan. Sprinkle them over the pork and serve.

Suggestions

A greater variety of vegetables can be used. For instance, green peas, broad beans, French beans or small pieces of cucumber could be added to the other vegetables, or used instead of them.

Wine

A red wine – Chinon, Bourgueil, a refreshing, young Gigondas or Madiran.

Lamb with Crayfish

Sauté d'agneau aux écrevisses

For 4 people

800g *(1¾ lb)*	boneless lamb, shoulder or neck
	salt, freshly ground pepper
4 tbsps	oil of arachide (refined peanut oil)
1 tbsp	butter
1	large carrot, diced
1	small onion, diced
24	live crayfish (for substitute, see Note)
1–2 tbsps	olive oil
3 tbsps	cognac
2	medium tomatoes, chopped
3	cloves of garlic, crushed
	bouquet garni of half a bay leaf, thyme, and parsley stalks
350ml *(12 fl. oz)*	chicken stock

Equipment

large *sauteuse* or deep frying pan, about 28cm *(11 in)* in diameter, with cover · skimmer or slotted spoon · large mixing bowl
To serve: 4 heated plates

The lamb

Cut the lamb into 4cm *(1½-in)* cubes and season generously with salt and pepper. Heat the oil of arachide in a *sauteuse* or deep frying pan, add the lamb and cook over a moderate heat for 5–6 minutes, turning to brown on all sides. When it is richly browned, stir in the butter, carrot and onion, and continue cooking for 3 minutes to brown the vegetables lightly. Drain the contents of the pan in a strainer over the sink. Pour off the fat from the pan. Reserve the meat and vegetables.

The crayfish

Hold each crayfish by its head, just in front of the tail, with the head pointing downwards. Grasp the central fin of the tail right at its base and bend it back towards the head, twisting gently, and pull it straight out (the string-like intestine will come out with it). Place the crayfish in a colander, rinse under cold running water and drain.

Heat the olive oil in the pan the lamb was cooked in until it is very hot. Add the crayfish, cover and cook for about 7 minutes, shaking the pan often. When all the crayfish are red, lift them out of the pan with a skimmer or slotted spoon and leave until cool enough to handle.

Separate the crayfish tails from the heads. Remove the meat from each tail and reserve. Save 20 heads for the sauce and 4 for decoration.

To cook and serve the lamb

Return the lamb, carrots and onion to the pan, heat over a low heat, add the cognac, boil for 30 seconds and add the tomatoes, garlic and *bouquet garni*. Boil over a moderate heat for about 5 minutes or until all the water in the tomatoes has evaporated. Add the 20 crayfish heads and the chicken stock, season lightly with salt and pepper, cover the pan and simmer gently for 45 minutes, stirring occasionally.

Remove the lamb from the pan and reserve. Strain the sauce into a mixing bowl, pressing the crayfish heads and vegetables with a wooden spoon to extract all their juices. Discard the heads and vegetables, and place the strained sauce in a clean pan with the lamb and crayfish tails.

Heat gently to warm the meat and sauce, taste for salt and pepper, then divide the lamb, crayfish and sauce between the plates. Decorate each plate with one of the reserved crayfish heads and serve.

Suggestions

A 1.4kg *(3-lb)* chicken, cut into 8 pieces, can be used instead of lamb.

Home-made pasta (see p.225), is excellent with this dish.

Note

A 1kg *(2¼-lb)* lobster may be used instead of the crayfish. Boil it for 9 minutes in salted water, timing from the moment the water comes back to the boil. Remove the tail and claw meat from the shell and cut it into slices. Chop the head into several pieces and use as described for the crayfish heads.

Wine

Bouzy or a young claret.

Sweetbreads Pierrette

Ris de veau pierrette

For 4 people

700g *(1½ lb)*	veal sweetbreads
½	small ripe avocado

For the stock

1 tbsp	butter
225g *(½ lb)*	chicken necks, wings or giblets, cut into pieces
5	shallots, sliced
1	medium tomato, seeded and diced
350ml *(12 fl. oz)*	water
	salt, freshly ground pepper

	For the sweetbreads
1 tbsp	butter
1	carrot, diced
1	onion, diced
50ml *(2 fl. oz)*	double cream
100ml *(4 fl. oz)*	whipping cream

	For the sauce
2 tsps	butter (for the shellfish)
8	uncooked Dublin Bay prawns, peeled
2	tomatoes, peeled, seeded and diced
1½ tbsps	butter
2	large basil leaves, finely chopped

Equipment

large bowl · small bowl · medium saucepan · deep frying pan or *sauteuse*, 26cm *(10½ in)* in diameter · small frying pan · wire whisk
To serve: heated serving dish

Preliminary preparations

The night before cooking the sweetbreads, place them in a large bowl of cold water and refrigerate overnight. Change the water at least once.

Drain the sweetbreads and cut off the outer membrane that surrounds them, as well as any fat or reddish spots. Reserve the sweetbreads on a plate and keep the parings for making the stock.

The stock

In a medium saucepan, melt a tablespoon of butter and add the parings from the sweetbreads and the chicken parts. Brown lightly, add the shallots and tomato, and cook over a moderate heat for about 9 minutes or until everything has browned nicely and some of the juices have caramelised on the bottom of the pan. Add the water, scraping the bottom of the pan to dissolve the juices, season lightly with salt and pepper and simmer, uncovered, for 25 minutes. Strain the stock and skim off the fat; there should be 175ml *(6 fl. oz)* of stock left.

The sweetbreads

Pat the sweetbreads dry in a teatowel.

In a deep frying pan or *sauteuse*, melt the butter and add the carrot and onion. Cook gently for 2 minutes to soften them slightly. Push the vegetables to the side of the pan and place the sweetbreads in the middle. Over a moderate heat, brown the sweetbreads lightly on all sides (if necessary, add a little more butter to keep them from sticking) for about 3 minutes. Add the cream, scraping the bottom of the pan to dissolve any meat juices stuck to it, lower the heat and simmer very gently, uncovered, for 15 minutes. Turn the sweetbreads over, add the stock, bring to the boil and simmer gently for 10 minutes more.

168

To finish the sauce and serve

Melt 2 teaspoons of butter in a small frying pan. When very hot, add the peeled Dublin Bay prawns and brown them lightly all over. This should take from 3–5 minutes, depending on their size. Reserve.

Rub the pulp of the avocado through a sieve with a wooden spoon; there should be 2 tablespoons of avocado purée.

Lift the sweetbreads out of the pan and place them on a serving dish. Whisk into their cooking liquid, in the following order, the diced tomatoes, the avocado purée and the butter. Taste for salt and pepper, then add the Dublin Bay prawns and basil. The sauce should be very hot, but do not allow it to boil. Pour it over the sweetbreads and serve immediately.

Suggestions

An equal weight of calves' or lambs' brains may be used instead of sweetbreads. Mint may be used instead of basil.

Wine

A red Bandol or a Chiroubles.

Pork with Orange and Lemon

Sauté de porc aux fruits

For 4 people

For the marinade

	juice of 2 oranges
	juice of 2 lemons
½ tsp	cinnamon
¼ tsp	dried, powdered oregano
2	cloves of garlic, crushed
	salt, freshly ground pepper
800g *(1¾ lb)*	boneless shoulder of pork, cut into 12 pieces

For the sauce

2 tbsps	oil of arachide (refined peanut oil)
40g *(1½ oz)*	butter
2	large tomatoes, peeled, seeded and chopped
	bouquet garni of thyme, parsley stalks and a bay leaf
175ml *(6 fl. oz)*	chicken stock
	salt, freshly ground pepper

Equipment

large mixing bowl · wire whisk · skimmer or slotted spoon · *sauteuse* or deep frying pan, 24cm *(9½ in)* in diameter, with cover
To serve: heated serving dish

To marinate

The day before cooking the pork, whisk together in a large bowl the orange and lemon juices, cinnamon, oregano and garlic. Season the pieces of pork and add them to the bowl; the liquid should just cover the pork (if not, use a smaller bowl). Cover with aluminium foil and refrigerate overnight.

To cook

An hour before cooking, remove the meat from the refrigerator. Lift the pork out of the marinade with a skimmer or slotted spoon and drain it in a sieve over the bowl containing the marinade. Dry the pork.

Heat the oil in a *sauteuse* or deep frying pan. When very hot, add the pork and brown over a high heat for about 2 minutes, stirring frequently. Add the butter, lower the heat and brown over a moderate heat for 5 minutes longer.

Remove the pork with the slotted spoon and drain. Pour off the fat in the pan and dry it with paper towels. Pour the marinade into the pan, place over a moderate heat and stir, scraping the bottom of the pan with a wooden spoon to dissolve any meat juices stuck to it. Boil for about 2 minutes or until the liquid has reduced by half, add the tomatoes, *bouquet garni*, stock and a little salt and pepper. Add the pork, cover and simmer gently for 30 minutes.

To serve the pork

Skim off any fat on the surface of the cooking liquid. Remove the *bouquet garni*, season the sauce generously with salt and pepper and serve.

Suggestions

Duck may be used instead of pork, and grapefruit juice instead of the combined orange and lemon juices.

Either rice or spinach would be an excellent accompaniment for this dish, and wedges of orange and lemon may be placed on each plate as a garnish.

Wine

A young, fresh red wine, such as a red Sancerre or a Saumur-Champigny.

Sweetbreads with Five Vegetables

Ris de veau aux cinq légumes

For 4 people

700g *(1½ lb)*	veal sweetbreads

For the vegetables

2 tbsps	butter
2	medium carrots, cut into julienne strips
10cm *(4-in)*	piece of cucumber, peeled and cut into julienne strips
2	small courgettes, unpeeled, cut into julienne strips
4	large white button mushrooms, cut into julienne strips
	salt, freshly ground pepper
1 tsp	sugar
100g *(4 oz)*	fine French beans, cut in half, blanched for 4 minutes and drained

For the sweetbreads

	salt, freshly ground pepper
2 tbsps	butter

Equipment
large bowl · large frying pan · roasting tin
To serve: 4 heated plates

Preliminary preparations
The night before cooking the sweetbreads, put them into a large bowl of cold water and refrigerate until the next day. Change the water at least once.

The next day, drain the sweetbreads and pat them dry with a towel. Use a sharp knife to remove the surrounding membrane, fat and reddish spots from the sweetbreads.

Pre-heat the oven to 450°F/230°C/Reg. 8.

The vegetables
In a large frying pan, melt 1 tablespoon of butter. Add the carrots and cook over a moderate heat for 3 minutes, shaking the pan several times. Add the rest of the butter; when it has melted, add the cucumber, courgettes and mushrooms. Season with salt, pepper and the sugar. Stir the vegetables together, cook for 4 minutes, add the blanched French beans, cook for 2 minutes and reserve.

The sweetbreads
Season the sweetbreads with salt and pepper.

Melt 2 tablespoons of butter in a roasting tin. Brown the sweetbreads until well coloured on all sides (allow about 5 minutes), then place in the oven and roast for 5 minutes more, turning the sweetbreads over once halfway through the cooking time.

To serve
Quickly reheat the vegetables if necessary. Slice the sweetbreads on a board and arrange them on the heated plates. Season lightly, place the vegetables over the sweetbreads and serve.

Suggestions
Wild mushrooms (chanterelles, ceps and so on) may be used instead of ordinary mushrooms.

Both the vegetables and the sweetbreads may be perfumed with a pinch of saffron and a pinch of curry powder.

Wine
Médoc, a red Coteaux Champenois or a red Sancerre.

Sweetbreads with Little Glazed Onions
Ris de veau aux petits oignons confits

For 4 people

700g *(1 ½ lb)*	veal sweetbreads
	For the sauce
1 ½ tbsps	butter
5	whole peppercorns
4	very large shallots, finely chopped
1	large tomato, diced
3 tbsps	cognac
2 tbsps	red wine vinegar
350ml *(12 fl. oz)*	brown chicken stock
1 tsp	cornflour
50g *(2 oz)*	butter, at room temperature, cut into cubes

                        For the onions
450g *(1 lb)*   button onions, peeled
     1 tbsp   butter
                 salt, freshly ground pepper
     ½ tsp   sugar

                 For the sweetbreads
                 salt, freshly ground pepper
     2 tbsps   butter

Equipment
large bowl · 3 medium saucepans · wire whisk · small frying pan ·
roasting tin
To serve: 4 heated plates

Preliminary preparations
The night before cooking the sweetbreads, place them in a large bowl of
cold water and refrigerate until the next day. Change the water at least
once.

The sauce
Drain the sweetbreads and pat them dry with a cloth. Use a paring knife
to remove the surrounding membrane, fat and reddish spots from the
sweetbreads. Keep all the parings for making the sauce.

Heat 1 tablespoon of butter in a medium saucepan over a moderate heat.
Add the parings from the sweetbreads, stir and brown for about 5
minutes. Add the peppercorns, shallots and tomato and cook for 3
minutes over a high heat to evaporate the moisture from the tomato. Add
the cognac and vinegar, reduce by boiling for 2 minutes over a moderate
heat, then add the stock and bring to the boil. Lower the heat and simmer
the sauce very slowly for 15 minutes, skimming off any foam that surfaces.

To thicken the sauce, mix the cornflour with a little water and pour this
mixture into the sauce very slowly, whisking constantly. Bring to a boil,
still whisking, lower the heat and simmer for 10 minutes. Strain the sauce
into a clean saucepan, pressing on the vegetables to extract all their
juices. Add salt and pepper if needed, skim off the fat, and reserve.

The onions
Cook the onions in boiling salted water for 10 minutes, then drain. Place
them in a small frying pan with the butter and brown over a moderate
heat. Season with salt, pepper and sugar, lower the heat and cook slowly
for 12 minutes, shaking the pan frequently.

The sweetbreads
Pre-heat the oven to 450°F/230°C/Reg. 8.

Heat 2 tablespoons of butter in a roasting tin and brown the sweetbreads until well coloured on all sides (allow about 5 minutes). Place in the oven and roast for 5 minutes, turning the sweetbreads over halfway through the cooking time.

To finish the sauce and serve the sweetbreads
While the sweetbreads are in the oven, heat the sauce over a low heat and whisk in the cubes of butter. Taste for salt and pepper and remove from the heat.

Place the sweetbreads on a board and cut them into ½cm (¼-in) slices. Pour any juices into the sauce and season the slices. Place the onions on the plates, pour the sauce round the outside, place the slices of sweetbreads on top of the onions and serve immediately.

Suggestions
The whites of small leeks may be used instead of small onions. Brains may be used instead of sweetbreads.

Serve with home-made pasta (see p.225) or spinach.

Wine
Côte de Beaune.

Veal Kidneys with Roast Shallots
Rognons de veau aux échalotes roties

For 4 people

For the shallots

700g (1½ lb)	shallots, unpeeled
	salt, freshly ground pepper
2 tsps	sugar
3 tbsps	butter at room temperature, cut into cubes

For the stock

1½ tbsps	butter
700g (1½ lb)	chicken wings or giblets, chopped into large pieces
1	large carrot, diced
1	large onion, chopped
1	stick of celery, chopped
	bouquet garni of 1 sprig of thyme, half a bay leaf and 2 parsley stalks
4	small tomatoes, chopped
4	large mushrooms, chopped
	salt, freshly ground pepper
475ml (16 fl. oz)	water

For the kidneys

125g *(¼ lb)*	fresh pig's caul fat (see Note)
2	veal kidneys, weighing about 350g *(12 oz)* each, outer membrane and fat removed
1 tsp	butter
6 tbsps	double cream or *crème fraîche* (see p.290)
	salt, freshly ground pepper

Equipment

oval or rectangular oven dish, 40cm *(16 in)* long (for the shallots) · small saucepan · large saucepan · skimmer or slotted spoon · liquidiser or *mouli-légumes* · 2 mixing bowls · scissors · small oven dish, 30cm *(12 in)* long (for the kidneys) · wire whisk
To serve: 4 heated plates and a sauceboat

The shallots

Pre-heat the oven to 425°F/220°C/Reg. 7.

Line a large oven dish with aluminium foil, spread the shallots over the bottom of the dish in a single layer, sprinkle with salt, pepper and sugar, and dot with the softened butter. Cover with aluminium foil and bake for 30 minutes. Turn the shallots over, lower the oven temperature to 350°F/180°C/Reg. 4 and bake for 30 minutes more.

Set aside 20 of the largest shallots for garnish. Cut the root ends off the remaining shallots and press to force the cooked pulp from the skins. Chop the pulp to a paste and reserve in a small saucepan.

The stock

Melt 1½ tablespoons of butter in a large saucepan, add the chicken wings or giblets and brown for about 10 minutes. Add the carrot, onion, celery and *bouquet garni*, and cook over a moderate heat for 4 minutes. Add the tomatoes and mushrooms, season lightly with salt and pepper, and simmer to evaporate any moisture. Add the water, bring to the boil, skim from time to time with a skimmer or slotted spoon and simmer, uncovered, for 45 minutes to 1 hour. Strain the stock, pressing on the vegetables with a wooden spoon to extract all the liquids. You will need 225ml *(8 fl. oz)* of stock once the surface fat has been removed. Place the skimmed stock in the saucepan with the chopped shallot pulp and reserve.

The kidneys

Soak the pig's caul in a large bowl of warm water for about 10 minutes before using. Drain it, squeeze out the water, then spread it out and pat it dry with a towel. Cut it with scissors into 2 large squares.

Pre-heat the oven to 425°F/220°C/Reg. 7.

Season the kidneys generously with salt and pepper and wrap each one in pig's caul. Put them in an oven dish with a teaspoon of butter and roast for 10 minutes. Turn the kidneys over and roast for 8 minutes more (they should be pink inside). After the kidneys have been turned over, wrap the whole shallots reserved earlier in a piece of aluminium foil and reheat them in the oven while the kidneys finish cooking.

To finish the sauce and serve the shallots

Whisk the cream into the stock–shallot mixture and simmer for 12 minutes. Season with salt and pepper if needed, pour the sauce into a liquidiser and blend until smooth, or work it through a *mouli-légumes*.

Remove the kidneys and whole shallots from the oven. Place the kidneys on a board, remove any pieces of fat remaining, cut them into thin slices and season with salt and pepper.

Place a little of the shallot sauce on each of the hot plates, arrange the slices of kidney on top, garnish each plate with 5 whole shallots and serve.

Suggestions

A simpler version of the sauce can be made by eliminating the stock and heating the chopped shallots with cream before liquidising (this is quicker but not as good).

Veal sweetbreads can be soaked overnight, then prepared exactly as described for the kidneys.

The roast shallots could be served with roast pork, roast chicken or duck.

Note

Pig's caul fat should be used if possible, but a tablespoon of lard can be rubbed on each kidney before roasting if caul fat is unavailable. In this case, baste the kidneys 2 or 3 times while roasting.

Wine

A Côtes du Rhône, such as red Hermitage; a Nuits-Saint-Georges, Beaune, Saint-Emilion, or Château Figeac.

Veal Kidneys Berkeley
Rognons de veau Berkeley

For 4 people

2	whole veal kidneys, weighing about 350g *(12 oz)* each, or 3–4 smaller kidneys, outer membrane and fat removed
	salt, freshly ground pepper
2 tbsps	oil of arachide (refined peanut oil)
8	shallots, chopped
2	medium carrots, cut into large julienne strips
½ tsp	thyme leaves
2	medium tomatoes, chopped
6 tbsps	madeira
350ml *(12 fl. oz)*	water
325ml *(11 fl. oz)*	whipping cream
2	generous tbsps *mousse de foie gras* (for substitute, see Note)
5 tsps	pale Dijon mustard

Equipment
oval or rectangular oven dish, 30cm *(12 in)* long · skimmer or slotted spoon · small mixing bowl · wire whisk
To serve: heated serving dish or 4 heated plates, and a sauceboat

The kidneys
Pre-heat the oven to 425°F/220°C/Reg. 7.

Lightly season each kidney. Heat 2 tablespoons of oil in an oven dish and brown the kidneys over a moderate heat for 4 minutes, turning frequently. Remove the kidneys from the pan with a skimmer or slotted spoon, and reserve on a plate, covered with aluminium foil.

Add the shallots and carrots to the oven dish, sprinkle with the thyme and brown for 3 minutes. Add the tomatoes and cook over a moderate heat for 3 minutes longer. Place the kidneys on top of the vegetables and roast for 12 minutes. Place the kidneys on a plate, cover with aluminium foil and keep hot in the oven with the door ajar while making the sauce.

The sauce
Place the oven dish over a moderate heat and boil the vegetables and cooking liquid for 3 minutes or until all the liquid has evaporated. Add the madeira and boil for 2 minutes, scraping the bottom of the pan to dissolve any meat juices caramelised on the bottom. When the madeira has reduced by half, add the water and boil for about 7 minutes. Add the cream, stir and simmer for about 5 minutes to thicken the sauce. Reserve.

In a small mixing bowl, beat the *mousse de foie gras* with the mustard until a smooth paste is formed. Strain the sauce gradually on to the mixture, whisking to combine. Taste the sauce and add salt and pepper if needed. The sauce can be gently reheated, but it should not boil.

To serve
Remove the kidneys from the oven; they can be served whole on a serving dish with the sauce in a sauceboat, or sliced (season the slices) and served on individual plates with the sauce underneath them.

Suggestion
Sweetbreads, first soaked overnight, can be cooked exactly as described for the kidneys.

Note
Tinned *foie gras* mousse is used in making the sauce, but an acceptable substitute can be made with chicken livers. Heat a tablespoon of butter in a small frying pan, add 3 chicken livers, 1 finely chopped shallot and a pinch of thyme. Cook over a high heat for about 2 minutes, pour off the fat, deglaze the pan with a teaspoon of sherry, then pour everything into a liquidiser and blend to a fine purée. Cool before using for the sauce.

Wine
Volnay, Médoc or Saint-Julien.

Calf's Head in Champagne Robert Courtine
Courtinandise

For 5–6 people

For the stock

1.1kg *(2½ lb)*	breast of veal and bones, sawn into pieces
1	bottle champagne (or other dry white wine)
2 tbsps	olive oil
1 tsp	butter
	salt, freshly ground pepper
2	carrots, coarsely chopped
2	sticks of celery, coarsely chopped
	bouquet garni of thyme, bay leaf and parsley stalks
2	onions, diced
450g *(1 lb)*	tomatoes, diced
1	clove of garlic, crushed
1 litre *(1½ pints)*	water

For the calf's head and foot

675g *(1½ lb)*	boned calf's head
1	whole calf's foot
1	lemon, cut in half
650g *(1½ lb)*	small carrots, 'turned' into olive-shaped pieces or cut into quarters
400g *(14 oz)*	young turnips, prepared like the carrots
400g *(14 oz)*	celeriac, prepared like the carrots
	flour (for sealing the casserole)
	salt, freshly ground pepper

For the onions

2 tsps	butter
250g *(9 oz)*	button onions, peeled
	salt, freshly ground pepper
½ tsp	sugar

Equipment

roasting tin · skimmer or slotted spoon · 2 large pans, 4½-litre *(8-pint)* capacity each · small mixing bowl · large frying pan · medium saucepan · large casserole, with lid · pastry brush · small frying pan, with lid

The veal stock

Pre-heat the oven to 425°F/220°C/Reg. 7.

Bone the breast of veal, place the bones in a roasting tin and roast for 45 minutes, turning frequently to brown. Remove from the oven, lift out the bones with a skimmer or slotted spoon, place them in a large pan and reserve. Pour off any fat in the roasting tin.

Pour a glass of the champagne into the roasting tin, scraping the bottom of the tin with a wooden spoon; pour into a bowl and reserve.

Cut the meat from the breast of veal into large cubes.

Heat the olive oil and butter in a large frying pan, add the pieces of veal, season generously with salt and pepper, and brown on all sides over a moderate heat. Lower the heat and simmer for 6 minutes. Remove the veal from the pan with a skimmer or slotted spoon and place in the pan with the bones.

Add the carrots and celery to the frying pan and simmer for 6 minutes to soften, then add them to the pan with the veal. Place the pan over a moderate heat, add the *bouquet garni* and the onions and simmer for 3 minutes. Add the tomatoes and garlic and boil rapidly for about 5 minutes to evaporate most of the liquid given off by the vegetables. Add the champagne remaining in the bottle and that used to deglaze the roasting tin. Bring to the boil, add the water and bring back to simmering point.

The calf's head and foot

Cut the head into 10–12 pieces. Leave the calf's foot whole. Rub both with lemon, place them in a large pan and add enough cold water to cover them by several inches. Bring to a boil, boil rapidly for 2 minutes, drain and cool under cold running water.

Add the head and foot to the simmering stock, lower the heat, cover the pan and simmer for 1 hour, skimming frequently.

Cook the carrots, turnips and celeriac for 3 minutes in a large pan of rapidly boiling water, drain, and cool under running water.

Lift the pieces of calf's head out of the stock and place them in a large casserole with the carrots, turnips and celeriac. Bone the foot, cut it into four large pieces and add it to the head. Strain the stock, pressing on the vegetables and meat to extract their juices (do not discard the meat; see Note), and ladle enough of the strained stock into the casserole almost to cover the meat. Taste and season generously with salt and pepper. Seal the casserole with a mixture of flour and water (for instructions, see Note under Chicken with 40 Cloves of Garlic, p.185), then bake for 30 minutes.

To finish and serve the *Courtinandise*

Melt 2 teaspoons of butter in a small frying pan, add the button onions, salt, pepper and sugar. Shake the pan and cook the onions over a moderate heat for a minute or two, then add enough water almost to cover the onions (they should not float). Half cover the pan and boil rapidly to evaporate the water and glaze the onions (allow about 10 minutes).

Remove the casserole from the oven, pry open the lid of the casserole, add the onions and serve (preferably with champagne).

Note

Any remaining stock can be reheated with the pieces of veal used in making it to make a small stew. Bind the cooking liquid with egg yolks and cream, add a little lemon juice and you have one of the many versions of *blanquette de veau*. (A few baby carrots, onions and button mushrooms can be added as well.)

Wine

Champagne or Lirac.

Sweetbreads with Red Peppers, Courgettes and Aubergines

Ris de veau à la crème de poivrons

For 4 people

800g *(1¾ lb)*	veal sweetbreads

For the sauce

1½ tbsps	butter
10	peppercorns, coarsely crushed
4 tbsps	sherry vinegar
475ml *(16 fl. oz)*	double cream or *crème fraîche* (see p.290)
2	large red peppers, coarsely chopped
	salt, freshly ground pepper

For the sweetbreads

2 tbsps	butter
9	silver onions, thinly sliced
2	medium red peppers, seeded and cut into julienne strips
1	medium courgette (do not peel), seeds removed, cut into julienne strips
1	small aubergine (do not peel), seeds removed, cut into julienne strips
	salt, freshly ground pepper
1 tbsp	oil of arachide (refined peanut oil)
1 tbsp	butter

Equipment

large bowl · 2 medium saucepans · liquidiser or food processor · sieve · small saucepan · wire whisk · large frying pan · roasting tin
To serve: heated serving dish or 4 heated plates

Preliminary preparations

The night before cooking the sweetbreads, place them in a large bowl of cold water and refrigerate until the next day. Change the water at least once.

The sauce

Drain the sweetbreads and pat them dry in a towel. With a small knife, carefully remove the outer membrane as well as any fat or reddish spots. Save these parings for the sauce. Reserve the sweetbreads on a plate.

In a medium saucepan, heat 1½ tablespoons of butter. When very hot, add the sweetbread parings and the peppercorns and cook, stirring frequently, for 3 minutes or until the bits of meat begin to brown lightly. Add the vinegar and boil for 45 seconds, scraping the bottom of the pan to dissolve any meat juices.

181

Add the cream, stir and bring to the boil. Lower the heat and boil very gently for 25 minutes. Skim off any foam that surfaces while the sauce is cooking. Strain the sauce into a clean saucepan – there should be 200ml *(7 fl. oz)*.

Blend the peppers to a purée in a liquidiser or food processor. Transfer this purée to a fine sieve over a small saucepan and press it down well to extract all the juices. Place the pan over a low heat and simmer until you have about 1 tablespoon left. Whisk this essence of red pepper into the sauce and reserve.

The vegetable garnish

Melt 2 tablespoons of butter in a large frying pan. When hot, add the onions, lower the heat and cook for 2 minutes or until soft and transparent – they should not brown. Add the juliennes of pepper, cook for 2 minutes over a moderate heat, stirring frequently, then add the courgette and aubergine, sprinkle with salt and pepper and cook for 2 minutes more, stirring frequently. Reserve.

The sweetbreads

Pre-heat the oven to 450°F/230°C/Reg. 8. Season the sweetbreads on both sides with salt and pepper.

Heat the oil in a roasting tin. When very hot, add the butter and when it has melted add the sweetbreads. Brown over a moderate to high heat on all sides (allow about 5–6 minutes), then place in the oven and roast for 10 minutes more, turning the sweetbreads over halfway through their cooking time.

To serve the sweetbreads

Cut the sweetbreads into slices about ½cm *(¼ in)* thick and season with salt and pepper.

Reheat the vegetables if necessary and place them in the centre of the serving dish or the plates. Spoon the sauce over and around the vegetables, arrange the slices of sweetbread on top, reheat briefly in the oven if necessary and serve immediately.

Wine

Médoc or young Côte de Beaune or a Côtes du Rhône such as Côte Rôtie.

POULTRY
AND
GAME

Chicken with 40 Cloves of Garlic
Poulet aux 40 gousses d'ail

For 4 people

For the garlic

2 tbsps	olive oil
	salt, freshly ground pepper
½ tsp	sugar
40	large cloves of garlic (about 4 large heads), separated but unpeeled

For the chicken

100ml *(4 fl. oz)*	olive oil
1	chicken, weighing 1.4kg (3 lb)
	salt, freshly ground pepper
2 tbsps	parsley, finely chopped
2 tbsps	chervil, finely chopped
2 tbsps	chives, finely chopped
2 tbsps	coriander leaf, finely chopped
2 tsps	basil, finely chopped
1 tsp	thyme leaves
½	bay leaf
80g *(4 oz)* approx.	flour (for sealing the casserole)

Equipment
large oval casserole, with lid · pastry brush

The garlic
Pour 2 tablespoons of olive oil on to a plate, season with salt, pepper and sugar, and roll the unpeeled cloves of garlic in the mixture to coat them completely.

To cook
Pre-heat the oven to 425°F/220°C/Reg. 7.

Heat the remaining olive oil in an oval casserole. Season the chicken generously inside and out with salt and pepper and place it in the casserole. Distribute the cloves of garlic around the chicken, sprinkle the herbs over everything, seal the casserole (see Note) and bake for 1 hour.

To serve the chicken
Take the casserole to the table and break the seal in front of your guests. Cut the chicken into pieces, sprinkle each piece with a little salt and pepper, spoon the herbs and garlic over the chicken, and serve. Each person should split the cloves of garlic open with a knife and eat the creamy inside as a vegetable.

Note
Add enough water to the flour to make a soft dough. Roll the dough between the palms of your hands, or on the table, to form a sausage (or 3–4 smaller sausages) long enough to go around the edge of the casserole. With a pastry brush dipped in water, dampen the rim of the casserole, place the sausage(s) around the edge and press down to hold in place. Lightly brush the dough with water, put the lid of the casserole into place, press it down and fold any excess dough up over the edge of the lid, pressing on it as you do so.

Wine
Côtes du Rhône, Madiran, Passe-Tous-Grains or red Coteaux d'Aix.

Chicken Dufour
Poulet Maître Dufour

For 4 people

	fritter batter (see p.238)
1	small chicken, weighing about 1kg *(2¼ lb)*, with liver, heart and gizzard
1	cooked lamb's brain (see Note), cut into 1cm *(½-in)* cubes (optional)
	salt, freshly ground pepper
2 tbsps	butter
1	onion, coarsely chopped
1	carrot, coarsely chopped
	bouquet garni
½	chicken stock cube
225ml *(8 fl. oz)*	whipping cream
1	small or ½ large, ripe avocado
	oil of arachide (refined peanut oil), for deep frying

Equipment
cleaver or poultry shears · small saucepan · deep frying pan or *sauteuse*, 24cm *(9½ in)* in diameter · large saucepan or deep fryer · deep-frying thermometer · wire whisk
To serve: heated serving dish

Preliminary preparations
Cut the legs, neck and wings from the chicken. Cut the drumsticks from the thighs and reserve on a plate.

With a large knife or cleaver or shears, separate the back from the breast and reserve on another plate with the wings and neck.

With a cleaver or poultry shears, split the breast by cutting through the breastbone. Cut each half breast in two and reserve with the legs.

Clean the gizzard and cut it into 4 pieces. Remove any greenish parts from the liver and cut it into four, cut the heart in half and place all of this on a third plate with the pieces of lamb's brain.

The chicken and the avocado

Season the legs and breasts with salt and pepper. Melt a tablespoon of butter in a deep frying pan or *sauteuse*, add the onion, cook for 1–2 minutes to soften, then add the carrot, a little salt and pepper, and simmer for 3–4 minutes. Add the remaining butter, raise the heat and add the chicken legs and breasts, stiffen over a low heat for 3–4 minutes without browning, add the back, wings and neck, the *bouquet garni* and enough liquid to come halfway up the pieces of chicken. Add half a stock cube, bring to the boil, cover the pan, lower the heat and simmer for 11 minutes. Turn the breasts and legs over after about 6 minutes.

Lift the legs and breasts out of the pan, skim off any scum that has surfaced and boil the liquid with the bones and vegetables until it has almost completely evaporated. Add the cream, place the legs and breasts back in the pan and simmer for 5 minutes. Cover and keep hot.

Peel the avocado, remove the stone, and purée the pulp by working it through a sieve with a wooden spoon. Place the purée in a small saucepan, cover and reserve for making the sauce.

The fritters

Heat the oil to 375°F/190°C in a large saucepan or deep fryer. Dip the pieces of lamb's brain, chicken liver, gizzard and heart into the batter and drop them into the hot oil. Fry for 3–4 minutes or until golden brown, then drain on paper towels while finishing the sauce.

To finish the sauce and serve the chicken

Place the chicken legs and breasts on a serving dish or divide them among 4 plates, with a piece of breast and a piece of leg on each one. Keep hot.

Spoon off as much fat as you can from the surface of the cooking juices, then strain them into the pan containing the avocado purée. Press gently on the bones and vegetables to extract their juices. Whisk the avocado sauce over a very low heat until very hot (but not boiling), taste for salt and pepper, and pour into a sauceboat. Spoon a little of the sauce over the chicken, place the fritters on a separate small dish and serve, with the sauce on the side.

Note

To prepare the lamb's brain, soak it for 2 hours in cold water, changing the water several times. Then, with your fingers, carefully peel off the thin membrane that surrounds it. Place 500ml *(16 fl. oz)* of water, 2 tablespoons of vinegar and a pinch of salt in a small saucepan, bring to a boil, add the lamb's brain and poach for 5 minutes. Drain on a cloth and allow to cool completely before cutting it into pieces.

Wine

A strong white Côtes du Rhône such as Hermitage.

Roast Pigeon with Broad Beans and Mangetout Peas
Pigeons rôtis aux fèves et aux pois gourmands

For 4 people

For the stock

4	young farmed pigeons, weighing about 350g *(¾ lb)* each (for substitute, see Note)
I tsp	butter
400ml *(14 fl. oz)*	water
	salt, freshly ground pepper

For the pigeon

	salt, freshly ground pepper
I tbsp	oil of arachide (refined peanut oil)
I tbsp	butter

For the vegetables

12	button onions, peeled
2 tbsps	butter
900g *(2 lb)*	broad beans, shelled and with the skin around each bean removed
225g *(8 oz)*	mangetout peas, strings removed
	salt, freshly ground pepper
¼ tsp	fresh rosemary leaves, finely chopped
½ tsp	sugar

Equipment

small saucepan · mixing bowl · kitchen string · oval or rectangular roasting tin, 33cm *(13 in)* long · medium saucepan · large frying pan
To serve: 4 heated plates and a sauceboat

The stock

Cut the neck and wings off each pigeon (or use 225g (½ lb) of chicken wings). Heat a teaspoon of butter in a small saucepan, add the wings and necks, and brown for 3–4 minutes. Add the water, bring to the boil, stirring to detach the meat juices stuck to the bottom of the pan and boil for 15 minutes or until the liquid has reduced almost by half. Strain the stock into a measuring jug; there should be 175ml (6 fl. oz) below the layer of fat on the surface. Spoon off the fat, season with salt and pepper and reserve in a bowl.

The pigeons

Pre-heat the oven to 425°F/220°C/Reg. 7. Season the pigeons generously inside and out with salt and pepper and truss them for roasting.

Heat the oil and butter in a roasting tin, add the pigeons and brown over a moderate heat for 6 minutes, then roast for 12 minutes, basting several times.

The vegetables

Boil the onions in a saucepan of rapidly boiling water for 4 minutes, then drain.

Melt 2 tablespoons of butter in a large frying pan, add the broad beans and mangetout peas and sauté over a moderate heat for 2 minutes. Season with salt and pepper, lower the heat and cook for 4 minutes, covered, stirring occasionally. Add the onions, rosemary, sugar, salt and pepper and sauté for 4 minutes more, uncovered.

To finish and serve the pigeons

Remove the string from the pigeons. Place the vegetables on plates and place the pigeons on top. Pour all the fat from the roasting tin, add the stock, bring quickly to a boil, stirring to detach any caramelised meat juices, then strain the sauce into a sauceboat. Serve, with the sauce on the side.

Note

A 1.6kg (3½-lb) duck may be used instead of the pigeons. It will take a bit longer to brown before roasting, and duck should roast for 30 minutes rather than 12 minutes, or longer if you like it a little more cooked.

Wine

Côte Rôtie, Volnay, Chambolle-Musigny.

Roast Pigeon with Leeks
Pigeons aux poireaux confits

For 2 people

1kg *(2¼ lb)*	leeks, white part only
2	young farmed pigeons, weighing about 350g *(12 oz)* each
	salt, freshly ground pepper
1½ tbsps	plus 1 tsp butter
2 tsps	sugar
	water

Equipment
large saucepan · kitchen string · large oval or rectangular oven dish, 30–33cm *(12–13 in)* long · smaller oven dish, 25–28cm *(10–11 in)* long · bowl
To serve: 2 heated plates

Preliminary preparations
Cut the white of each leek into pieces about 5cm *(2 in)* long and cut each piece in half lengthwise. Separate the leaves and wash in cold water. Drain well, then boil for 3 minutes in rapidly boiling salted water. Drain, cool under running water, drain again and reserve.

Cut the neck and wings off each pigeon, season each bird inside and out with salt and pepper, then tie them with string to hold the legs close to the body.

The leeks and pigeons
Pre-heat the oven to 475°F/220°C/Reg. 7.

Heat 1½ tablespoons of butter in a large oven dish, add the leeks, season generously with salt and pepper, stir in the sugar and sauté for 6–7 minutes or until all the liquid in the pan has evaporated. Reserve.

In a smaller oven dish, heat 1 teaspoon of butter, brown the pigeons, their giblets and necks over a moderately high heat for about 6 minutes, turning frequently to avoid burning.

Place both the oven dishes in the oven and cook for 12 minutes. Turn the birds over halfway through the cooking time; the leeks should become slightly caramelised and glazed.

To finish and serve the pigeons
Turn the oven off and place the pigeons on top of the leeks to keep warm inside the oven while making the sauce.

Place the necks and giblets on a plate and pour all the fat from the pigeons' oven dish.

Put the necks and giblets back in the oven dish, place over a high heat, add the water and boil rapidly for 4 minutes to make a light sauce. Add salt and pepper as needed, then strain into a bowl.

Remove the leeks and pigeons from the oven, untruss the birds, divide the leeks between the plates, place a pigeon on top of each, spoon the sauce over and serve.

Note

If possible, cut the birds into quarters after they are cooked and serve this way, rather than whole. Although slightly more complicated, the presentation is nicer and the birds are much easier to eat.

Wine

A Côte Rôtie, Volnay or Echézeaux.

Pigeons Peking Style
Pigeons pékinois

For 4 people

4	young farmed pigeons, with their giblets, weighing about 350g *(¾ lb)* each (for substitute, see Note)

For the marinade

500ml *(16 fl. oz)*	white wine
175ml *(6 fl. oz)*	light corn syrup
175ml *(6 fl. oz)*	dark corn syrup
6 tbsps	soy sauce

For the stock

1 tsp	butter
225g *(½ lb)*	chicken necks, wings or giblets
2	tomatoes, chopped
4	shallots, chopped
	salt, freshly ground pepper
	water

For the lime and ginger julienne

	zest of 2 limes, cut into fine julienne strips
8cm *(3-in)*	piece of fresh ginger, peeled and cut into fine julienne strips
	water
50g *(2 oz)*	caster sugar

Equipment

kitchen string · large wide bowl · 2 medium saucepans · small
saucepan · wire whisk · large oval roasting tin, 33–35cm *(13–14 in)*
long
To serve: 4 heated plates and a sauceboat

To marinate

The day before, cut the neck and wing tips off each bird and reserve them
for making the stock.

Truss the birds for roasting.

In a bowl large enough to hold the pigeons in one layer, whisk the wine,
the corn syrups and the soy sauce together thoroughly for 3–4 minutes to
mix the ingredients well. Place the pigeons in the marinade and cover the
bowl. Refrigerate for 24 hours to marinate (if the birds are not completely
covered by the marinade, turn them over every 6–8 hours).

Remove the bowl from the refrigerator an hour or two before cooking the
pigeons.

The stock

In a medium saucepan, melt a teaspoon of butter, add the reserved necks,
giblets, wing tips and the chicken parts, and sauté quickly to brown. Add
the tomatoes and shallots, season lightly, and boil for about 5 minutes or
until almost all the liquid given out by the tomatoes has evaporated. Add
the water, bring to simmering point and cook, uncovered, for 25–30
minutes. Strain the stock into a clean saucepan, pressing on the meat
and vegetables to extract all the juices; there should be 175ml *(6 fl. oz)* of
stock left. Skim off any fat and reserve the stock.

The lime and ginger julienne

Place the julienne of lime zest and ginger in a small saucepan with the
water and sugar, bring to the boil, lower the heat and simmer very slowly
for 25 minutes. Drain the julienne and place in the saucepan with the
strained stock.

Place the saucepan over a very low heat and simmer for 20 minutes.
Reserve.

The pigeons

Pre-heat the oven to 450°F/230°C/Reg. 8.

Lift the pigeons out of the marinade, then pour half the marinade into a
roasting tin. On top of the stove, bring the marinade to the boil, then
place the pigeons in the tin on their sides. Roast for 8 minutes, turn the
birds over and roast for 8 minutes on the other side. Turn the birds on to
their backs and roast for a final 10 minutes. Untie the birds, place them
on a dish and put them back into the turned-off oven with the door ajar.

To finish the sauce and serve the pigeons

Place the roasting tin back over a high heat and boil the cooking liquid for 3 minutes. Measure out 150ml (¼ pint) of the reduced liquid and add it to the saucepan with the stock, lime and ginger. Reheat if necessary.

Place a pigeon on each plate, spoon some of the sauce over each one and serve, with the rest of the sauce in a sauceboat.

Suggestions

Serve the pigeons accompanied by either fresh green peas or soy bean sprouts that have been sautéed in a little oil and seasoned with salt, pepper and a touch of soy sauce.

Note

Duck may be used instead of pigeons. Buy one weighing about 1.5kg (3¼ lb), cut off the wing tips and neck, and marinate as described for the pigeons. Roast for 1 hour and 20 minutes, turning and basting every 10–15 minutes to brown evenly on all sides. Because of the longer cooking time, there is no need to boil and reduce the cooking liquid. Skim the fat off before measuring and adding it to the stock, lime and ginger mixture. Carve the duck, place a piece on each plate and serve as described for the pigeons.

Wine

A Côtes du Rhône – red Hermitage, or a red Burgundy – Moulin-à-Vent.

Stuffed Duck Legs with Pasta
Jambonnettes de canard

For 4 people

2	ducks, weighing 2kg (4½ lb) each

For the stuffing

100g (¼ lb)	pork back fat
2	duck (or 4 chicken) livers
6 tbsps	crème fraîche (see p.290) or double cream
1 generous tsp	parsley, finely chopped
1 generous tsp	chervil, finely chopped
1 generous tsp	chives, finely chopped
½ tsp	thyme leaves
1 tbsp	cognac
	a pinch of quatre épices (see p. 162)
	salt, freshly ground pepper

For the stock

3	medium tomatoes, chopped
1	small carrot, finely chopped
1	small onion, finely chopped
1	stick of celery, finely chopped
2	cloves of garlic, crushed
	bouquet garni of parsley, thyme, a bay leaf and a leek leaf
1 tbsp	tomato paste
1¾ litres *(3 pints)*	chicken stock
	salt
15	whole peppercorns

For cooking the ducks' legs

2 tbsps	oil
	salt, freshly ground pepper
1 tbsp	butter
10	shallots, finely chopped
1	large stick of celery, finely chopped
1 generous tsp	peppercorns, coarsely crushed
475ml *(16 fl. oz)*	red wine
½ tsp	thyme leaves
	home-made pasta (see p.225)

Equipment

small boning knife · mincer or food processor · large mixing bowl · trussing needle · kitchen string · cleaver · large *sauteuse* or casserole, 25–28cm *(10–11 in)* in diameter · small saucepan
To serve: 4 heated plates and a sauceboat

To stuff the legs

Remove the legs from the ducks; remove the breast meat as well and reserve for making either Preserved Duck (see p.196) or one of the recipes for duck breasts (see p.197 and p.203). Save the wings, neck and carcass of one of the ducks for making the stock for this recipe.

Place the duck legs, skin-side down, on a board and with a small knife slit them lengthwise on the inner side. Carefully de-bone first the thigh, then the drumstick (do not cut them apart). Be careful not to cut or puncture the skin.

Carefully cut away half of the duck meat from each leg, horizontally and as evenly as possible. Place this meat, with the pork back fat and duck livers, in a mincer or food processor and mince, not too finely. Transfer the mixture to a bowl and add the cream, herbs, cognac and *quatre épices*; season generously and mix with a spoon for several minutes.

Using a trussing needle and kitchen string, fasten the lower end of each drumstick. Spread the legs out on a clean surface, skin-side down, and season the meat lightly. Spread a quarter of the stuffing over each leg, then fold the legs in half lengthwise so that the edges touch. Using the needle and string, sew the edges together, enclosing the stuffing, and making 4 approximately triangular pouches. Reserve on a plate while making the stock.

The stock

Chop the reserved duck carcass, wings and neck into pieces with a cleaver. Place them in a large saucepan and brown over a low heat for about 10 minutes (no fat need be added). Add the tomatoes and boil for about 8 minutes, stirring frequently, to evaporate their water, then add the carrot, onion, celery, garlic and *bouquet garni*. Simmer for 8 minutes longer to soften the vegetables, then add the tomato paste, stock, a little salt and the peppercorns, and simmer uncovered for 90 minutes. Skim off any foam that surfaces. Strain the stock; there should be about 450ml *(¾ pint)* and spoon off any fat from its surface. Reserve.

To cook the legs

Heat 2 tablespoons of oil in a casserole large enough to hold all 4 legs in a single layer with a little space around them. Season with a little salt and pepper, prick each one once with a trussing needle and place them in the hot oil. Brown evenly over a moderate heat for about 8 minutes, turning them over with a wooden spoon. Place on paper towels to drain, and reserve.

Pour away the fat from the casserole and place the pan back over a moderate heat. Heat the tablespoon of butter, add the shallots, celery and peppercorns, and simmer for about 5 minutes or until the shallots are soft. Add the wine, raise the heat and boil rapidly for 14 minutes or until all but about a tablespoon of the wine has evaporated.

Pre-heat the oven to 425°F/220°C/Reg. 7.

Place the duck legs in the casserole with the reduced wine mixture and add the stock reserved earlier (the legs should be half-covered by the liquid). Add the thyme leaves, cover the casserole and bake for 32 minutes.

To serve the stuffed ducks' legs

Place the legs on a board.

Strain the cooking liquid into a measuring jug and skim off the fat. If there is more than 300ml *(½ pint)*, pour the liquid into a clean saucepan and boil rapidly to reduce it to that amount.

Carefully remove the string from each leg.

Spoon a little of the sauce on to each plate, then pour the rest of the sauce into a sauceboat. Place a stuffed leg on each plate and serve with home-made pasta (see p.225) – the perfect accompaniment for the taste of both the duck and the sauce.

Wine

A red Burgundy, Mazis-Chambertin or Latricières-Chambertin.

Preserved Duck
Confit de Canard

For about 700g (1½ lb)

1	duck, weighing about 1.5kg *(3¼ lb)*
1	clove of garlic, cut in half
50g *(2 oz)*	coarse salt
1 tsp	thyme leaves
1 tbsp	peppercorns, coarsely crushed
1.5kg *(3¼ lb)*	goose or duck fat

Equipment

mixing bowl · large casserole · 2 1-litre *(2-pint)* preserving jars (glass or stoneware)

Salting the duck

The day before cooking, cut the legs off the duck and separate the thighs from the drumsticks.

Cut off the breast meat and wings, each side in one piece, then cut these pieces in half across the middle of the breast. Rub each piece of duck with garlic.

Mix the coarse salt, thyme and pepper in a bowl and rub each piece of duck with this mixture, pressing it in well. Shake off any excess salt, place the duck on a plate, covered loosely, and refrigerate for 24 hours before cooking.

Cooking the duck

Wipe each piece of duck with a cloth and reserve.

Melt the goose fat in a large casserole. When hot, place the pieces of duck in it (they should be completely covered) and simmer very gently for 1 hour over a very low heat. Then skim off any scum that has appeared and simmer for 30 minutes more. Test the duck to see if it has cooked through: if the meat comes easily away from the bone, it is done; if not, cook for a bit longer and test again.

Storing the duck

Lift the duck out of the fat and place the pieces in the jars (in each jar, place the long piece with the wing in first, upright, then fit in the other half of the breast and a thigh and drumstick. Pour or ladle the fat through a sieve into the jar until the duck is covered, then cover the jars and store in the refrigerator. The preserved duck can be kept for several months if left untouched.

To use the duck

Preserved duck is used in several recipes in this book, generally one jar 350g *(¾ lb)* at a time.

To remove the duck from the jar, place the jar in a slow oven to melt the fat, remove the pieces and drain thoroughly before following the cooking instructions given in any recipe.

Suggestions

Goose or pork can be preserved in the same way. Use an equal weight of fat and meat to preserve (if preserving pork, use lard). Goose fat can be obtained in tins from Hobbs & Co., 30 South Audley Street, London W1.

Wine

Madiran, Cahors or red Coteaux d'Aix.

Duck Breasts with Honey and Thyme
Magrets de canard au miel et à la fleur de thym

For 4 people

2	ducks, weighing 1.8–2kg *(4–4½ lb)* each (see Note)

For the stock

1 tsp	butter
1 tbsp	oil
1	onion, finely chopped
2	carrots, finely chopped
	bouquet garni of thyme, parsley and a bay leaf
1	stick of celery, finely chopped
2	medium tomatoes, chopped
1	small clove of garlic, crushed
5	mushrooms, chopped
	salt, freshly ground pepper
1 litre *(1½ pints)*	water

For the sauce

2 tbsps	honey
¼ tsp	thyme leaves and flowers
3 tbsps	red wine vinegar
½ tsp	salt
	freshly ground pepper

For the duck breasts

	salt, freshly ground pepper
2 tbsps	butter
2 tbsps	honey
l tsp	thyme leaves or flowers

Equipment

cleaver · large stock pan · skimmer · small bowl · small saucepan · large frying pan
To serve: 4 heated plates and a sauceboat

Preliminary preparations

Cut the legs from each duck and reserve for use in other recipes (see Note). Remove each breast, keeping your knife close to the bone to make thick steaks. Remove the skin from each duck breast and trim off all but a very thin layer of fat.

Cut off the wings and chop the duck carcasses into pieces with a cleaver; reserve for making the stock.

The duck stock

Heat the butter and oil in a large pan, add the duck bones and wings and brown for about 8 minutes (be careful not to let them burn). Add the onion, carrots, *bouquet garni*, celery, tomatoes and garlic and cook for 4 minutes. Add the mushrooms and a little salt and pepper and cook for 4 minutes more. Pour in the water, bring to the boil and reduce gently, uncovered, for 40 minutes, skimming off any scum that surfaces. Strain the stock into a smaller pan (do not press on the bones or vegetables) and reduce; there should be 325ml *(½ pint)* of stock below the layer of fat on the surface. Use a spoon to remove all the fat, pour the stock into a small bowl and reserve.

The sauce

Heat the honey and the thyme leaves and flowers in a small saucepan; cook until the honey turns a deep brown and begins to caramelise. Add the vinegar, stirring to mix together well. Add the strained duck stock, lower the heat and simmer very slowly for 10 minutes. Taste for salt and pepper and keep the sauce hot while cooking the steaks.

To cook and serve the duck

Season the duck lightly with salt and pepper.

Heat 2 tablespoons of butter in a large frying pan, add the duck breasts, fat-side down, and brown over a moderate heat for 2 minutes. Turn them over and cook for 2 minutes longer, then spread ½ tablespoon of honey over each one, sprinkle with ¼ teaspoon of thyme leaves or flowers and cook for 2–3 minutes (they should be slightly rare).

Drain the duck breasts for a few seconds on a paper towel and place each one on a heated plate. Serve immediately, with the sauce on the side.

The breasts can also be served cut into fine slices, in which case season the slices lightly with salt and pepper before serving.

Note
Only the breast meat and carcasses are used in this recipe. Save the legs for making Preserved Duck (see p.196) or Stuffed Duck Legs with Pasta (see p.193).

Wine
A red Côtes du Rhône, a Saint-Joseph, or a Côtes de Provence.

Wild Duck with Spinach Salad and Oranges
Canard sauvage rôti, salade d'épinards crus et oranges

For 4 people

For the salad

450g *(1 lb)*	fresh young spinach, stems and ribs removed
3	medium oranges, preferably seedless
1 tbsp	each of chopped parsley, chervil and chives
3	shallots, finely chopped

For the vinaigrette

1 tsp	wine vinegar
1 tbsp	sherry vinegar
4 tbsps	oil of arachide (refined peanut oil)
	salt, freshly ground pepper

For the ducks

2	wild ducks, weighing about 700g *(1½ lb)* each when cleaned (see Note)
2 tsps	butter
	salt, freshly ground pepper

Equipment
large mixing bowl · small mixing bowl · wire whisk · large roasting tin
To serve: 4 heated plates

The salad
Cut the spinach into 5mm *(¼-in)* strips and place in a large mixing bowl.

Peel the oranges *à vif*, paring off the orange peel and white pith with a sharp knife, then cut out each section from between the membranes. Remove any seeds if necessary. Add the segments of orange, the herbs and shallots to the spinach and reserve.

Make a vinaigrette by whisking together the 2 vinegars, the oil and a little salt and pepper. Reserve.

The ducks
Pre-heat the oven to 410°F/210°C/Reg. 6½.

Season each duck inside and out, then place them on their sides in a large roasting tin. Place a teaspoon of butter on each duck and roast for 13 minutes. Turn the ducks so that they rest on the other side and roast for 25 minutes more, basting them with their juices 2–3 times.

To finish and serve the duck
Cut the legs and breasts off each duck. Cut the drumsticks from the thighs and slice the breast meat into fine slices. Season them lightly with salt and pepper.

Add the vinaigrette to the spinach salad and toss to mix. Divide the salad among the plates, place half a duck (thigh, drumstick and slices of breast meat) on each plate and serve immediately.

Note
One ordinary duck weighing about 1.8kg *(4 lb)* can be used instead of the 2 wild ducks. Cook the duck for 1¼ hours, resting it on each breast, then on each leg and finally on the back as it roasts. Carve as described, but in this case each person will get only half a leg and half a breast.

Suggestions
The oranges could be replaced by finely chopped orange or lemon peel. The thighs can be spread all over with mustard and cooked for a further 7–8 minutes to finish them.

Wine
Château Chalon. Vin jaune du Jura (at its best with any dish including oranges).

Duckling with Sherry Vinegar Sauce and Stuffed Turnips

Sauté de canard au vinaigre de Xérès

For 2 people

1	duckling, weighing 1.25kg *(2¾ lb)*

For the stock

2 tbsps	oil of arachide (refined peanut oil)
1	small carrot, coarsely chopped
1	small onion, coarsely chopped
1	medium tomato, coarsely chopped
½	stick of celery, coarsely chopped
3	cloves of garlic, cut in half horizontally
½ tsp	whole coriander seeds
½ tsp	peppercorns, coarsely crushed
	bouquet garni of thyme, a bay leaf, parsley stalks and a leek leaf
3 tbsps	sherry vinegar
1½ tbsps	dry white wine
1.25 litres *(2 pints)*	chicken stock
¼ tsp	tomato paste
1 tsp	coarse salt
½ tsp	Dijon mustard
1½ tbsps	butter, at room temperature

For the turnips

4	small round turnips, together weighing about 350g *(¾ lb)*
1	shallot, finely chopped
2 tsps	parsley, finely chopped
	salt, freshly ground pepper
2 tsps	butter

Equipment

cleaver or poultry shears · large casserole · bowl · wire whisk · medium saucepan · small saucepan · melon baller · large saucepan · mixing bowl · small frying pan · 2 small roasting tins
To serve: 2 heated plates

Preparing the duck

Cut the legs off the duck and reserve. Remove the backbone, neck and wings and reserve.

Cut the breast in half lengthwise with a cleaver or poultry shears. Chop the back, wings and neck into small pieces.

The stock

Heat the oil in a large casserole, add the duck back, wings and neck and brown over a moderate heat, stirring frequently, for about 15 minutes. Lift the pieces of duck out of the casserole, pour off all the fat and lightly blot the bottom of the casserole with paper towels to remove any excess fat. Place the pieces of duck back in the casserole with the carrot, onion, celery, tomato, garlic, coriander seeds, peppercorns and *bouquet garni* and cook over a moderate heat for about 3 minutes to soften the vegetables. Add the vinegar and wine, boil rapidly for 4–5 minutes, then add the stock, tomato paste and salt. Boil for 35 minutes, or until the liquid has reduced to 225ml *(8 fl. oz)*. Strain the stock into a bowl, pressing on the vegetables and bones to extract all their juices. Skim off any fat. Whisk in the mustard and reserve 6 tablespoons of the finished stock in a small saucepan for making the sauce.

Place the rest of the stock in a small roasting tin for cooking the stuffed turnips.

The turnips

Cut a thin slice off the bottom of each turnip so that it will stand upright. Peel the turnips thinly and use a melon baller to hollow them out (be careful not to puncture the sides or bottom). Drop the hollowed-out turnips into a large saucepan of lightly salted boiling water, boil for 3 minutes, cool under running water, drain and leave to dry, inverted on a towel, while making the stuffing.

Bone the duck legs and discard the skin and bones. Chop the meat coarsely and place it in a mixing bowl with the chopped shallot and parsley. Season with salt and pepper and stir well.

Heat the butter in a small frying pan. Make 4 little balls with the seasoned chopped duck and fry them for about 4 minutes to brown on all sides. Remove them from the pan and drain on paper towels.

When the balls of stuffing are cool enough to handle, place one in each of the hollowed-out turnips and place in the roasting tin with the stock.

To cook

Pre-heat the oven to 425°F/220°C/Reg. 7.

Season the duck breasts with salt and pepper. Place them in a small roasting tin without any butter or oil and roast for 10 minutes; turn the pieces over and return to the oven together with the turnips. Cook for 10 minutes more, then remove everything from the oven. Drain the duck breasts carefully.

To finish the sauce and serve the duck

Heat the stock, reserved earlier, until warm, then whisk in 1½ tablespoons of softened butter, little by little, to finish the sauce (do not allow to boil).

202

Skin and bone the duck breasts and cut the meat into thin slices. Garnish each plate with the slices of duck and 2 stuffed turnips, cover lightly with the sauce and serve.

Suggestion
The duckling could be replaced with a young goose.

Wine
Red Burgundy, either Mercurey or Santenay, or a Côtes du Rhône or Saint-Emilion.

Duck Breasts with Orange Zest and Green Peppercorns
Magrets de canard au zeste d'orange et poivre vert

For 4 people

2	ducks, weighing 1.8–2kg *(4–4½ lb)* each

For the stock (see Suggestions)

2 tsps	butter
2 tsps	oil of arachide (refined peanut oil)
3	small carrots, diced
3	small onions, diced
1	stick of celery, diced
4	tomatoes, diced
5	medium mushrooms, quartered
2	cloves of garlic, crushed
	bouquet garni of thyme, parsley, a bay leaf and 2 green leek leaves
15	whole peppercorns
1¾ litres *(3 pints)*	chicken stock

For the duck breasts

	zest of 1 orange, cut into long, fine julienne strips
	salt
3 tbsps	bottled green peppercorns
1 tsp	butter
1 tsp	oil of arachide (refined peanut oil)

Equipment
cleaver (optional) · large pan or *sauteuse* · frying pan · skimmer or slotted spoon · 2 small saucepans · 2 small bowls · large frying pan · ladle
To serve: heated serving dish and a sauceboat

Preliminary preparations

With a large knife, cut the wings and legs off the ducks. They will not be used in this recipe; save them for making Preserved Duck (see p.196), or, if you prefer, the legs may be used for making Stuffed Duck Legs with Pasta (see p.193).

Carefully remove the breast meat from the bones, leaving as little meat on the carcasses as possible. If the duck is very fatty, remove the skin and some of the fat so that the meat is covered by a layer of fat about 3mm (⅛ in) thick. Reserve the breasts on a plate.

Cut the tail off each carcass and discard. Chop the carcasses into pieces with a cleaver or a large knife.

The sauce

In a large pan or *sauteuse*, heat a teaspoon each of butter and oil until very hot. Add the pieces of duck carcass and brown them on all sides, stirring frequently. Be careful not to let them burn. When brown, lower the heat and cook slowly for 20 minutes, stirring occasionally.

Heat the remaining teaspoon of butter and oil in a frying pan. When very hot, add the carrots, onions and celery. Cook over a moderate heat for 5 minutes or until the vegetables begin to brown, stirring frequently.

When the duck bones have cooked for 20 minutes, add to them the cooked vegetables, the tomatoes, mushrooms, garlic and *bouquet garni*. Stir together well, add the peppercorns and cook, stirring, for 4 minutes. Add the chicken stock, bring to the boil, season lightly, and simmer for 1 hour and 20 minutes, skimming frequently.

When the stock is ready, strain it, pressing on the bones and vegetables with a wooden spoon to extract all the juices. There should be 600ml (1 pint) of stock once all the fat has been skimmed off the surface.

Place the degreased stock in a small saucepan over a moderate heat and boil for about 15 minutes or until the sauce has reduced to 300ml (½ pint). Reserve.

The orange zest and green peppercorns

Place the julienne of orange zest in a small saucepan, cover with cold water, bring to the boil and boil for 1 minute. Drain, cool under running water and drain again. Reserve in a small bowl.

Reserve quarter of the green peppercorns on a small plate for cooking the duck breasts. Place the remaining peppercorns in a bowl and reserve.

The duck breasts

Season the duck breasts on both sides with salt. Spread out the green peppercorns reserved for the breasts and squash them under the blade of a large knife. Spread the crushed peppercorns over both sides of the duck breasts, pressing down into the meat with the knife blade.

Heat the butter and oil in a large frying pan until almost smoking, then add the duck breasts fat-side down. Cook over a high heat for 2 minutes, turn them over and cook for 4 minutes more. Drain on paper towels and keep hot while finishing the sauce.

To finish the sauce and serve the duck breasts

Place the sauce over a moderate heat and bring just to the boil, add three-quarters of the orange zest, lower the heat and simmer for 3 minutes.

Pour all the fat from the frying pan the duck breasts cooked in and blot the bottom of the pan with a paper towel. Place the pan back over the heat and add a ladleful of the sauce, scraping the bottom of the pan with a wooden spoon to dissolve all the caramelised meat juices. Add the contents of the pan to the sauce.

The duck breasts can be served either whole or sliced. If sliced, sprinkle each slice with a little salt and pepper before serving.

Place the breasts on a dish, strain the sauce into a sauceboat, stir in the reserved orange zest and green peppercorns and serve immediately.

Suggestions

If you don't want to make the stock, pour 250ml *(9 fl. oz)* cream into the frying pan the duck breasts cooked in, after pouring off the fat and patting the pan dry. Bring to the boil, add salt, pepper and three-quarters of the orange zest, and boil for 3 minutes or until the sauce has thickened slightly. Strain, stir in the remaining zest and peppercorns and serve as described. You could replace the green peppercorns with a mixture of black and white peppercorns.

Wine

A red Burgundy or Côtes du Rhône, a Provençal wine, a Saint-Emilion or a vin jaune du Jura.

Roast Rabbit with Stuffed Cabbage

Lapin rôti et choux farcis

For 4 people

4	generous tbsps chives, finely chopped
3 tbsps	softened butter
2kg *(4½-lb)*	farmed rabbit
350g *(12 oz)*	pig's caul fat

For the sauce

2 tsps	butter
1	small carrot, chopped
1	small onion, chopped
1	small *bouquet garni* of half a bay leaf and a sprig of thyme
8 tsps	madeira
½ litre *(17 fl. oz)*	double cream or *crème fraîche* (see p.290)

For the cabbage

2 tsps	butter
2	shallots, finely chopped
1	medium tomato, peeled and chopped
2	medium mushrooms, chopped
	salt, freshly ground pepper
12	whole perfect cabbage leaves, ribs trimmed
4 tsps	cooking oil (for the rabbit)
2 tsps	butter (for the cabbage)

Equipment

2 small bowls · cleaver · medium, deep frying pan or *sauteuse* · small saucepan · small frying pan · large saucepan · oval or rectangular oven dish, 33–35cm *(13–14 in)* long (for the rabbit) · oval or rectangular oven dish, 30cm *(12 in)* long (for the cabbage) · wire whisk
To serve: heated serving dish or 4 heated plates, and a sauceboat

Preliminary preparations

Place the chives and butter in a bowl and beat together with a wooden spoon, then place in a wire sieve over a mixing bowl. Rub the chives and butter through the sieve with the wooden spoon and reserve for finishing the sauce, scraping the underside of the sieve to retrieve all the butter.

Cut the rabbit in half just below the rib cage. Cut the hind end into 3 pieces (2 legs and the saddle) and reserve. De-bone the fore end of the rabbit. Save the bones for making the sauce. Dice the meat and reserve.

Soak the pig's caul in warm water for 20 minutes, drain and pat dry with a clean cloth.

The sauce

Chop the reserved rabbit bones into pieces with a cleaver. Melt 2 teaspoons of butter in a deep frying pan or *sauteuse*, add the bones and brown over a moderate heat for 8 minutes. Add the carrot, onion and *bouquet garni*, simmer for 5 minutes, add the madeira and boil for 5 seconds; stir in the cream. Lower the heat and simmer for 15 minutes. Remove 4 tablespoons of the sauce and reserve for the stuffing, then cook the remaining sauce for 5–10 minutes more or until there is about 250ml *(9 fl. oz)* of liquid left. Spoon off any fat that surfaces, strain the sauce into a small saucepan and reserve.

The stuffing

Melt 2 teaspoons of butter in a small frying pan, add the shallots and cook for 2 minutes to soften, then add the diced rabbit, tomato, mushrooms and a little salt and pepper. Cook over a moderate heat for about 5 minutes or until all the liquid given out by the meat and vegetables has evaporated. Add the 4 tablespoons of sauce reserved earlier, bring to the boil and pour into a bowl to cool before stuffing the cabbage leaves.

The cabbage

Boil the cabbage leaves in a large saucepan of rapidly boiling salted water for 6 minutes, drain, cool under running water, drain again and spread the leaves out on a cloth to dry.

Place a quarter of the stuffing in the centre of a cabbage leaf and fold in the edges of the leaf to cover it. Place a second leaf over the opening at the top and wrap it around. Finish by enclosing the package in a third leaf, making the cabbage roll as round as possible.

Take between half and two-thirds of the pig's caul and cut it into 4 squares. Wrap each stuffed cabbage roll in a square of pig's caul so that it will hold its shape, and reserve.

To cook

Pre-heat the oven to 425°F/220°C/Reg. 7.

Wrap the saddle and each of the 2 rabbit legs in the remaining pig's caul cut into squares. Heat the oil in the larger oven dish, add the saddle and legs, and brown, turning frequently, for about 4 minutes. Roast for 5 minutes.

While the rabbit is roasting, heat 2 teaspoons of butter in the smaller oven dish and brown the stuffed cabbage over a moderate heat for 2–3 minutes, turning often. Place in the oven and cook the cabbage with the rabbit for 12 minutes, turning both over after 6 minutes. At the end of the 12 minutes, remove the saddle from the oven but continue cooking the legs and cabbage for 6 minutes more.

To finish the sauce and serve

Remove the pig's caul from the rabbit and slice all the meat. Place it on a plate with the cabbage, cover with aluminium foil and keep warm in the oven with the door ajar while finishing the sauce.

Heat the sauce, but do not allow to boil. Taste, add salt and pepper if needed, and whisk the chive butter, little by little, into the sauce.

Either serve the rabbit and cabbages on a serving dish, with the sauce on the side, or place a cabbage on each of 4 plates, arrange the rabbit meat around or next to it, spoon the sauce over the rabbit and serve.

Suggestions

Parsley or tarragon can be mixed with the butter and sieved as described for the chives to make a different sauce. Since tarragon is quite strong, use only half as much.

A chicken or guinea fowl could be cooked in the same way.

A finely diced truffle or a little *foie gras* could be added to the cabbage stuffing.

The herb butter could be replaced by a large spoon of mustard.

Note

If pig's caul is unavailable, tie the stuffed cabbages with kitchen string and add 2 tablespoons of lard to the butter in the oven dish used to cook them. Also add 2 tablespoons of lard to the oven dish used for the rabbit; baste both the meat and the cabbages as they roast, if lard is used instead of caul fat.

Wine

Côte Rôtie, or Burgundy such as red Chassagne. If you are using tarragon, drink a Côtes du Rhône or a Côtes de Provence.

Guinea Fowl Poached in Tea
Pintadeau au thé noir

For 2 people

1kg *(2¼-lb)*	guinea fowl (for substitutes, see Suggestions)
2½ litres *(4½ pints)*	water
2 generous tbsps	China, Indian or Ceylon tea
1½ tsps	coarse salt
1	large carrot, diced
1	large turnip, diced
140g *(5 oz)*	fine French beans, diced
100g *(4 oz)*	shelled peas
100ml *(4 fl. oz)*	double cream or *crème fraîche* (see p.290)
1½ tsps	tea leaves (for the sauce)
	salt, freshly ground pepper

Equipment

large pan, 4½-litre *(8-pint)* capacity, with lid · large mixing bowl · large pan · large saucepan · large frying pan or *sauteuse* · skimmer or slotted spoon
To serve: large heated serving dish or 4 heated plates

The guinea fowl
Cut the neck and wing tips off the bird and reserve.

Bring the water to a boil in a large pan. Place the tea in a large mixing bowl, pour the boiling water over it, cover with aluminium foil and leave to infuse for 10 minutes.

Strain the tea back into the pan used to boil the water, add the coarse salt and bring to a boil. Add the guinea fowl, its neck and wing tips, cover the pan and simmer for 25 minutes (11 minutes per pound). If the bird is not completely covered by the tea, turn it over halfway through the cooking time.

The vegetables
Bring a large pan of lightly salted water to a boil, add the carrot, turnip, beans and peas, and boil for 6 minutes, cool under running water and drain. Reserve.

The sauce
Carve off the breasts and legs of the guinea fowl, remove the skin and reserve.

Cut the carcass into 3 or 4 pieces, removing any fatty parts, and place it in a saucepan with the skin from the legs and breasts, the neck and the wings. Add 350ml (12 fl. oz) of the cooking liquid and boil rapidly for 4–5 minutes or until the liquid has reduced by half. Add the cream and simmer 7 minutes longer.

To finish and serve the guinea fowl
Remove the sauce from the heat. Add 1½ teaspoons of tea leaves, stir, cover the pan and allow to infuse for 1 minute. Strain the sauce into a large frying pan or *sauteuse*, pressing on the bones and tea to extract as much flavour as possible. Skim off any fat that surfaces, place the vegetables and pieces of guinea fowl in the sauce and heat gently for 3–4 minutes to warm through.

With a skimmer or slotted spoon, lift the pieces of guinea fowl and vegetables out of the pan and place them on a large serving dish or individual plates; taste the sauce, add salt and pepper if needed, spoon it over the piece of guinea fowl and serve at once.

Suggestions
A small chicken or turkey, or an equal weight of veal can be cooked and served in this way.

Wine
Why not drink tea?

Guinea Fowl En Croûte

Pintadeau rôti en croûte

For 4 people

2	guinea fowl, weighing about 650g *(1½ lb)* each, or one weighing 1.4kg *(3 lb)* (for substitute, see Note)
225g *(8 oz)*	back fat, beaten flat, for larding (see Note)
	salt, freshly ground pepper
90g *(4 oz)*	pork back fat, diced (see Note)
2 tsps	butter
3	shallots, finely chopped
3	medium mushrooms
1 tbsp	cognac
2 tsps	parsley, finely chopped
2 tsps	chervil, finely chopped
2 tsps	chives, finely chopped
	a pinch of *quatre épices* (see p.162)
3 tbsps	double cream or *crème fraîche* (see p.290)
4 tsps	oil of arachide (refined peanut oil)
375ml (13 fl. oz)	water
250g *(9 oz)*	puff pastry (see p.242)
1	egg, beaten

Equipment

cleaver · kitchen string · oval or rectangular roasting tin, about 33cm *(13 in)* long · mincer or food processor · mixing bowl · medium saucepan · large saucepan · small saucepan · rolling pin · pastry brush · baking sheet
To serve: 4 heated plates and a sauceboat

Preliminary preparations

Cut the legs and wings from each bird. Cut off the lower half of the backbone and reserve. Use a cleaver to separate the rest of the back from the breasts.

Lightly salt and pepper the breasts, wrap them in barding fat and tie with string. Place in a roasting tin and reserve.

Remove the skin from the legs, de-bone them, cut the meat into 5mm *(¼-in)* cubes and reserve.

Use the cleaver to chop the bones into small pieces and reserve with the backs and wings.

The stuffing

Mince half the leg meat with the pork back fat in the mincer or food processor. Mix this with the remaining cubes of meat and reserve.

210

Melt the butter in a saucepan, add the shallots and cook over a low heat for 3–4 minutes to soften, then add the mushrooms, salt and pepper and cook for 4 minutes more, stirring frequently, or until all the moisture from the mushrooms has evaporated. Cool and transfer to the bowl with the meat, stir in the cognac, herbs, salt, pepper, *quatre épices* and cream, and reserve.

The sauce
Heat the oil in a large saucepan and add the bones, wings and backs of the birds. Lower the heat and brown slowly for 30 minutes, stirring frequently (do not allow to burn).

Remove everything from the pan and pour off all the fat; gently pat the bottom of the pan dry with a paper towel. Return the bones, wings and backs to the pan, add the water and bring to a boil, scraping the bottom of the pan to dissolve the meat juices stuck to it. Boil for 10 minutes or until the liquid has reduced by about half, strain into a clean saucepan, spoon off the fat that surfaces, and reserve.

The pastries
On a lightly floured table, roll out the pastry into a rectangle about 20 × 35cm *(8 × 14 in)*. Using a saucer 13 cm *(5 in)* across as a guide, cut out 2 circles with a pointed knife or pastry wheel. Pack the scraps of pastry into a ball and roll them out again into a rectangle the same size as before. This time, cut about 5mm *(¼ in)* away from the edge of the saucer to make 2 circles 14cm *(5½ in)* in diameter. Brush any excess flour from the pastries.

Place the 2 smaller circles on a lightly buttered baking sheet. With a pastry brush, draw a narrow border of beaten egg around the rims of the pastries, being careful not to let any egg drip over the edge. Place half the stuffing on each circle, spreading it out as much as possible but staying inside the ring of egg. Cover the stuffing with the 2 larger circles, pressing them down all around the edges so that they stick to the bottoms. Lightly brush the surface of each finished pastry with the beaten egg and refrigerate for 25 minutes before baking.

To cook and serve the guinea fowl and pastries
Pre-heat the oven to 425°F/220°C/Reg. 7.

Bake the prepared breasts and pastries for 15 minutes. Remove the pastries, then turn the breasts over and bake for 10 minutes more.

Remove the barding fat and skin from the breasts and cut the meat lengthwise into thin slices; season the meat lightly.

Reheat the sauce; season with salt and pepper to taste.

Cut each pastry in half and place half on each plate. Arrange the slices of breast meat in front of the cut side of the pastries and serve immediately, with the heated sauce on the side.

Note
An equal weight of salt pork or bacon, placed in cold water, brought to a boil and drained, may be used to replace either the back fat or the barding fat, or both.

Two pheasants, or a 1.4kg *(3-lb)* chicken may be used instead of guinea fowl.

Wine
A full red Burgundy or claret, a Pommard or a Saint-Julien.

Fricassee of Rabbit with Tarragon and Garlic
Fricassée de lapin à l'estragon et à l'ail

For 4 people

For the rabbit

1.9kg *(4¼-lb)*	rabbit
8	large sprigs of fresh tarragon
	salt, freshly ground pepper
1 tbsp	oil of arachide (refined peanut oil)
2 tsps	butter
50ml *(2 fl. oz)*	tarragon vinegar
4	medium tomatoes, peeled, seeded and chopped
350ml *(12 fl. oz)*	double cream or *crème fraîche* (see p.290)

For the garlic

16	large cloves of garlic, unpeeled
¼ litre *(9 fl. oz)*	milk
1 tbsp	butter
	salt, freshly ground pepper
1 tsp	sugar

Equipment
2 large frying pans, one with lid · slotted spoon · small saucepan · small frying pan · wire whisk
To serve: large heated serving dish

Preliminary preparations
Only the saddle and hind legs of the rabbit are used in this recipe. Cut the rabbit in half just below the rib cage (use the fore end of the rabbit for stock). Cut the legs from the saddle. Cut each hind leg in half and cut the saddle crosswise into 4 pieces.

Remove the tarragon leaves from their stalks and reserve. Tie the stalks of the tarragon in a bunch.

The rabbit

Season the rabbit generously. Heat the oil in a large frying pan and add the rabbit. When it starts to brown, add the butter, lower the heat and brown on all sides for about 10–15 minutes, shaking the pan often to avoid sticking. With a slotted spoon, remove the rabbit from the pan and reserve.

Pour all the fat from the pan and pat it dry with a paper towel. Add the tarragon vinegar, stirring to detach any caramelised meat juices on the bottom of the pan, and place over a high heat. Boil the vinegar for about 30 seconds or until it has almost completely evaporated, add the tomatoes and the bunch of tarragon stems and cook slowly for 4 minutes. Add the cream, salt and pepper, then add the rabbit, cover the pan and simmer for 15 minutes.

The garlic

Place the cloves of garlic in a saucepan, add the milk and bring to a boil. Boil gently for 4 minutes and drain.

Heat the butter in a small frying pan, add the garlic, salt, pepper and sugar. Cook over a very low heat for 15 minutes, stirring often, to brown and caramelise the garlic on all sides without burning.

To serve the rabbit

Lift the pieces of rabbit out of the sauce with the slotted spoon and place them on a plate. Measure the sauce; if there is more than 375ml (13 fl. oz), simmer it to reduce to that amount, then strain it into a clean pan. Taste for salt and pepper, then heat the rabbit in the sauce.

Place the rabbit on a serving dish, spoon the sauce over it, and sprinkle with the freshly chopped tarragon. Place the caramelised cloves of garlic around the rabbit and serve.

Home-made pasta (see p.225) makes an excellent accompaniment to this dish.

Suggestions

Instead of rabbit you can use any kind or poultry or veal. The garlic can be replaced by shallots.

Fresh basil or fennel may be used instead of tarragon; in this case use ordinary wine vinegar, preferably made from white wine. Alternatively, season the fricassee with curry powder or paprika.

Wine

A red Provençal wine or a Côtes du Rhône, a young Bourgeuil or a Côte de Beaune.

Pheasant Pastries
with Pears and Spinach
Tourte de faisan

For 2 people

200g *(7 oz)*	puff pastry (see p.242)
1	small egg
1	pheasant, weighing about 575g *(1¼ lb)*, cleaned (see Note)
	salt, freshly ground pepper
125g *(¼ lb)*	chicken giblets
1 tsp	butter
2 tbsps	madeira
150ml *(¼ pint)*	warm water

For the pears

1 tsp	butter
1	large pear, weighing about 225g *(8 oz)*, peeled, cored and cut into 8 wedges
	salt, freshly ground pepper
½ tsp	granulated sugar
2 tbsps	cognac
5 tbsps	double cream or *crème fraîche* (see p.290)

For the spinach

1 tsp	butter
225g *(½ lb)*	fresh spinach, stems and ribs removed
	salt, freshly ground pepper

Equipment
rolling pin · pastry brush · baking sheet · small roasting tin · 2 wooden spoons · cake rack · cleaver or large knife · small saucepan, with lid · 2 small frying pans, with lids
To serve: 2 heated plates and a sauceboat

Preliminary preparations
On a lightly floured worktop, roll out the pastry into a large rectangle about 14 × 28cm *(5½ × 11 in)*. Using a plate as a guide, cut out 2 circles 12cm *(5 in)* wide. With a pastry brush, brush off any excess flour, then place the circles of pastry on a baking sheet, leaving plenty of space between them.

Beat a small egg with a pinch of salt and brush each circle with a little of it – do not allow the egg to drip over the edge of the dough, as this will prevent it from rising properly.

Allow the pastry to rest in the refrigerator for 15 minutes before baking.

The meat, the pastries and the sauce
Pre-heat the oven to 425°F/220°C/Reg. 7.

Cut off the neck and wing tips of the pheasant. Season the bird lightly inside and out.

Heat a teaspoon of butter in a roasting tin, add the chicken giblets, the wing tips and neck of the pheasant, and the pheasant itself. Lay the pheasant on its side and brown for 2 minutes, then, using 2 wooden spoons, turn the bird over and brown for 2 minutes on the other side.

Place the pheasant, still on its side, in the oven and roast for 6 minutes. Turn the bird on to its other side, place the pastries in the oven and bake for 7 minutes. Place the pheasant upright and finish baking the pastries and the pheasant for 9 minutes more.

When done, remove the pheasant and pastries from the oven and reduce the oven heat to 350°F/180°C/Reg. 4. Place the pastries on a rack to cool and put the pheasant on to a board.

Pour any fat from the roasting tin, but leave the wings and giblets. Cut the leg and breast meat into thin slices, place it on a plate and cover with aluminium foil. Keep warm.

Use a cleaver or large knife to chop the pheasant bones into large pieces, and put them back in the roasting tin. Cook the bones for about 2 minutes over a low heat, add the madeira and boil rapidly until it has completely evaporated. Add the warm water, scraping the bottom of the tin with a wooden spoon and simmer for 11 minutes. Strain the liquid into a saucepan, taste for salt and pepper, cover and reserve.

The pear and spinach garnish
Heat a teaspoon of butter in a small frying pan, add the pear wedges in one layer, salt and pepper lightly, sprinkle with the sugar and brown lightly over a moderate heat for about 2 minutes. Add the cognac and boil to evaporate it completely, add the cream and boil for 2 minutes longer. Cover and keep the pears warm while cooking the spinach.

Melt a teaspoon of butter in another frying pan, add the spinach, salt and pepper. When the spinach has melted down, cook for 2 minutes, stirring frequently, cover and reserve.

To serve the pastries
Run the tip of a knife around the top of each pastry and lift the tops off carefully. Place the pastries back into a 350°F/180°C/Reg. 4 oven for about 3 minutes to reheat (the pheasant can also be reheated if kept covered with foil – allow about 5 minutes).

Reheat the sauce prepared with the pheasant bones and pour it into a sauceboat.

Remove the pastries from the oven and place one on each plate. Divide first the spinach, then the pears between them, placing the pears and their sauce on a bed of spinach inside the pastries. Finish filling the pastries with the pheasant – it should form a mound. Place the tops on the pastries and serve, with the sauce on the side.

Note
Any game bird may be used instead of pheasant. Roast as described, allowing about 16 minutes per pound.

If preferred, the rectangle of pastry can be cut in half to form 2 squares, rather than circles. Trim all the edges to ensure even rising.

Wine
Pomerol or Chambolle-Musigny.

Haunch of Venison Baked in Clay
Cuissot de marcassin du mendiant

For 6–8 people

1	haunch of venison or wild boar, weighing about 1.5–2kg *(3½–4½ lb)*
125g *(¼ lb)* approx.	pork back fat for larding (use about 10 per cent of the weight of the meat)
1	large carrot, diced
2	small onions, diced
5	shallots, diced
1	stick of celery, diced
½	head of garlic (cut horizontally)
10	whole peppercorns
2	cloves
8	coriander seeds, coarsely crushed
6	juniper berries, coarsely crushed
	bouquet garni of thyme, rosemary and parsley
1¼ litres *(2¼ pints)*	red wine
6 tbsps	wine vinegar
	salt, freshly ground pepper
1 tbsp	oil of arachide (refined peanut oil)

For the sauce

6 tbsps	cognac
2 tbsps	madeira
3	medium tomatoes, seeded and chopped

For the herb butter

2 tbsps	parsley, finely chopped
2 tbsps	chives, finely chopped
2 tbsps	chervil, finely chopped
½ tsp	sage, chopped
½ tsp	savory, chopped
½ tsp	rosemary, chopped
½ tsp	thyme, chopped
1	bay leaf, broken
100g *(4 oz)*	softened butter

Equipment

larding needle · oval enamelled cast-iron casserole, about 4½-litre *(8 pint)* capacity, with lid · small square of muslin · large bowl · skimmer or slotted spoon · wooden mortar and pestle · greaseproof paper · kitchen string · 2kg *(4½ lb)* potter's clay · roasting tin or oven dish · hammer
To serve: sauceboat and a large carving board with a channel to collect the juices

To marinate

Three days before cooking, bone the venison and remove the large tendon at the base of the leg. Keep the bones and trimmings.

Cut the back fat into long thin strips and use a larding needle to lard the venison with it.

Place the bones, trimmings and the venison in an enamelled cast-iron casserole with the carrot, onions, shallots, celery and garlic. Tie the peppercorns, cloves, coriander seeds and juniper berries in a square of muslin and place next to the meat. Add the *bouquet garni*, wine and vinegar, cover the casserole and refrigerate for a total of 72 hours, turning the meat after the first 36 hours.

Preliminary cooking and sauce

Several hours before cooking, lift the meat out of the marinade and place it in a colander over a large bowl to drain completely. Strain the marinade; discard the spices in the muslin and the *bouquet garni*, but reserve the liquid and the vegetables for later use.

Pre-heat the oven to 500°F/260°C/Reg. 10. Season the venison generously with salt and pepper.

Heat 1 tablespoon of oil in the casserole in which the meat marinated. Put the meat in and spread the bones and vegetables from the marinade around the meat. Roast for 30 minutes to brown the meat, turning it once while roasting. Put the meat on to a board to cool.

Place the casserole, with the vegetables and bones still in it, on top of the stove, add the cognac and madeira and boil for 1 minute, scraping the bottom of the casserole to detach the meat juices stuck to it. Add the tomatoes and the strained liquid from the marinade and simmer for about 1½ hours, skimming off any foam that surfaces. Strain the sauce into a saucepan and spoon off all the fat that surfaces; there should be 375ml *(13 fl. oz)* of sauce. Taste for salt and pepper, and reserve.

The herb butter

Place all the herbs in a mortar and pound to a paste, add the softened butter and mix it into the herbs. Reserve at room temperature.

To bake and serve the venison

Pre-heat the oven to 425°F/220°C/Reg. 7.

Spread the herb butter all over the now cooled venison. Wrap the meat in a large sheet of greaseproof paper to enclose it completely. Fold up the ends of the paper and tie the package with kitchen string, at the ends and around the middle.

Spread out a damp teatowel on the table. Place the clay in the centre of it and with your hands press it out into a circle about 5mm *(¼ in)* thick and large enough to completely cover the venison. Place the venison in the centre of the clay and lift the corners of the towel to encase the venison, pressing and smoothing the edges of the clay together to seal them. Use your fingers or a knife blade to smooth out the clay and eliminate any cracks. (Keep the moist towel wrapped around it until ready to bake. Place the venison in a roasting tin or oven dish. With a skewer or trussing needle, make 2 holes in the top of the clay (one at each end) to allow steam to escape, and bake for 1 hour.

When the meat has finished cooking, reheat the sauce and pour it into a sauceboat. Use a hammer to break open the hardened shell of clay and remove the larger pieces. Then cut open the paper and carve the meat, spooning as much of the herb butter as possible over each plateful. Serve the sauce separately.

Suggestions

The ideal accompaniments for this dish are sweet potato purée (see p.227) and Turnip Darphin (see p.228). Prepare the vegetables while the meat is baking in the clay and serve them in vegetable dishes.

Note

The sauce may be made and the venison roasted and wrapped in clay several hours in advance. Clay can be bought from art shops, or dug out of the ground in clay-soil areas.

Wine

A good Burgundy – Chambertin, Clos de Bèze or Romanée.

218

VEGETABLES AND GARNISHES

Spinach au Gratin
Gratin d'épinards

For 3–4 people

For the spinach

575g *(1¼ lb)*	fresh young spinach, stems removed (see Note)
1 tbsp	butter
	salt, freshly ground pepper

For the mushrooms

2 tsps	butter
450g *(1 lb)*	mushrooms, sliced
	salt, freshly ground pepper
3 tbsps	madeira
250ml *(9 fl. oz)*	double cream or *crème fraîche* (see p.290)
½	clove of garlic (for the dish)
	melted butter (for the dish)
1	egg yolk

Equipment
2 large frying pans or *sauteuses* · oval gratin dish, 25cm *(10 in)* long, or round dish 21cm *(8½ in)* in diameter · pastry brush

The spinach
Heat a tablespoon of butter in a large frying pan or *sauteuse*, add as much spinach as the pan will hold, stir constantly and, as the spinach melts down, add more to the pan. When all the spinach has been added and has melted down, season with salt and pepper and cook over a moderate heat for 3–4 minutes, stirring frequently. Remove from the heat and reserve.

The mushrooms
Melt 2 teaspoons of butter in a large frying pan and add the mushrooms, stirring constantly at the beginning to avoid burning. When the mushrooms begin to give off their juices, season them lightly with salt and pepper, and cook for about 2 minutes or until their liquid has evaporated and they are nicely browned. Add the madeira, boil until it has evaporated, then add the cream and boil rapidly for 1 minute. Remove the pan from the heat and reserve.

To cook and serve the spinach
Pre-heat the grill.

Rub a gratin dish with half a clove of garlic, then brush the dish lightly with melted butter. Reheat the spinach if necessary and cover the bottom of the dish with it.

Stir the egg yolk into the mushroom—cream mixture, taste for salt and pepper, and pour over the spinach, spreading it out so that the spinach is entirely covered. Place under the grill for 1–2 minutes or until the surface has browned, then serve immediately.

Suggestions
An equal weight of lettuce or Swiss chard leaves may be prepared as described for the spinach.

This dish is excellent with any grilled meat or fish.

Note
If the spinach you buy has thick, dark-green leaves, rather than small, tender, light-green ones, parboil it for 2 minutes in rapidly boiling salted water, drain, cool under cold running water and press dry in the palms of your hands before preparing it as described.

Archestrate Potatoes
Pommes de terre Archestrate

For 2 people

250g *(9 oz)*	large, starchy potatoes
2 tbsps	butter
	salt, freshly ground pepper

Equipment
small frying pan (preferably non-stick), 24cm *(9½ in)* in diameter, or an enamelled cast-iron gratin dish · spatula
To serve: heated serving dish

Preliminary preparations
Peel, wash and dry the potatoes. Slice very, very thinly, as if making potato crisps, and reserve.

Melt the butter in a frying pan or gratin dish, remove the pan from the heat, and tip and turn to coat the bottom evenly with the butter.

To cook and serve the potatoes
Away from the heat, lay the potato slices in the pan one by one, making a circle around the edge. Place the potatoes so that each slice covers half of the preceding one. Continue making concentric, overlapping circles, until the bottom of the pan is covered, then make a second layer in the same way, using half the slices of potato.

222

Salt and pepper the top of the potatoes, place the pan over a moderate heat and cook for 2 minutes, then lower the heat and cook for 4 minutes longer. Shake the pan gently to avoid sticking. When the bottom potatoes have browned, use a spatula to turn over the 'pancake', season again with salt and pepper, and cook for 5 minutes or until the second side has browned. Slide on to a heated dish and serve (if using a gratin dish, the potatoes may be served in it, if preferred).

Make one 'pancake' for each person. This is the perfect accompaniment to all grilled meat.

French Beans Eventhia
Haricots verts Eventhia

For 4 people

400g *(14 oz)*	thin French beans
4½ tbsps	olive oil
3	medium onions, finely sliced
3	large tomatoes, peeled, halved and seeded
	salt, freshly ground pepper
3	sprigs of thyme

Equipment
large mixing bowl · large frying pan, with lid
To serve: vegetable dish

Preliminary preparations
Trim the ends off the beans, wash the beans in cold water and leave to soak in a large bowl of cold water for about 5 minutes.

To cook and serve the beans
Heat the olive oil in a large frying pan, add the onions, stir, and cook over a low heat for 5 minutes or until transparent but not browned.

Lift the beans out of the cold water with your hand, shake them once over the sink, then add them to the pan (the water remaining on the beans will be enough to cook them). Cook the beans over a low heat for 5 minutes, then take the tomato halves and squeeze them in your hand over the pan; let the juice from the tomatoes and their pulp fall into the pan. Season with salt and pepper, add the thyme, stir, cover and cook over a very low heat for 1 hour or a little more.

Remove the thyme and serve in a vegetable dish.

Suggestions
Fresh snap beans or yellow beans can be cooked in this way.

Mixed Vegetables au Gratin
Gratin arlequin

For 4 people

2	medium potatoes
2	medium carrots
2	medium turnips
½	clove of garlic
	salt, freshly ground pepper
375ml *(13 fl. oz)*	double cream or *crème fraîche* (see p.290)
120g *(4 oz)*	grated cheese, Emmenthal or Gruyère
2 tbsps	butter

Equipment
deep, round gratin dish, 21cm *(8½ in)* in diameter

To make and serve the gratin
Pre-heat the oven to 350°F/180°C/Reg. 4.

Peel the vegetables and cut them into thin slices. Wash the slices thoroughly and dry them in a towel.

Rub the gratin dish all over with the garlic, then cover the bottom of the dish with about a quarter of the sliced vegetables mixed together. Season with salt and pepper, add a quarter of the cream and sprinkle with a quarter of the grated cheese. Make 4 layers in this manner and top the last layer of cheese with nuts of butter.

Bake for 25 minutes, lower the temperature to 325°F/170°C/Reg. 3 and continue baking for 30 minutes more or until the surface of the dish is golden brown. Serve immediately.

Potatoes au Gratin
Gratin de pommes de terre

For 4–5 people

1kg *(2¼ lb)*	waxy potatoes
1	clove of garlic, cut in half
	salt, freshly ground pepper
350ml *(12 fl. oz)*	double cream or *crème fraîche* (see p.290)
120g *(4 oz)*	grated Gruyère or Emmenthal cheese
2 tbsps	butter

Equipment
oval gratin dish, 33–35cm *(13–14 in)* long

To bake and serve the gratin

Pre-heat the oven to 400°F/200°C/Reg. 6.

Peel the potatoes and cut them into slices about 2–3mm (⅛ in) thick. Wash in cold water, drain and pat dry in a towel.

Rub the gratin dish with the halves of garlic, then cover the bottom of the dish with about a quarter of the potato slices. Sprinkle with salt and pepper, pour a quarter of the cream over them and sprinkle with a quarter of the cheese. Make 4 layers in this manner, dotting the last layer of cheese with the butter.

Bake the potatoes for 20 minutes, then lower the oven to 325°F/170°C/Reg. 3 and bake for 25 minutes more or until tender and golden brown. Serve immediately.

Suggestions

Try using sliced turnips or celeriac instead of potatoes.

Home-made Spinach Pasta
Pâtes fraîches aux épinards

For 8 people as a garnish

450g (1 lb)	fresh spinach, stalks removed
750ml (1¼ pints)	water
300g (11 oz)	plain flour
1½ tsps	salt
2	whole eggs
4	egg yolks
1 tbsp	oil
1 generous tbsp	butter
	salt, freshly ground pepper

Equipment

heavy-duty liquidiser or food processor · saucepan · small bowl · large mixing bowl · large, very sharp knife, or pasta machine · broom handle or clean cloth · large saucepan
To serve: heated serving dish

The green colouring

Place 250ml (9 fl. oz) of water in a liquidiser or food processor with one-third of the spinach and blend to a fine purée. Strain into a saucepan, stirring and pressing on the residue left in the sieve to extract all the liquid. Do the same with the remaining water and spinach.

225

Bring the spinach liquid to a boil: a thick foam will rise to the surface. Boil for 45 seconds, then strain. There should be about 2 tablespoons of green colouring matter left in the sieve. Place this in a bowl and refrigerate. Discard the liquid.

The dough

In a large mixing bowl place the flour, salt, eggs, egg yolks, oil and green colouring. Mix all the ingredients together, then knead the dough by hand until a smooth, rather stiff dough of a uniform green colour is formed. If preferred, the dough can be made using a mixer equipped with a dough hook (run the machine in short bursts).

Form the dough into a ball, cover and allow to rest for 15 minutes.

Cutting the pasta

The pasta dough may be cut either by hand or using a pasta machine.

By hand. On a lightly floured surface, roll out the dough into a very thin sheet, turning it to ensure even rolling. Allow the dough to dry until it feels leathery but the edges are not yet brittle (about 20–30 minutes), then roll it up into a sausage and make noodles by cutting the sausage into slices about ½cm (¼ in) wide, using a large, very sharp knife.

With a manually operated pasta machine. Divide the ball of dough into 4 pieces. Flatten each piece between the palms of your hands, flour it lightly, and run it through the machine on the widest setting. Run it through the successive settings to number 4 or 5 (do not make the dough *too* thin) and allow the sheets of dough to dry for 20–30 minutes or until leathery. Insert the handle at the proper cutter width and run the dough through to form noodles.

Whether cutting the noodles by hand or with a machine, allow them to dry, either by draping them over a broom handle set between 2 chairs or by placing them in loose bunches on clean teatowels over the backs of chairs. If the sheets of dough have dried correctly, the noodles will not stick together.

To cook and serve the noodles

Bring a large pan of salted water to a boil. Add the noodles and boil for 2–3 minutes (they should be cooked *al dente*: tender, but firm to the bite). Drain them in a colander, rinse very rapidly under cold water and drain again.

Place the butter in the pan over a very low heat, add the noodles, season with salt and pepper, and toss to heat the noodles and melt the butter. Serve immediately.

Suggestions

A spoonful of truffle juice may be added to the pan with the butter and tossed with the noodles just before serving.

The green colouring may be made with watercress or lettuce instead of spinach. Use 3 bunches of watercress or 450g *(1 lb)* of lettuce.

If preferred, 2½ tablespoons of carrot juice or mushroom purée may be added instead of the colouring to the ingredients used in making the dough.

Sweet Potatoes Puréed with Apples and Bananas
Purée de patates douces

For 6–8 people

2 tbsps	butter
1	large apple, peeled, cored and cut into 8 slices
2	pinches of paprika
1	small banana, sliced
	juice of 1 small orange
	juice of 1 small lemon
150g *(5 oz)*	sugar
475ml *(16 fl. oz)*	water
1.4kg *(3 lb)*	sweet potatoes, peeled and diced
3 tbsps	double cream or *crème fraîche* (see p.290)
	salt, freshly ground pepper

Equipment
small frying pan · mixing bowl · large saucepan, with lid · *mouli-légumes* or potato masher · medium saucepan
To serve: heated serving dish

The sweet potatoes
Place the orange and lemon juices in a large saucepan with the sugar, bring to the boil and cook for about 13 minutes or until the sugar has caramelised. Add the water and sweet potatoes, bring to the boil, pressing the sweet potatoes down into the liquid, lower the heat and cook, covered, stirring occasionally, for 30–35 minutes or until soft.

The apple and banana
Melt 1 tablespoon of butter in a small frying pan, add the slices of apple and brown, turning once, for about 4 minutes. Season with paprika, transfer to a bowl and reserve.

227

Add 1 tablespoon of butter to the pan, brown the slices of banana on both sides for about 4 minutes, season with paprika and transfer to the bowl with the apple. Reserve.

To purée and serve the sweet potatoes
Using a *mouli-légumes* or potato masher, purée the potatoes and their liquid with the apple and banana. Pour the purée into a saucepan and, over a very low heat, stir in the cream. Taste for salt and pepper, heat through, transfer to a serving dish and serve.

Suggestions
The banana may be omitted. This purée is the perfect accompaniment for all sorts of game (see Haunch of Venison Baked in Clay, p.216).

Turnip Darphin
Darphin de navets

For 4 people

575g *(1 ¼ lb)*	turnips
225g *(½ lb)*	potatoes
	salt, freshly ground pepper
6 tbsps	butter

Equipment
grater · mixing bowl · small saucepan · 2–4 small, non-stick frying pans, 10cm *(4 in)* in diameter · pastry brush
To serve: large serving dish

Preliminary preparations
Clarify the butter as described for Potato Pancakes (see p.229).

Peel, wash and dry the turnips and potatoes, then grate them coarsely. Place them in a mixing bowl, season generously with salt and pepper, mix well together and reserve.

To cook
Make individual pancakes exactly as described for Potato Pancakes but, when cooking the second side, do not lower the heat and cook for only 3 minutes or until just cooked through.

Suggestion
Celery root (celeriac) may be used instead of turnips.

Potato Pancakes
Galettes de pommes de terre rapées

For 2 people

450g *(1 lb)*	waxy potatoes
	salt, freshly ground pepper
	nutmeg
3 tbsps	butter

Equipment
small saucepan · vegetable grater · 2 small non-stick frying pans, 10cm
(4 in) in diameter · pastry brush for basting
To serve: heated serving dish

Preliminary preparations
Clarify the butter by melting it in a small saucepan and spooning off any
foam that surfaces. Reserve.

Peel, wash and dry the potatoes. Grate them coarsely, season generously,
add a little nutmeg and cover. Reserve.

To cook
Butter the small frying pans generously using a brush, and heat over a
moderate heat until the butter is almost smoking. Add a handful of
grated potatoes to each pan, shake the pan for a few seconds to make
sure they don't stick, then flatten the pile of potatoes with the back of a
spoon to make a pancake 5mm *(¼ in)* thick. With the brush, dab a little of
the butter over each pancake and cook over a moderate heat, shaking the
pan often, for 3–4 minutes or until the bottom of each pancake has
browned. Flip each pancake out on to a plate, browned-side up. Lightly
brush each pan with a little more butter, then slide the pancakes back,
uncooked-side down, and lower the heat. Brown on the second side for
4–5 minutes, then slide the pancakes out on to a paper towel to drain for
a few seconds. Place them on a hot serving dish and keep hot while
making the remaining pancakes (there will be 2–3 pancakes per person,
depending on the thickness).

Suggestions
Freshly chopped herbs, such as parsley, chives and tarragon, and a few
finely shredded mushrooms may be added to the grated potatoes before
cooking.

If desired, one sizeable pancake may be made in a larger frying pan,
preferably non-stick.

BREADS, PASTRIES AND BATTERS

Bread Rolls
with Walnuts and Raisins
Pains aux noix et aux raisins

For 5 rolls

6g *(¼ oz)*	fresh baker's yeast or a generous ¼ tsp dried baking active yeast
120ml *(4 fl. oz)*	lukewarm milk
1½ tbsps	granulated sugar
½	egg, beaten
200g *(7 oz)*	plain white flour
¾ tsp	salt
2 tbsps	melted butter
40g *(1½ oz)*	sultanas
40g *(1½ oz)*	raisins
40g *(1½ oz)*	walnut halves

Equipment
2 mixing bowls · wire whisk · wooden spoon or electric mixer with dough hook · baking sheet · very sharp knife ·
To serve: bread basket

The dough
Place the yeast in a mixing bowl (if using fresh yeast, break it into small pieces). Whisk in the warm milk, leave for about 15 minutes, then whisk again. When the yeast has completely dissolved, whisk in the sugar. Add the beaten egg, stirring it in with a wooden spoon, then stir in the flour and salt.

Knead the dough, either by hand or using a mixer equipped with a dough hook, for 4–5 minutes or until it forms a ball, then knead in the melted butter. When the butter has been mixed in, knead in the raisins, sultanas and nuts. If the dough is too wet, knead in more flour.

Transfer the finished dough to a mixing bowl and cover with aluminium foil. Put it in a warm place (in the oven with the pilot light on, for example) to rise for 1½–2½ hours or until doubled in size. With lightly floured hands, punch the dough down, form it once again into a ball, cover with foil and refrigerate for 35 minutes.

To make and bake the rolls
Pre-heat the oven to 400°F/200°C/Reg. 6. Lightly grease a baking sheet.

On a lightly floured worktop roll the dough out into a sausage about 5cm *(2 in)* thick. Cut the dough into 5 equal pieces, then roll each piece into a ball between the palms of your hands.

Place the rolls on the baking sheet with plenty of space between them. Leave them in a warm place for 30–45 minutes or until doubled in size.

With a very sharp knife, slit the top of each roll, then immediately place the baking sheet in the oven. Bake for 10 minutes at 400°F/200°C/Reg. 6, lower the oven to 350°F/180°C/Reg. 4 and bake for a further 25 minutes. When done place the rolls in a basket until ready to serve.

Walnut and raisin dinner rolls are delicious with cheese, especially goat's cheeses.

Lady's Finger Sponge for Charlottes
Biscuit à la cuillère

For lining a 15cm *(6¼-in)* charlotte mould

3	egg yolks
4½ tbsps	caster sugar
3	egg whites
6 tbsps	plain white flour, sifted (measure before sifting)

Equipment

mixing bowl · wire whisk · wooden spatula · baking sheet · flexible rubber scraper · flexible metal spatula · large cake rack · 15cm *(6¼-in)* charlotte mould

The batter

Whisk the egg yolks and 1½ tablespoons of sugar together in a mixing bowl until the mixture is smooth and has lightened in colour.

In another bowl, beat the egg whites until firm but not stiff, add 3 tablespoons of sugar, and continue beating until very stiff. Using a wooden spatula, fold a quarter of the egg whites into the egg-yolk mixture, then fold in the remaining egg whites. When smooth, lightly fold in the sifted flour; the finished batter should be perfectly smooth and creamy.

To bake

Pre-heat the oven to 400°F/200°C/Reg. 6. Butter and flour a baking sheet lightly.

With the handle of the wooden spatula, draw a rectangle 19 × 35cm *(7½ × 13½ in)* in the centre of the baking sheet.

234

Scrape the batter from the bowl into the centre of the rectangle using a flexible rubber scraper. With a flexible metal spatula, spread the batter out so that it fills the rectangle, then smooth the surface.

Bake for 15–20 minutes or until the top is golden brown and it begins to resist when pressed lightly.

Remove the pastry and detach it from the baking sheet with a flexible metal spatula. Slide it on to a cake rack and allow to cool completely.

To cut

When cool, place the pastry on a table. Set a 15cm *(6¼-in)* charlotte mould on it at one corner, as close to the edge as possible. With a sharp knife cut out a circle, using the bottom of the mould as a guide.

Cut the rest of the pastry into straight bands about 2½cm *(1-in)* wide, then cut each band in half crosswise; you should have 14 bands measuring about 2½ × 9cm *(1 × 3 ½ in)* each (plus a few left-over ends).

When making a charlotte, the circle and bands are used to line the mould with the browned upper sides touching the mould.

Note

This method of baking and cutting the pastry is much easier than the traditional method of making individual lady's fingers with a pastry bag; it also makes lining the bottom of the mould very simple.

Bread Rolls
Pain

For 8 rolls

For the starter

6g *(¼ oz)*	fresh baker's yeast or a generous ¼ tsp dried active baking yeast
6 tbsps	warm water
1 generous tbsp	honey
115g *(4 oz)*	plain white bread flour
4 tsps	rye flour
	generous ¼ tsp salt

For the dough

	a scant 10g *(½ oz)* compressed baker's yeast or ¾ tsp dried active baking yeast
180ml *(6 fl. oz)*	warm water
280g *(10 oz)*	plain flour
2 tbsps	rye flour
¾ tsp	salt

Equipment

medium mixing bowl · wire whisk · large mixing bowl · electric mixer with dough hook (optional) · large bowl · baking sheet · roasting tin · very sharp knife or razor blade · pastry brush · cake rack

The starter

The night before making the bread, place the yeast in a medium mixing bowl (if using fresh yeast, break it into small pieces) and add the warm water. Set aside for about 5 minutes, whisking occasionally. When the yeast is completely dissolved, stir in the honey, the 2 flours and the salt. Beat vigorously with a wooden spoon to form a smooth sticky dough, then cover the bowl with aluminium foil and leave overnight at room temperature.

The dough

The next day, the starter should have doubled in size and bubbles should have formed on the surface. With a spoon, stir down the starter and form it more or less into a ball in the bottom of the bowl.

In a large mixing bowl, make the dough. Dissolve the yeast in the water as described above, then stir in the 2 flours and the salt. Beat for just long enough to mix all the ingredients together thoroughly and form a dough. Place the starter in the bowl with the dough.

If using a mixer with a dough hook, beat the dough and starter together for about 3 minutes, making sure they are perfectly mixed.

If kneading by hand, knead for 5–7 minutes on a lightly floured worktop, stretching and folding the dough over on itself to mix and make it perfectly smooth and elastic.

The finished dough should be soft but not sticky. Form it into a ball, flour it lightly, place it in a clean, large bowl and cover with aluminium foil. Leave in a warm place (about 75–80°F) for about 1½ hours or until the dough has doubled in size.

To make and bake the rolls

Pre-heat the oven to 425°F/220°C/Reg. 7. Lightly grease a baking sheet.

Lightly flour the worktop, then transfer the dough to it. Punch the dough down, shape it into a ball and divide it into 2 equal parts with a sharp knife. Roll each half of the dough into a sausage shape about 5cm *(2 in)* thick and 15cm *(6 in)* long and cut each sausage into 4 pieces. Form each piece into a little oblong roll about 10cm *(4 in)* long and place them on the baking sheet, leaving at least 5cm *(2 in)* between them. Cover with a towel and leave to rise in a warm place for 15–20 minutes or until the rolls have nearly doubled in size.

Fill a roasting tin half full of water and bring to a boil over a high heat; place it in the bottom of the oven (the steam will keep the rolls from drying out and make them brown better).

With a very sharp knife or a razor blade, make 5 shallow slits in the top of each roll, cutting at an angle and holding the blade at a slight tilt.

Bake the rolls for 6 minutes at 425°F/220°C/Reg. 7, lower the oven to 400°F/200°C/Reg. 6, and bake for 25 minutes. With a pastry brush, brush the top of each roll with a little of the water in the roasting tin, then bake for 15 minutes more. Test to see whether the rolls are done: pick one up and tap the bottom with your knuckles; if a hollow sound is produced, the rolls are done; if it makes a dull thump, bake them longer. Cool on a cake rack.

Suggestions
Cumin rolls are made exactly as described above, but after slitting the top of the rolls, brush them with a little warm water and sprinkle each one generously with cumin seeds. Bake as described. These rolls are especially good with Munster cheese.

Sweet Flan Pastry with Ground Almonds
Pâte sablée amandine

For 275g (10½ oz) pastry (for a 20cm (8-in) tart)

115g *(4 oz)*	plain white flour
75g *(3 oz)*	ground almonds
5 tbsps	butter, softened and broken into pieces
½	a beaten egg
150g *(5 oz)*	caster sugar
¼ tsp	vanilla essence

Equipment
food processor (optional) · 2 bowls · wire whisk

To make the pastry with a food processor
Place the flour, almonds and butter in a food processor. Using the chopping blade, run the machine for 3 minutes.

Beat the egg with the sugar and vanilla in a bowl until the mixture becomes very pale. Add this to the pastry mixture and run the machine for 2 minutes more.

Remove the pastry from the processor, form it into a ball, place in a bowl, cover with a folded teatowel and refrigerate for at least 2 hours before using as described in specific recipes.

To make the pastry by hand

Beat the egg with the sugar and vanilla until the mixture becomes very pale.

Place the flour and almonds in a bowl or on a worktop, mix together and make a well in the centre. Place the bits of butter on the flour and place the egg mixture in the well. Rapidly mix everything together with a pinching motion.

When all the ingredients have been more or less mixed together, *fraiser* the dough: with the heel of your hand, smear bits of the dough across the worktop and away from you. When all the dough has been crushed in this way, scrape it off the table with a plastic scraper, pack all the pieces loosely together and *fraiser* once more, bit by bit.

Form the finished pastry into a smooth ball, place in a bowl, cover with a folded teatowel and place in the refrigerator for at least 2 hours before using.

Note

This pastry is very fragile. Rather than rolling it out, the ball of pastry may be flattened with your hand, placed in the mould or tart tin and pressed in with your fingers.

The pastry becomes very hard in the refrigerator, so it is best to leave it at room temperature for at least 15 minutes before using it.

Fritter Batter and Basic Deep-frying Technique
Pâte à beignets (principe et suggestions)

For 4 people (see Suggestions)

25g *(1 oz)*	fresh baker's yeast or 15g *(½ oz)* dried baking yeast
250ml *(8 fl. oz)*	beer
¾ tsp	salt
175g *(6 oz)*	flour, measured and then sifted
	cooking oil

Equipment

mixing bowl · wire whisk · deep fryer or large saucepan · deep-frying thermometer · fork · skimmer or slotted spoon · salt shaker or sugar dredger
To serve: heated serving dish

238

The batter
Dissolve the yeast in 2 tablespoons of beer (if using fresh yeast, crumble it into small pieces), then whisk in the rest of the beer and add the salt. Add the sifted flour all at once, whisking rapidly to dissolve it and to make a smooth batter. Cover the bowl and set aside at room temperature for at least 3 hours.

Preliminary preparations
Half fill a large saucepan or deep fryer with cooking oil. Heat it to 375°F/190°C (this should take about 15 minutes). Line a large flat dish with several thicknesses of paper towel for draining the fried food.

Have ready a fork for dipping the food into the batter, a skimmer or slotted spoon, a heated serving dish and a salt shaker or sugar dredger, according to whether you are making sweet or savoury fritters. Pat the food to be fried with a towel to remove any excess moisture.

Cooking
When the oil is hot, drop the pieces of food into the fritter batter; make sure they are completely coated. One by one, lift the pieces out of the batter with the fork and drop them into the hot oil. (Fritters must be dropped into the oil one at a time, or they will stick together in a huge mass.) Depending on the size of the pan and the size of the fritters, anything from about 8–20 fritters may be fried at a time. Do not crowd them; if the fritters must be cooked in several batches, pre-heat the oven to 250°F/130°C/Reg. ½ and keep the finished ones hot while cooking the rest.

When the fritters are golden brown on one side, turn them over using the fork, the skimmer or slotted spoon; it generally takes about 2–3 minutes to brown each side. If they brown much faster than this, lower the heat – the oil is getting too hot. If it takes much longer, raise the heat – the oil is not hot enough and the fritters may be greasy.

When the fritters are nicely browned on each side, lift them out of the oil with the skimmer or slotted spoon and drain them on the paper towels. Place them on a serving dish and sprinkle with salt (savoury fritters) or sugar (sweet fritters).

Suggestions
The following suggestions for meat, fish or fruit fritters are for 4 people.

Meat or fish
450g–700g *(1–1½ lb)* of calf's or lamb's brains, or firm filleted fish such as
    monkfish cut into 2½cm *(1-in)* cubes.
20–24 sea scallops or 700g *(1½ lb)* queen scallops

Fruit

about 450g *(1 lb)* pears or apples, peeled, cored and cut into wedges or slices, or bananas, sliced
about 900g *(2 lb)* melon or pineapple, peeled, seeded or cored, and cut into wedges or slices
about 450g *(1 lb)* strawberries, stalks removed and left whole

Note

Oil used for deep frying may be used several times if strained and stored. It should be discarded when it begins to turn dark (slightly brownish) or to smell strong.

The same oil may be used for frying meat or fruit, but oil used for fish should only be used for fish.

Brioche
Brioche fine

For 1 brioche, serving 4–6 people

For the yeast starter

10g	a scant *(½ oz)* fresh baker's yeast or ½ tsp dried active baking yeast
2 tbsps	warm milk
4½ tbsps	plain white bread flour

For the dough

200g *(7 oz)*	plain white bread flour
2 tbsps	granulated sugar
½ tsp	salt
2	eggs
125g *(4 oz)*	softened butter, broken into pieces
1	egg, beaten with a pinch of salt (to brush on the brioche)

Equipment

bowl · wire whisk · 2 large mixing bowls · mixer with dough hook · brioche mould (see Note) · pastry brush · trussing needle or skewer · cake rack

The yeast starter

Place the yeast in a small bowl (if using fresh yeast, break it into small pieces) and stir in the warm milk. Allow to sit for 5–10 minutes, then whisk. When the yeast has completely dissolved, stir in the flour and mix until perfectly smooth. Form the dough into a mound in the bottom of the bowl, cover with aluminium foil and set in a warm place (75–80°F) to rise for about 20 minutes; the dough should double in size.

The dough

Put the flour, sugar, salt and eggs in a large mixing bowl. Mix together with a wooden spoon, then beat the dough vigorously for 1–2 minutes or until it forms a ball around the spoon. If possible, replace the spoon with a mixer equipped with a dough hook and continue beating the dough for 3–5 minutes or until smooth; otherwise beat by hand for 7–8 minutes. Add the yeast starter and beat for 2 minutes or until it has been completely incorporated. Beat in the butter piece by piece; it should take about 3–4 minutes to add all the butter and mix it completely with the dough, which will have become very creamy.

Place the dough in a large clean bowl and cover with a thickly folded towel or aluminium foil. Place in a warm place for 2½–4 hours or until the dough has doubled in volume (the rising time varies greatly depending on the yeast; fresh yeast acts more quickly than dried).

When the dough has finished rising, beat it down with a wooden spoon, cover once again and refrigerate for 2–2½ hours. At the end of this time, it should be rounded on top. Punch it down with your hands and proceed either to shape and bake it, or cover and refrigerate overnight.

To shape, bake and serve the brioche

Press the dough into a lightly buttered brioche mould (see Note). If you have left the dough overnight, work it with your hands to warm it up a bit before placing it in the mould. The mould should be about half filled.

Leave the dough to rise in a warm place for about 2½ hours or until it has risen about 2cm (¾ in) above the top of the mould.

Pre-heat the oven to 400°F/200°C/Reg. 6.

When the dough has finished rising, paint the top with the beaten egg, using a pastry brush, and bake for 8 minutes. Lower the oven to 375°F/190°C/Reg. 5 and bake for 35–40 minutes more or until the brioche is a rich golden brown and a trussing needle or skewer plunged into the centre comes out clean and hot. (If the top darkens too much while the brioche is baking, cover it lightly with aluminium foil.)

Turn the brioche out on to a cake rack as soon as it comes from the oven. Serve it either warm or cool, or cut it into slices, toast them and serve with a compôte of fruit or a fruit salad.

Suggestion

Add a little chopped candied peel to the dough before the butter.

Note

A brioche may be moulded to almost any shape. A cylindrical brioche (brioche mousseline) is made in a cylindrical mould; a 1-litre (2-lb) tin is a good substitute for a mousseline mould. This shape is used when making a brioche for the Hot Guava or Apple Charlottes (see p.269 and p.272).

A loaf tin may also be used. The brioche will be prettier if the dough is divided into 4 or 6 pieces, each piece rolled into a ball, and the balls laid in the tin next to each other.

A Parisian brioche is made in a round, fluted tin brioche mould. Divide the dough into 2 pieces, one about 3 times the size of the other. Roll each one into a ball. Place the large one in the mould and make an indentation in the centre. Set the small ball into this depression. This is the brioche most often seen in French pastry shops.

Puff Pastry
Pâte feuilletée

For 1kg *(2¼ lb)* pastry

550g *(19 oz)*	flour (see Note)
480g *(17 oz)*	unsalted butter
1½ tsps	salt
250ml *(9 fl. oz)*	water

Equipment
bowl · sharp knife · food processor · plastic film · rolling pin · pastry brush

Making the pastry
Place the flour in the processor bowl, add the salt and sprinkle in 80g *(3 oz)* of the butter, cut into small cubes. Run the processor for 45 seconds, then add the water through the opening in the top; continue running the machine for ½–1 minute more or until the pastry has formed itself into a ball. Do not run the machine for too long, or the pastry will become elastic and hard to work.

Form the pastry into a ball, flatten it and chill it in the refrigerator for at least 2 hours.

Rolling out the pastry
Place the remaining butter, chilled, between 2 sheets of plastic film and flatten it by thumping it a few times with a rolling pin. Then continue flattening it with the palm of your hand until it forms a square or rectangle 15 × 15cm *(6 × 6 in)*, 1¼–2cm *(½–¾ in)* thick.

Lightly flour the worktop. Roll out the chilled pastry into a square 35cm × 35cm *(14 × 14 in)*. The centre of the square of pastry should be considerably thicker than the edges.

With a pastry brush, brush any excess flour off the surface of the pastry. Place the butter in the centre and carefully fold 2 sides of the pastry over it; the pastry should overlap. Brush off any flour, then fold the other 2 sides of the pastry over the butter, pressing them down.

Lightly flour the worktop and the top and underside of the pastry, then place it back on the worktop.

Place the rolling pin in the centre of the block of pastry and roll away from you. Lift the rolling pin up, place it back in the centre and roll away from you again. Replace the rolling pin in the centre and this time roll towards you. Repeat this motion and continue in this way, always placing the rolling pin in the centre of the pastry and rolling either away from or towards you, until you have a long band of pastry a little less than 1½cm *(½ in)* thick. It should be slightly thicker in the centre than at the ends. Periodically lift it up to make sure it is not sticking to the worktop, flour the worktop and pastry lightly, and continue.

When you have a long band of pastry – about 20 × 65cm *(8 × 25 in)*, brush off any excess flour. Fold the top end of the rectangle towards you, leaving the bottom third of the pastry exposed. Brush it lightly, then fold the bottom end over, covering the first third. Brush it again and turn it by 90°, so that the sides now become the ends. You have just given the pastry its first 'turn'.

Give it a second rolling and folding and turning, exactly as you did before. It has now had two turns.

Place the folded pastry on a plate, cover with aluminium foil or plastic film, and refrigerate for at least 30 minutes.

Give the pastry 2 more turns as described above, chill for 30 minutes, then give it 2 final turns – a total of 6 turns. After a final rest of 30 minutes, it is ready to be rolled out and cut into the desired shapes.

Once the pastry has been cut, allow it to rest for at least 20 minutes.

Note

Although any flour may be used in making puff pastry, a mixture of 3 parts plain flour to 1 part strong flour gives the best results.

Puff pastry freezes very well, which is why the recipe given here is for making larger amounts than are ever called for at one time. Cut the pastry into sections of the desired weights, depending on the recipes you intend to try eventually. Then either roll out and cut each section into the desired shapes, place flat in freezer bags (or in one bag in several layers separated by sheets of plastic) and freeze; or simply put each section in a plastic bag and freeze. In the second case, remove the pastry from the freezer and place in the refrigerator for 24 hours before cutting. If using puff pastry that was cut before being frozen, it may be placed directly in the oven or thawed for 15–20 minutes before baking. If placing directly in the oven, allow 1–2 minutes extra cooking time.

When rolling out the pastry prior to cutting it, do not hesitate to roll in any direction, or to fold the pastry if necessary; each recipe gives directions on how to roll out and cut the pastry.

When actually cutting the shapes, it is important to remember: puff pastry will not rise properly unless the edges are cleanly cut; use a large, very sharp knife; never drag it through the pastry to cut it, but press down straight or use a slight rocking motion. If cutting around a saucer to obtain a circle, cut with the tip of the knife, using an up-and-down sawing motion.

Once the shapes are cut, turn them upside down so that the fold in the pastry will be on the bottom; this is to ensure even rising.

Puff pastry should always be kept in the refrigerator unless actually being rolled out, because if it becomes too warm the butter softens and breaks through the pastry. For this reason it is always best to work in a cool kitchen; do not even attempt to make puff pastry if the room temperature is above 80°F, and if it is above 70°F don't be surprised if it is a little difficult to work with.

If, for one reason or another, the butter does break through the pastry, don't panic. Simply flour the broken place copiously and place the pastry in the refrigerator to chill for about 15 minutes before continuing. Flour the worktop lightly and continue rolling the pastry out. The best way to avoid accidents is to check the bottom of the pastry often, and flour the table whenever it seems necessary. As long as the pastry slides slightly on the worktop as it is being rolled out, there is no problem. Check it immediately if it stops moving.

Puff pastry will keep for about 4 days in the refrigerator, tightly wrapped in aluminium foil. Any scraps should be saved and packed into a ball; when rolled out, the pastry will still rise, and is excellent for making Spiced Palmiers (see p.288) or tart bottoms.

DESSERTS

Pears Poached with Blackcurrants
Poires fraîches pochées au cassis

For 4 people

4	large or 8 small pears, weighing 1 kg *(2 lb)*
½	lemon
400g *(14 oz)*	blackcurrants, fresh or tinned
775g *(27 fl. oz)*	water
700g *(1½ lb)*	caster sugar
1	vanilla pod, split in half
3 tbsps	crème de cassis (see Note)

Equipment
spoon, melon baller or apple corer · liquidiser · fine sieve · large saucepan
To serve: large serving bowl

The pears
Peel the pears. If large, cut them in half and scoop out the core with a spoon or melon baller. If small, core them with an apple corer and leave them whole. Rub the pears with half a lemon to prevent discolouration.

The blackcurrants
Set aside half of the blackcurrants for later use. Place the remaining half in a liquidiser (with 6 tablespoons of their syrup, if tinned) and blend to a purée. Strain the purée into a large saucepan, rubbing on the seeds and skins with a wooden spoon to extract all the juice.

To cook and serve the pears
Add the water, sugar, vanilla pod and crème de cassis to the blackcurrant purée and bring to a boil, stirring until the sugar is dissolved. Add the pears, bring back almost to the boil, lower the heat and simmer for 12 minutes. Add the reserved blackcurrants and cook for 5 minutes more. Pour into a large serving bowl and allow to cool.

Chill in the refrigerator for at least 2 hours before serving.

Suggestion
If desired, vanilla ice-cream can be served at the same time as the pears.

Note
Crème de cassis, a speciality of Dijon, is a sweet blackcurrant liqueur (not the syrup). It is sold by most good wine merchants or grocers.

Wine
Dry champagne.

Stuffed Pears Colette Dufour
Poires Colette Dufour

For 4 people

4	scoops pistachio ice-cream

For the pears

4	pears
½	lemon
2 litres *(3½ pints)*	water
½	vanilla pod, cut in half lengthwise
180g *(5 oz)*	caster sugar

For the stuffing

80g *(3 oz)*	walnut halves
3 tbsps	light brown sugar

For the sauce

150ml *(5 fl. oz)*	milk
2 tbsps	caster sugar
130g *(4 oz)*	unsweetened cocoa powder
1½ tbsps	softened butter

Equipment
apple corer · large saucepan · liquidiser or food processor · small saucepan · wire whisk · ice-cream scoop
To serve: 4 chilled dessert plates and a sauceboat

Preliminary preparations
The pears must be poached and allowed to cool completely before stuffing. It is best to poach the pears a day ahead of time; otherwise allow at least 3 hours for them to cool.

Peel the pears and rub each one with the half lemon to avoid discolouration. Use an apple corer to remove the central cores. Place the water, vanilla pod and sugar in a large saucepan and bring to the boil, stirring to dissolve the sugar. Add the pears, lower the heat and simmer for 15 minutes or until tender. Remove from the heat and leave the pears in their cooking liquid to cook completely.

Stuffing the pears
Place the walnut halves and sugar in a liquidiser or food processor and grind to a paste.

Remove the pears from their liquid and drain completely on a cloth or towel. Place them upright on a large plate and carefully fill each one with walnut paste, pushing in as much of the paste as possible without breaking the pear. Place the stuffed pears in the freezer while making the chocolate sauce (see Note).

248

The chocolate sauce

Heat the milk, sugar and cocoa powder in a saucepan until boiling, whisking constantly, then whisk in the butter. Remove the pan from the heat and stir with a spoon for 1–2 minutes, then pour the sauce into a sauceboat.

To serve the pears

Place a scoop of pistachio ice-cream on each chilled dessert plate. Make a depression in the centre of each one, stand the pears upright in the ice-cream and serve, with the chocolate sauce on the side.

Note

The pears can be stuffed several hours in advance. If prepared more than ½ hour in advance, reserve them in the refrigerator, not in the freezer.

Wine

A white Côtes-du-Jura.

Tropical Fruit Salad
Salade de fruits éxotiques

For 6–8 people

For the syrup

1	clove
½ tsp	Chinese five-spice mixture
	zest of 2 limes
	zest of 2 oranges
	zest of half a lemon
1½	vanilla pods, split in half lengthwise
1½	bulbs fresh lemongrass (citronella), diced (see Note)
1 tsp	fresh ginger, chopped
3	coriander seeds
150g *(5 oz)*	sugar
1 litre *(1¾ pints)*	water

For the salad

1	ripe mango
12	ripe (wrinkled) passion fruits
3	large or 6 small kiwi fruits, peeled and sliced
½	fresh, ripe pineapple, cut into chunks
	leaves from a large sprig of mint, cut into thin strips

Equipment

large saucepan
To serve: large serving bowl

The syrup

Place all the ingredients for the syrup in a large saucepan. Bring to a rolling boil, immediately remove from the heat and allow to cool completely.

The fruit salad

With a knife, peel the mango, cut the pulp away from the stone, dice it and place it in a serving bowl. Cut the passion fruits in half, scoop out the seeds and transfer the fruits to the bowl with the mango. Add the sliced kiwis and pieces of pineapple, strain the cold syrup over the fruit, and chill for at least 2 hours.

At the last minute, sprinkle with the strips of mint and serve.

Note

In general, the ingredients used in this salad can be found in speciality shops dealing in products from South-East Asia.

Lemongrass (citronella) is a pale green aromatic grass with reedy leaves about a foot long growing from a bulbous base. It is often sold dried, but for this recipe it is preferable to buy it fresh. The term 'bulb' used in the ingredients list refers to the whole plant (bulb and leaves).

Wine

Dry champagne.

Pineapple Eventhia
Ananas Eventhia

For 4 people

1	ripe pineapple, weighing about 900g *(2 lb)*
150g *(5 oz)*	fresh raspberries
100ml *(4 fl. oz)*	*crème fraîche* (see p.290) or double cream, chilled
2 tbsps	icing sugar
8	small or 4 regular scoops of rum-flavoured ice-cream
250g *(9 oz)*	fresh strawberries

Equipment

liquidiser or food processor · fine sieve · large mixing bowl, chilled · wire whisk · pastry bag with star-shaped nozzle (see Note)
To serve: 4 dessert plates

The pineapple

Cut the pineapple into quarters lengthwise. Remove the core from each piece and cut the flesh away from the skin; be careful not to damage the skins, as they will be used to serve the dessert.

Dice the pineapple flesh, place it on a plate and chill it in the freezer while making the raspberry cream (see Note).

The pink *crème Chantilly*

Purée the raspberries in a liquidiser or food processor, then work the purée through a sieve to eliminate all the pips.

Place the cold *crème fraîche* or double cream in a chilled mixing bowl, add the icing sugar and the strained raspberry purée and whisk until the cream stands in peaks.

To serve the pineapple

Place each pineapple skin on a plate. Spoon some of the diced pineapple on to each one, top each with 2 small or 1 large scoop of ice-cream, and place the remaining pieces of pineapple and the strawberries over and around the ice-cream. Using a pastry bag, decorate with a ribbon of the pink *crème Chantilly*. Serve immediately.

Note

The pineapple can be prepared up to several hours in advance. In this case, place the diced flesh in the refrigerator, not in the freezer.

If you do not have a pastry bag, the raspberry cream can simply be served in a sauceboat on the side.

Wine

Dry champagne.

Pears with Ginger Cream and Chocolate Mousse
Poires pochées, crème au gingembre

For 4 people

For the pears

4	small or 2 large pears
	zest of 1 lime, finely grated
½ litre *(17 fl. oz)*	water
300g *(11 oz)*	caster sugar

For the ginger cream

3	egg yolks
3 tbsps	caster sugar
250ml *(9 fl. oz)*	milk
½ tsp	powdered ginger

For the mousse

100g *(4 oz)*	dark semi-sweet chocolate (*Chocolat Menier* is ideal)
2 tsps	softened butter
4 tsps	Scotch whisky
3	egg whites
2	drops lime juice
2 tsps	caster sugar

Equipment
large saucepan · large mixing bowl · wire whisk · medium saucepan · double boiler
To serve: 3 serving bowls

The pears
If using small pears, leave them whole; core them with an apple corer, then peel them. Large pears should be peeled, cut into halves and their cores cut out with a spoon.

Place the grated lime zest in a saucepan with the water and sugar. Bring to the boil, lower the heat and simmer for 20 minutes. Add the pears and simmer for 20 minutes more. Remove from the heat and leave the pears to cool completely in the liquid.

The ginger cream
Beat the egg yolks with the sugar until smooth and pale in colour. Heat the milk and ginger in a saucepan, then whisk into the egg yolks. Continue to cook and cool the cream exactly as described for the vanilla custard in Floating Island (see p.261)

The mousse
Melt the chocolate in a double boiler. When melted, stir in the butter and Whisky, remove from the heat and allow to cool until no longer warm to the touch.

In a mixing bowl, beat the egg whites and the lime juice until foamy, add the sugar and beat until very stiff. Carefully fold the egg whites into the chocolate, then transfer to a serving dish and chill for at least 1–2 hours before serving.

To serve the pears
Drain the pears and place them in a serving dish.

Place the ginger cream in another bowl, then bring the 3 dishes (pears, cream and mousse) to the table. Everyone should serve himself, taking a little of each.

Note
Everything must be made at least 3–4 hours in advance in order to have time to cool. If you prefer, you can prepare everything up to 24 hours in advance.

Wine
A Condrieu or a vigorous Alsace.

Caramel Mousse
Mousse au caramel

For 4 people

250g *(9 oz)*	lump sugar
I tsp	lemon juice
I ½ tbsps	water
5	eggs, separated
	scant ½ tsp gelatine powder
I ½ tsps	warm water
325ml *(11 fl. oz)*	cream or *crème fraîche* (see p.290), whipped until stiff
	a few drops of lemon juice (for the egg whites)

Equipment
small saucepan · 2 mixing bowls · wire whisk or electric beater
To serve: soufflé mould or 4 small individual dishes

The caramel
In a saucepan, place the sugar, lemon juice and 1½ tbsps of water. Bring to the boil and cook over a very low heat for 10–15 minutes or until the syrup is a pale golden colour. Swirl the pan to obtain even colouring and watch very carefully to make sure that it doesn't darken too much.

Place the egg yolks in a mixing bowl and beat them lightly. Moisten the gelatine with 1 ½ teaspoons of warm water.

When the caramel is ready, remove the pan from the heat and wait for a few seconds for it to stop bubbling. Then, beating the egg yolks vigorously with a whisk or electric beater, pour the hot caramel on to them in a very thin, steady stream; a thick, creamy mixture should form. As soon as all the caramel has been added, add the gelatine. Continue beating for another 5 minutes or until the mixture has cooled completely.

To finish and serve the mousse

Using a wooden spatula, fold the whipped cream into the caramel mixture. When perfectly mixed, add a few drops of lemon juice to the egg whites, beat until very stiff and fold them into the mixture; the final mixture should be perfectly smooth.

Pour the mousse into a large soufflé dish or 4 small dishes and refrigerate for several hours before serving.

Suggestion

About 50g *(2 oz)* of chopped almonds, walnuts or hazelnuts may be beaten into the caramel after the gelatine has been added.

Wine

A rosé d'Anjou.

Chocolate Mousse
Mousse au chocolat

For 4 people

175g *(6 oz)*	dark semi-sweet chocolate *(Chocolat Menier* is ideal)
2 tsps	butter, cut into cubes
6 tbsps	*crème fraîche* (see p.290) or double cream
1 tsp	curaçao (see Suggestions)
3	egg yolks
4 tbsps	caster sugar
4	egg whites
	a few drops of lemon juice (for the egg whites)

Equipment

large double boiler · mixing bowl · wire whisk or electric beater
To serve: serving dish

The chocolate

Melt the chocolate in the top of a large double boiler. Check from time to time to make sure that the water in the bottom of the double boiler never boils (remove from the heat if necessary).

When the chocolate has melted, stir it with a wooden spoon to make it perfectly smooth. Stir in the butter a cube at a time. Stir in the cream little by little, then add the curaçao. The mixture should be smooth and creamy. Remove the chocolate from the heat, stir in the egg yolks and 2 tablespoons of sugar and allow to cool until no longer warm to the touch.

To make and serve the mousse

In a mixing bowl, place the egg whites and lemon juice. Beat until very stiff, folding in 2 tablespoons of sugar. Fold a quarter of the egg whites into the chocolate, then fold in the rest; the finished mixture should be perfectly smooth and even.

Pour the mousse into a serving dish and chill for 1–2 hours before serving.

This mousse should be eaten the day it is made.

Suggestions

Whisky, brandy or other alcohol may be used instead of curaçao to flavour the mousse.

If desired, 50–75g (2–3 oz) chopped walnuts may be folded into the mousse with the egg whites.

Savoy Pears with Toasted Brioche

Poires savoyardes, brioche toastée

For 4 people

4	large pears
½	lemon
2 tbsps	butter
100g (4 oz)	caster sugar
5 tbsps	pear liqueur (eau-de-vie de poire)
175ml (6 fl. oz)	crème fraîche (see p.290) or double cream
20	peppercorns, coarsely crushed in a mortar
8	slices brioche (see p.240), 1½cm (½ in) thick

Equipment

large frying pan · 2 wooden spoons
To serve: large plate and 4 dessert plates

The pears

Peel the pears, core them and cut each one into 6 slices, rubbing each piece with half a lemon to keep it from turning brown.

Melt the butter in a large frying pan, add the pears and roll in the butter to coat each wedge. Add the sugar, raise the heat, and cook for 5 minutes, turning the pears carefully with 2 wooden spoons to caramelise them lightly on all sides. Add the liqueur and light; when the flame has died out, add the cream and peppercorns, stir and simmer very slowly over a low heat for 12 minutes.

To finish and serve the pears

Toast the slices of brioche under the grill. They brown very quickly – ½–1 minute on each side should be enough – so watch very carefully.

Place the toasted brioche on a plate. Place the pears and their sauce on individual dessert plates and serve, with the brioche on the side.

Suggestion

Apples can be prepared exactly like the pears, in which case apple brandy (calvados) should be used.

Note

Although the brioche adds a nice touch, it is not absolutely essential to the taste of the dessert. Do not be afraid to eat the pieces of peppercorn – they are delicious with the pears and the sauce.

Wine

Dry champagne.

Strawberry Charlotte
Charlotte aux fraises

For 4–6 people

1 kg *(2¼ lb)*	ripe strawberries
2 tbsps	icing sugar
3½	sheets of leaf gelatine
3 tbsps	cold water
3	egg yolks
50g *(2 oz)*	caster sugar
1	quantity lady's finger sponge (see p.234)
4½ tbsps	strawberry *eau-de-vie* or Kirsch
100ml *(4 fl. oz)*	whipping cream or liquid *crème fraîche* (see p.290) whipped until stiff

Equipment

food processor or liquidiser · fine sieve · wire whisk · mixing bowl · saucepan · bowl · electric mixer (optional) · wooden spatula · large bowl (optional) · charlotte mould, 16cm *(6¼ in)* in diameter · pastry brush · ladle or large spoon
To serve: serving dish and a sauceboat

Preliminary preparations

Wash the strawberries and remove the stalks. Measure out 150g *(5 oz)* and pat them dry in a clean cloth or paper towel. Cut them into quarters and reserve in a bowl.

256

Purée the rest of the strawberries in a food processor or liquidiser, then strain through a fine sieve to remove all the seeds, stirring and rubbing the pulp to extract all the liquid. Measure the juice; there should be approximately 600ml (1 pint).

The strawberry sauce

Set aside 450ml (¾ pint) of the strawberry purée for making the strawberry cream. Pour the remaining purée into a sauceboat and add the icing sugar, whisking until the sugar is completely dissolved. Refrigerate until ready to serve.

The strawberry cream

Place the reserved strawberry purée in a saucepan and heat for 6 minutes over a low heat, stirring occasionally. Do not allow to boil.

Soften the gelatine in the water.

Beat the egg yolks and sugar together in a bowl until the mixture is creamy and light in colour. Add the hot strawberry purée, whisking constantly. Pour back into the saucepan, place over a low heat and cook, stirring constantly with a wooden spatula, for about 4 minutes or until the thick foam on the surface has disappeared (only a few bubbles will be left) and the mixture has thickened enough to coat the spatula lightly. Test by lifting the spatula straight out of the cream and letting the excess cream drip off. Draw a horizontal line in the cream on the spatula with your finger; if the top of the line holds its shape, the cream is done. Do not let the cream boil.

Pour the strawberry cream into a mixing bowl and whisk in the moistened gelatine. Allow to cool completely in the refrigerator (about 2 hours), whisking occasionally, or place the mixing bowl in a larger bowl filled with ice and water and whisk frequently until cold (about 15 minutes), changing the ice and water when necessary. The cream is ready when it is cold to the touch and as thick as thick custard or home-made mayonnaise.

The charlotte

Lightly butter the sides of the charlotte mould. Cut a circle of waxed paper to fit the bottom of the mould and put it in place. Lay a sponge circle, cut to fit, in the mould with the flat (bottom) side facing up.

With a pastry brush, paint the circle with some of the strawberry eau-de-vie or Kirsch. Brush the top side of the remaining sponge as well, cut into fingers and fit them together round the sides of the mould with the rounded (top) side touching the mould.

When the strawberry cream is cold, whisk it vigorously until perfectly smooth. Fold in the whipped cream with a wooden spatula; make sure the 2 creams are perfectly mixed together.

Ladle a quarter of the cream into the mould and cover it with one-third of the reserved quartered strawberries. Ladle in a second quarter of the cream, cover again with strawberries – and so on, finishing with a layer of cream (the completed charlotte will have 4 layers of cream and 3 layers of strawberries). Smooth the surface of the cream and refrigerate the charlotte for at least 7–8 hours.

To serve the charlotte

Slice off the top ends of the sponge fingers so that they are even with the cream.

Place a serving dish upside down over the charlotte mould and then invert everything so that the mould is sitting on the dish (see Note). Lift off the mould, peel off the paper and serve the charlotte with the strawberry sauce on the side.

Suggestion

An equal amount of raspberries may be used instead of strawberries (use whole raspberries for garnishing the charlotte).

Note

If the charlotte does not come out of the mould easily, dip it into a bowl of hot water, carefully run a knife around the edge and try again.

Wine

Champagne, a sweet wine or a fresh, fruity red.

Snow Eggs
Blancs en neige sur crème anglaise

For 4 people

For the custard

½ litre *(17 fl. oz)*	milk
½	vanilla pod, cut in half lengthwise
6	egg yolks
290g *(10 oz)*	caster sugar

For the snow eggs

2 tsps	lemon juice
6	egg whites
75g *(3 oz)*	caster sugar

For the caramel

6 tbsps	water
100g *(4 oz)*	granulated sugar

Equipment

saucepan · bowl · wire whisk · large deep frying pan or *sauteuse* · cake rack · large mixing bowl · electric beater (optional) · skimmer or slotted spoon · small saucepan
To serve: deep serving dish

The custard

Make the custard as described for the Floating Island (see p.261), using the measurements given here. Allow to cool completely.

The snow eggs

Place a deep frying pan or *sauteuse* over a moderate heat and fill it three-quarters full with water. Place a clean cloth on a cake rack (preferably one with 'feet').

In a mixing bowl, add the lemon juice to the egg whites and begin beating. When foamy, add a third of the sugar. Continue beating until the whites begin to stiffen, then add a second third of the sugar. When the egg whites form soft peaks, add the remaining sugar and beat until very stiff and smooth.

Dip an ordinary kitchen tablespoon into a bowl of water. When the water in the pan simmers, take a large spoonful of the egg white and place it in the water (hold the spoon down in the water – the egg white will float off). Place 3 or 4 of these 'eggs' in the pan and poach for 3 minutes, turn them over and poach for 3 minutes on the second side. Lift them out of the water with a skimmer or slotted spoon and drain on the cloth. Continue in this way until all the egg white has been used up.

To serve

Pour the cold custard into a deep serving dish and place the snow eggs delicately on top in a mound.

Place the water and sugar for the caramel in a small saucepan and boil for 6–8 minutes or until a golden caramel is formed. Swirl the saucepan to obtain an even colouring. Pour over the snow eggs in a thin stream and serve immediately.

Suggestion

A fruit sauce may be used instead of the vanilla custard.

Note

Any fruit may be used in making a fruit sauce. Use 450g *(1 lb)* of prepared fruit (i.e., peeled, seeded, and cut into pieces if necessary) and follow the directions and measurements given for the raspberry sauce for the Pear Charlotte (see p.278).

Lemon Mousse
with Flaming Cherries
Mousse au citron et aux cerises flambées

For 6 individual mousses

	zest of 3 lemons, finely chopped
2 tbsps	caster sugar
150ml (¼ pint)	dry white wine
1½ tbsps	lemon juice
4	sheets of leaf gelatine or 1 tbsp powdered gelatine
3 tbsps	cold water
3 generous tbsps	lemon jelly
7	eggs, separated
1 tbsp	caster sugar (for the egg whites)
48	cherries, tinned or stewed
3 tbsps	cherry syrup
2 tbsps	caster sugar (for the cherries)
6 tbsps	Kirsch

Equipment
saucepan · 2 mixing bowls · wire whisk or electric beater · frying pan
To serve: 6 small dishes or individual soufflé moulds

The mousses
Place the lemon zest in a saucepan with the sugar, wine and lemon juice. Bring to a boil, lower the heat and simmer slowly for 10 minutes.

Soak the gelatine with the water.

Remove the lemon mixture from the heat and whisk in the gelatine and lemon jelly until they have dissolved and the mixture is smooth.

Beat the egg yolks lightly in a mixing bowl, then pour the contents of the saucepan on to them, whisking constantly. Continue beating for about 5 minutes; the mixture should cool and thicken.

Beat the egg whites until very stiff; halfway through add the sugar. With a wooden spatula, fold a quarter of the egg whites into the cooled lemon mixture, then fold in the remaining whites; the final mixture should be perfectly smooth.

Divide the mousse among the small dishes or soufflé moulds and chill in the refrigerator for at least 2 hours before serving.

To serve the mousses
The mousses may either be turned out (dip each mould in boiling water for a few seconds) or served in the dishes or moulds.

Place the cherries and their syrup in a frying pan. Bring the liquid to a boil, add the sugar and continue cooking until the cherries caramelise slightly. Add the Kirsch and light with a match, pour the cherries over the mousses and serve immediately.

Suggestion
Orange mousses may be made in the same way, using oranges, orange juice and orange jelly.

Note
If making orange mousses, use the zest of 1½ oranges; the other measurements remain the same.

Wine
A chilled rosé.

Floating Island
Ile flottante aux pralines

For 4–5 people

For the pralines

100g *(4 oz)*	shelled almonds
6 tbsps	water
120g *(4½ oz)*	granulated sugar

For the custard

½ litre *(17 fl. oz)*	milk
½	vanilla pod, cut in half lengthwise
5	egg yolks
100g *(4 oz)*	caster sugar

For the 'island'

6 tbsps	water
40g *(1½ oz)*	caster sugar
	a few drops of lemon juice
6	egg whites
1 tbsp	caster sugar

Equipment
marble slab or baking sheet · 3 saucepans · baking sheet or roasting tin · flexible metal spatula · mortar, food processor or heavy-duty liquidiser · wire whisk or electric mixer · wooden spatula · roasting tin · non-stick cake tin, 20cm *(8 in)* in diameter, 5cm *(2 in)* deep
To serve: deep serving dish

The praline (see Note)

Pre-heat the oven to 350°F/180°C/Reg. 4.

Bring a saucepan of water to the boil, add the almonds and boil for 1 minute, drain, cool under running water and peel by squeezing them out of their skins. Dry the almonds on a cloth, then spread them out on a clean baking sheet or roasting tin and toast them in the oven for 8 minutes.

Place 6 tablespoons of water and 120g (4 oz) of sugar in a saucepan, melt the sugar and boil for 10–15 minutes or until a rich, dark caramel is formed. Swirl to obtain an even colour, then stir in the almonds with a wooden spoon; they should all be coated with the caramel. Pour them on to a lightly oiled marble slab or baking sheet and spread them out with the wooden spoon into an even layer. Allow to cool and harden.

Slide a flexible metal spatula under the almond brittle to detach it from the marble or baking sheet, break it into pieces and break into chips briefly in a mortar, food processor or liquidiser. Reserve in a bowl.

The custard

Place the milk and vanilla pod in a saucepan and heat over a low heat for 6 minutes; the milk should be almost boiling.

In a bowl, beat the egg yolks and sugar until very pale, then pour the hot milk on to them in a thin stream, whisking vigorously. Pour back into the saucepan and cook over a low heat for 5–6 minutes, stirring constantly with a wooden spatula. The foam on the surface should disappear, and the custard should thicken enough to coat the spatula lightly. To test, lift the spatula straight out of the custard and let any excess drip off, then draw a horizontal line on the spatula with your finger. If the top edge of the line of custard holds its shape, the custard is done. Do not allow the custard to boil.

Strain the custard into a bowl and allow to cool, whisking occasionally.

The 'island'

Pre-heat the oven to 350°F/180°C/Reg. 4.

Pour water about 1½cm (½ in) deep into a roasting tin and place it in the oven.

Boil 6 tablespoons of water and 40g (1½ oz) of sugar in a saucepan for 5–6 minutes or until a dark blond caramel is formed. Do not allow it to burn.

While the caramel is cooking, place the cake tin in the oven. When the caramel is ready, pour it into the tin and turn the tin in all directions to coat the bottom and sides completely (be very careful not to burn yourself when coating the sides).

Add a few drops of lemon juice to the egg whites and beat them until foamy, add a tablespoon of sugar and continue beating until the egg whites are very stiff and smooth.

Sprinkle the crushed almond brittle over the egg whites and fold it in. When the mixture is uniform, pour it into the caramelised mould and smooth the surface with a wooden spoon.

Place the mould in the roasting tin and bake for 45 minutes.

To serve the floating island
Remove the 'island' from the oven. Pour the custard into a deep serving dish. Run a knife around the edge of the 'island', then very carefully turn it out on to the custard; the island will float. Allow to cool for 15 minutes, then serve.

Note
If you like, you can use 200g *(7 oz)* ready-made nut brittle (almond or hazelnut).

The floating island may be made and turned out well in advance. It is equally good served cold or lukewarm.

Stuffed Peaches
Pêches farcies

For 4 people (see Note)

For the pastry cream

100ml *(4 fl. oz)*	milk
¼	vanilla pod, cut in half lengthwise
2	egg yolks
2 tbsps	caster sugar
1½ tbsps	plain flour
½ tsp	butter
35g *(1½ oz)*	slivered almonds
4	whole tinned peaches in syrup or fresh peaches poached in syrup (see Note)
2 tbsps	raspberry liqueur *(eau-de-vie de framboise)*

Equipment
saucepan, with lid · 2 mixing bowls · wire whisk · baking sheet · gratin dish, 20cm *(8 in)* long · trussing needle or large knitting needle · pastry bag with 1cm *(⅜-in)* nozzle · small saucepan
To serve: serving dish or 4 dessert plates

The pastry cream

Place the milk and vanilla pod in a saucepan and bring to the boil, remove from the heat, cover and leave to infuse for 9 minutes.

Beat the egg yolks and sugar until pale and creamy, then whisk in the flour. Bring the vanilla infusion back to the boil and add it gradually to the egg yolks and sugar, whisking constantly. Pour back into the saucepan and bring to the boil, whisking constantly. Boil for 30 seconds, whisk again, pour the cream into a clean mixing bowl and remove the vanilla pod. Rub the surface of the cream with the butter to keep a skin from forming, and leave to cool. Whisk once or twice and cover the bowl when the mixture is cold.

The almonds

Pre-heat the oven to 400°F/200°C/Reg. 6.

Spread the almonds out on a baking sheet; place in the oven for about 10 minutes, stirring about every 3 minutes, to brown them evenly. When golden brown, place in a bowl and allow to cool.

The peaches

Raise the oven temperature to 425°F/220°C/Reg. 7.

Drain the peaches. Place their syrup in a gratin dish and reserve.

Stone each peach by holding it in one hand and sticking a trussing needle or knitting needle into the bottom (pointed end) of the peach directly under the seed. Push gently; the seed will come out of the top of the peach without damaging it.

Stir the almonds into the pastry cream. Fill a pastry bag with the cream and fill each peach with it.

Bring the syrup from the peaches to the boil, then place the peaches in it. Bake for 12 minutes, basting once or twice.

To serve the peaches

Lift the peaches out of the syrup and place them on a serving dish or dessert plates.

Place 2 tablespoons of the syrup in a small saucepan; discard the remaining syrup. Bring the syrup in the saucepan to a rapid boil, add the liqueur and light with a match. Pour flaming over the peaches and serve immediately.

Suggestions

Pear *eau-de-vie* or Kirsch may be used instead of raspberry liqueur. Coarsely chopped walnuts or hazelnuts may be used instead of slivered almonds.

264

Note

In his restaurant, Alain Senderens would serve 2 peaches per person, rather than one (therefore, the proportions given here would be for 2 servings rather than for 4). This makes for a very filling dessert, but you can double all measurements for 4, if you like.

If you buy and poach fresh peaches, use 150ml *(½ pint)* of their syrup for the proportions given in the ingredients list when baking them in the oven.

Wine

Dry champagne.

Melon Fritters
with Fresh Strawberry Sauce
Beignets de melon au coulis de fraises

For 4 people

	fritter batter (see p.238)
450g *(1 lb)*	strawberries
2 tbsps	caster sugar
2	small cantaloupes or ogen melons, weighing about 450g *(1 lb)* each
2 litres *(3¼ pints)*	cooking oil
100g *(4 oz)*	icing sugar
	flour (for the baking sheet)

Equipment

mixing bowl · wire whisk · food processor or liquidiser · fine sieve · deep fryer or large saucepan · deep-frying thermometer · skimmer or slotted spoon · baking sheet
To serve: serving dish or 4 dessert plates, and a sauceboat

Preliminary preparations

Prepare the fritter batter at least 3 hours in advance.

The sauce

Wash the strawberries, remove their stalks and purée them in a food processor or liquidiser. Strain the purée into a bowl to remove the seeds, rubbing them with a wooden spoon to extract all the juice. Whisk in the sugar (more or less sugar may be added, according to taste). Pour the finished sauce into a sauceboat and chill until ready to serve.

The melon

Cut each melon in half and scoop out the seeds. Cut each half into 6–8 wedges about 2cm (¾ in) wide at the base and cut off the rind. Reserve the wedges on a plate.

The fritters

Fill a deep fryer or large saucepan halfway with cooking oil and heat to 375°F/190°C.

When the oil is hot, drop 2–3 wedges of melon into the batter. Make sure they are completely coated, lift them out one by one with a fork and drop them into the hot oil. Depending on the size of the fryer or saucepan, 8–12 wedges may be cooked at once. After 1–2 minutes, they should have browned on one side. Turn them over with a wooden spoon and brown on the other side, then lift them out of the oil with a skimmer or slotted spoon and place on paper towels to drain. Cook the remaining melon wedges in the same way; 2–3 batches should be enough to cook them all.

To glaze and serve the fritters

Pre-heat the grill. Place the icing sugar in a soup plate. Lightly flour a baking sheet.

When the fritters have drained, roll them one by one in the icing sugar, place them on the baking sheet and slide them under the grill for about 1 minute to glaze. Watch carefully to see that they brown but don't burn.

Place the fritters on a serving dish or dessert plates and serve immediately, with the strawberry sauce on the side.

Suggestion

Any fruit can be prepared in this way.

Caramelised Strawberries with Lemon Cream

Fraises caramélisées, crème anglaise au citron

For 4 people

For the lemon cream

	zest of 1 lemon
250ml (9 fl. oz)	milk or single cream
3	egg yolks
110g (4 oz)	caster sugar

For the strawberries

600g *(1 ¼ lb)*	strawberries
250g *(9 oz)*	lump sugar (for the caramel)
6 tbsps	water

Equipment
saucepan · wire whisk or electric beater · wooden spatula ·
bowl · baking sheet or aluminium foil · small saucepan ·
trussing needle or skewer
To serve: 4 dessert plates

The lemon cream
Chop the lemon zest finely, then place it in a sieve and rinse it under cold running water. Drain thoroughly.

Make the lemon cream exactly as described for the vanilla custard in the recipe for Floating Island (see p.261), but using the chopped lemon zest instead of vanilla and the other ingredients as listed here.

Strain the cream into a bowl and allow to cool to lukewarm, stirring occasionally.

The strawberries
Wash and remove the stalks of the strawberries, then set them on a cloth to dry. Lightly oil a baking sheet or a sheet of aluminium foil.

Place the sugar and water in a small saucepan. Heat, stirring until the sugar has dissolved, then boil rapidly until the syrup begins to turn a golden yellow. Swirl the saucepan to ensure an even colouring, then remove it from the heat.

Stick a strawberry on to a trussing needle or skewer, dip it into the caramel, swirl it if necessary to coat it all over, then set it down on the baking sheet. (Remove the needle or skewer by pushing lightly on the strawberry with the tip of a knife.) Continue in this manner until all the strawberries are coated – if the caramel thickens too much as it cools off, place it back over the heat for a few seconds, swirling the pan to distribute the heat evenly.

To serve the strawberries
If necessary, reheat the lemon cream to lukewarm, then pour it into the dessert plates. Arrange the strawberries on top of the cream and serve.

Suggestions
The lemon zest may be replaced by the zest of an orange. Raspberries may be used instead of strawberries.

Wine
Champagne.

Coffee Charlotte
Gâteau au café

For 4–6 people

3 generous tbsps	coffee beans
½ litre *(17 fl. oz)*	milk
6	egg yolks
125g *(4½ oz)*	caster sugar
4	sheets of leaf gelatine
3 tbsps	cold water
1	quantity lady's finger sponge (see p.234)
100ml *(4 fl. oz)*	cold strong coffee or 2 tsp instant coffee dissolved in 100ml *(4 fl. oz)* boiling water and allowed to cool
250ml *(9 fl. oz)*	double cream or *crème fraîche* (see p.290) whisked until stiff

Equipment
pestle and mortar or bowl and smaller bowl or glass · saucepan · mixing bowl · wire whisk or electric mixer · fluted brioche mould, 21cm *(8½ in)* in diameter, or charlotte mould, 16cm *(6¼ in)* in diameter
To serve: serving dish

The coffee cream
Crush the coffee beans coarsely in a mortar, or place them in a bowl and crush them with the bottom of a smaller bowl or a glass.

Place the crushed coffee beans in a saucepan, add the milk and heat gently for 8 minutes; at the end of this time, the milk should be almost boiling. Allow to simmer for 3 minutes more.
Beat the egg yolks and sugar in a mixing bowl until the mixture is pale yellow, then slowly strain the hot milk on to it, whisking constantly.

Pour the mixture back into the saucepan, finish cooking, add the gelatine and cool as described for the strawberry cream in the Strawberry Charlotte (see p.256).

The charlotte
Line the mould with the lady's finger sponge (brush the pastry with the cold coffee) exactly as described for the Strawberry Charlotte.

When the coffee cream is cold, whisk it until perfectly smooth, then fold in the whipped cream. Pour the finished cream into the mould, smooth the surface and chill for 7–8 hours.

To serve the charlotte
Trim the sponge fingers so that they are even with the cream, turn out the charlotte as described for the Strawberry Charlotte and serve.

Suggestions

The sponge fingers may be brushed with rum instead of coffee.

If desired, a few bits of left-over lady's finger sponge may be soaked in a mixture of coffee and rum. Pour half of the coffee cream into the mould, arrange the pieces of sponge on top, then pour in the rest of the cream and finish as described.

Wine

Coffee liqueur.

Hot Guava Charlottes with Kiwi Sauce
Charlottes chaudes aux goyaves, coulis de kiwis

For 4 individual charlottes

For the lemon zest

	zest of 1 lemon, cut into very fine julienne strips
	juice of 1 lemon
125ml *(4 fl. oz)*	water
2 tbsps	caster sugar

For the sauce

4	kiwi fruits (for substitute, see Suggestions)
	juice of 2 oranges
3½ tbsps	icing sugar

For the charlottes

8	guavas (for substitute, see Suggestions)
1 tbsp	butter
3½ tbsps	caster sugar
1	cylindrical brioche (see p.240), preferably one day old
5 tbsps	melted butter (for the baking sheet, moulds and brioche)
4 tbsps	apricot jam

Equipment

small saucepan · food processor or liquidiser · bowl · frying pan · 4 individual charlotte moulds, 8cm *(3 in)* in diameter or 4 soufflé moulds, 10cm *(4 in)* in diameter · baking sheet · pastry brush · roasting tin or oven dish
To serve: 4 dessert plates and a sauceboat

The candied lemon zest

Place the julienne of lemon zest in a strainer, rinse under cold running water, drain and place in a small saucepan. Add the lemon juice, water and sugar, bring to the boil, lower the heat and simmer, uncovered, for 40 minutes (there should be about a tablespoon of the liquid left). Reserve.

The kiwi sauce

Peel the kiwis, cut into pieces and purée in a food processor or liquidiser.

Place the purée in a bowl, stir in the orange juice and sugar, and whisk until the sugar is dissolved. Strain the sauce into a sauceboat and chill until ready to serve.

The guavas

With a potato peeler, peel the guavas and cut them into quarters. Scoop out the centres and seeds using a spoon.

In a frying pan, melt the butter, add the guavas and sprinkle them with the sugar. Cook over a moderate heat for 7 minutes, stirring frequently. The guavas will soften and brown lightly. Reserve.

Preparing the brioche

Pre-heat the oven to 425°F/220°C/Reg. 7.

Cut the brioche into slices about 3mm (⅛ in) thick. Trim 4 slices to line the bottoms of the moulds. Cut the edges off the remaining slices to make squares, then cut them into bands about 2cm (¾ in) wide and the height of the moulds. Make sure the bands line the sides of the mould perfectly, with no spaces between; the brioche will shrink slightly.

Remove the pieces of brioche from the moulds. Brush the baking sheet lightly with melted butter and place the brioche on it. Brush the moulds with a little butter and set them aside. Brush the pieces of brioche with the remaining butter and bake them for 5–7 minutes or until just beginning to turn golden brown.

Line the moulds with the warm brioche, starting with the circles that line the bottoms. It is important to line the moulds as soon as the brioche comes from the oven, as it becomes very brittle when cool.

To make and serve the charlottes

Place 3 pieces of guava in each lined mould, pressing on them as you do so. Add a tablespoon of apricot jam to each one, then divide the candied lemon zest among them and finish each charlotte with a second layer of guavas. Press on the contents of the moulds so that the charlottes will hold together; the moulds should be filled to the brim, or very close to it.

Place the charlottes in a large roasting tin or oven dish. Butter a sheet of aluminium foil large enough to cover all the charlottes at once and place it on top of them, buttered-side down. Bake for 20 minutes, lower the oven to 350°F/180°C/Reg. 4 and bake for 15 minutes more.

Turn the charlottes out on to dessert plates, pour a little of the kiwi sauce around them and serve immediately, with the rest of the sauce on the side.

Suggestions
The kiwi sauce may be replaced by a pineapple sauce made as for the Coconut Charlotte (see p.276). The guavas may also be replaced by the flesh of a large ripe pineapple, cut into chunks and prepared as described above.

If desired, ¼ teaspoon of cinnamon or Chinese five-spices mixture may be added to the guavas at the same time as the sugar.

Note
If the guavas sink when baking so that the ends of the brioche stick up above them, trim the brioche so that it will be even with the filling before turning the charlottes out.

Wine
Champagne or a rosé wine.

Winter Tart
Tarte d'hiver

For 6–8 people

275g *(10½ oz)*	sweet flan pastry with ground almonds (see p.237)
130g *(4½ oz)*	caster sugar
5 tbsps	softened butter, cut into small cubes
1	vanilla pod, cut in half lengthwise
¾ tsp	cinnamon
150g *(5 oz)*	chopped almonds
4	apples, peeled, cored and diced
	crème fraîche (see p.290) (for serving)

Equipment
rolling pin · tart tin, 20cm *(8 in)* in diameter · mixing bowl

To bake and serve the tart
Pre-heat the oven to 400°F/200°C/Reg. 6.

Roll out the pastry into a circle about 3mm *(⅛ in)* thick. Line the tart tin and cut off any excess pastry with a knife. Lightly press the pastry with your fingers to eliminate air pockets.

Put the sugar and butter in a mixing bowl and beat with a wooden spoon until creamy. Split open the vanilla pod and, using a knife, scrape its contents into the bowl. Beat in the cinnamon and chopped almonds to make a soft paste of uniform appearance.

Fill the tart tin almost completely with the diced apple, then cover the surface with pieces of the almond paste. With your fingers, push the bits of paste together to form a solid layer on top of the apples, then bake for 40 minutes (the surface of the tart should be golden brown when done). Cool for 10 minutes before serving warm, with a sauceboat of *crème fraîche*.

Suggestions
Chopped walnuts may be used instead of the almonds and diced pears instead of the apples.

Wine
Accompany with a rough farmhouse cider.

Hot Apple Charlottes
Charlottes aux pommes chaudes

For 4 individual charlottes

For the lemon zest

	zest of 1 lemon, cut into very fine julienne strips
	juice of 1 lemon
225ml *(8 fl. oz)*	water
2 tbsps	caster sugar

For the charlottes

1	cylindrical brioche (see p.240), preferably one day old
5 tbsps	melted butter (for the baking sheet, moulds and brioche)
8	medium apples 1.3kg *(2¾ lb)*
80g *(3 oz)*	butter
6 tbsps	caster sugar
4 tbsps	apricot jam
	crème fraîche (see p.290) for serving

Equipment
small saucepan · 4 individual charlotte moulds, 8cm *(3 in)* in diameter, or 4 soufflé moulds, 10cm *(4 in)* in diameter (about 225ml *(8 fl. oz)* capacity) · baking sheet · pastry brush · large frying pan · fork · large roasting tin or oven dish
To serve: 4 dessert plates and a sauceboat

The lemon zest and brioche

Make the candied lemon zest, cut and toast the brioche, and line the moulds exactly as described for the Hot Guava Charlottes (see p.269).

The apples

Peel and core the apples, then cut each one into 6 slices.

Melt the butter in a large frying pan, then add the apples in a single layer (if necessary, use 2 frying pans, or cook the apples in 2 batches, dividing the butter and sugar between them). Sprinkle with the sugar and cook for 5 minutes or until the first side has browned. Turn the pieces over with a fork and lightly brown the second side. Lower the heat and cook for about 5 minutes more to caramelise the sugar (do not allow it to burn).

To make and serve the charlottes

Pre-heat the oven to 350°F/180°C/Reg. 4.

Place 4 pieces of apple in each lined mould, wedging them tightly together. Spoon a tablespoon of apricot jam into each mould and cover with another layer of apples, divide the candied lemon zest among the moulds and finish filling them with a layer of apples. The apples should form a slight dome on top.

Place the charlottes in a large roasting tin or oven dish. Butter a sheet of aluminium foil large enough to cover all the moulds at once and place it on top of them, buttered-side down. Bake for 40 minutes.

When the charlottes are done, cut the ends of the brioche off, if necessary, so that it is even with the apples, then turn out the charlottes on to dessert plates and serve immediately, with *crème fraîche*.

Suggestions

Pears or bananas may be used instead of apples.

A cold vanilla custard, made as described for the Floating Island (see p.261), or a strawberry or raspberry sauce, made as described for the Pear Charlotte (see p.278), may be served instead of *crème fraîche*.

Note

If using pears or bananas, use 8 pears or 4 large bananas. Cut the pears like the apples; cut the bananas into slices about ½cm (¼ in) thick. Prepare as described for the apples.

Double cream, lightly whipped, may also be served instead of *crème fraîche*, but the incomparable taste of the *crème fraîche* is worth the effort of making it.

Wine

Serve with a farm cider or a sweet white wine – Jurançon, Monbazillac or a non-vintage champagne.

Lemon Tart
Tarte aux citrons

For 4–6 people

275g *(10½ oz)*	sweet flan pastry with ground almonds (see p.237)
	zest of 2 lemons, finely chopped
225ml *(8 fl. oz)*	cold water
	juice of 2 lemons
	juice of 2 oranges
2	eggs
60g *(2 oz)*	caster sugar
60g *(2 oz)*	ground almonds
65g *(2½ oz)*	melted butter

Equipment
pastry brush · rolling pin · tart tin, 20cm *(8 in)* in diameter · saucepan · bowl · wire whisk · mixing bowl

Preliminary preparations
Pre-heat the oven to 425°F/220°C/Reg. 7. Lightly butter the tart tin.

On a lightly floured worktop, roll out the pastry into a circle about 3mm *(⅛ in)* thick. Line the tart tin (if the pastry breaks, simply push the broken edges together with your fingers). Cut off any excess pastry and refrigerate the pastry case while making the filling.

The filling
Place the lemon zest in a saucepan, add the water, bring to the boil and boil for 5 seconds. Drain, cool under running water and drain again. Reserve in a bowl. Strain the lemon and orange juices into the bowl with the lemon zest.

Whisk the eggs lightly in a mixing bowl, then add the sugar, ground almonds, fruit juices and zest, and the melted butter. Mix well and pour into the lined tart tin.

To bake and serve the tart
Bake the tart for 15 minutes, lower the oven to 400°F/200°C/Reg. 6 and bake 15–17 minutes longer or until the blade of a knife plunged into the centre of the filling comes out clean and the pie crust has begun to brown.

Allow to cool for about 10 minutes. Serve warm.

Wine
A Provençal rosé.

Five Tropical Fruit Tartlets
Cinq tartelettes exotiques

For 4 people

200g *(7 oz)*	puff pastry (see p.242) or other pastry dough of your choice
1	small apple, cut into thin slices icing sugar (to sprinkle over the tartlets) softened butter (to dot over the apple tartlets)
1	small mango, peeled, seeded and cut into thin slices
1	small kiwi fruit, peeled and cut into thin slices
1	small pear, peeled and cut into thin slices half a 2½cm- *(1-in)-* thick slice of fresh pineapple, cut into thin slices *crème fraîche* (see p.290) (to serve with the tartlets)

Equipment

rolling pin · 7cm *(2¾-in)* round cutter · 2 baking sheets · tart tin, 20cm *(8 in)* in diameter · sugar dredger
To serve: 4 large dessert plates and a sauceboat

The pastry

Pre-heat the oven to 425°F/220°C/Reg. 7.

On a lightly floured worktop, roll out the pastry to a thickness of about 1½mm *(¹⁄₁₆ in)*, then cut out 20 circles with the cutter. It may be necessary to cut out about half of the circles, then form the scraps of pastry into a ball, roll it out and cut the rest.

Place 16 of the circles on a lightly buttered baking sheet. Butter a second baking sheet and place it, buttered-side down, over the rounds; this will keep the rounds from rising too much.

Place the 4 remaining rounds in a lightly buttered tart tin. Cover the surface of each one with apple slices, overlapping them so that none of the pastry is showing. Sprinkle with icing sugar, then dot each one with a few dabs of butter.

Bake the pastry rounds and the tartlets for 15 minutes, then remove the baking sheets from the oven and lift off the top sheet. Allow the apple tartlets to cook for 5 minutes more.

When the ungarnished pastry rounds have cooled, cover 4 of them with slices of mango, 4 with kiwi, 4 with pear and 4 with pineapple. In each case, the slices should overlap and there should be no pastry showing when finished.

To glaze and serve the tartlets

Pre-heat the grill.

Sprinkle the 16 raw fruit tartlets with icing sugar and place them under a moderate grill for about 2–3 minutes. The tops should colour slightly, but watch them carefully to see that they don't burn. Remove the tartlets and place the apple tartlets under the grill for about 45 seconds to warm them.

Place one of each kind of tartlet on each of 4 dessert plates and serve immediately, with *crème fraîche* on the side.

Note

Any left-over fruit may be used to make Tropical Fruit Salad (see p.249).

Wine

Monbazillac or Loupiac.

Coconut Charlotte with Pineapple Sauce
Charlotte au coco coulis d'ananas

For 4–6 people

For the coconut cream

1	whole coconut with milk inside (see Note)
½ litre *(17 fl. oz)*	milk
½ tsp	powdered ginger
100g *(4 oz)*	caster sugar
5	egg yolks
4	sheets of leaf gelatine
3 tbsps	water
1	quantity lady's finger sponge (see p.234)
175ml *(6 fl. oz)*	double cream or *crème fraîche* (see p.290) whisked until stiff
½	small ripe pineapple, weighing 900g *(2 lb)*
100g *(4 oz)*	icing sugar

Equipment

ice-pick · hammer · mixing bowl · food processor or heavy-duty liquidiser · wire whisk · *mouli-légumes* · saucepan · wooden spatula · charlotte mould, 16cm *(6¼ in)* in diameter
To serve: serving dish and a sauceboat

276

The coconut

The night before making the charlotte, remove the 'milk' from the coconut; with an ice-pick, pierce holes in 2 of the dents in the top of the coconut and pour the liquid into a mixing bowl; this is the coconut milk.

With a hammer, break the coconut open and pry off the hard outer shell with a sturdy knife. Cut the coconut meat into pieces about 2½cm *(1 in)* square, place one-third of them in a food processor or a heavy-duty liquidiser with one-third of the cow's milk, and purée. Add the purée to the coconut milk in the mixing bowl. Continue until all the coconut has been puréed and added to the bowl, stir in the ginger, mix well, cover the bowl and refrigerate overnight.

The coconut cream

The next day, place the coconut purée in a *mouli-légumes* and grind all the liquid through, as well as some of the pulp; you will need 450ml *(¾ pint)* for making the charlotte.

Place the coconut-flavoured milk in a saucepan with 50g *(2 oz)* sugar and bring to the boil. In a mixing bowl, beat the egg yolks with the remaining sugar until creamy and pale. Continue to make the coconut cream as described for the strawberry cream in the recipe for Strawberry Charlotte (see p.256), using the measurements given here.

Lining the charlotte mould

Line the mould with the lady's finger sponge as described for the Strawberry Charlotte (the sponge is used dry in this recipe).

Assembling the charlotte

When the coconut cream is cold, whisk it vigorously to make it smooth and fold in the whipped cream, mixing the 2 creams together perfectly. Pour the finished cream into the mould, smooth the surface and chill for at least 7 hours.

The pineapple sauce

Cut the pineapple in half. Only half will be used in this recipe; the rest can be used to make a Tropical Fruit Salad (see p.249), Five Tropical Fruit Tartlets (see p.275), or eaten as it is.

Remove the skin and core from the half pineapple and cut the flesh into chunks. Purée the flesh in a liquidiser or food processor, then strain it into a sauceboat, rubbing with a wooden spoon to extract all the juice. Whisk in the icing sugar and chill until ready to serve (more or less sugar may be added according to taste).

To serve the charlotte

Trim the tops of the lady's sponge fingers and turn the charlotte out as described for the Strawberry Charlotte. Serve, with the pineapple sauce on the side.

Suggestions

The whipped cream may be replaced by 2 stiffly beaten egg whites, and the ginger may be replaced by ¼ teaspoon of rum, or vanilla essence.

A handful of finely chopped *unsalted* cashews can be added to the lady's finger sponge at the same time as the egg whites.

Note

If fresh coconut is unavailable, 225g *(8 oz)* of desiccated (grated) coconut, plus 175ml *(6 fl. oz)* boiling water, may be used instead. Mix this with the milk and ginger, and proceed as described for fresh coconut.

Wine

A sweet wine, or champagne.

Pear Charlotte
Charlotte aux poires

For 4–6 people

8	pear halves, stewed or tinned in light syrup
2	fresh pears
	juice of 1 lemon
¼	vanilla pod, cut in half lengthwise
5½	sheets of leaf gelatine
3 tbsps	cold water
6	egg yolks
75g *(3 oz)*	caster sugar
1	quantity lady's finger sponge (see p.234)
1 tsp	pear liqueur *(eau-de-vie de poire)* (optional)
1	egg white
1 tbsp	caster sugar
450g *(1 lb)*	raspberries
150g *(5 oz)*	icing sugar

Equipment

2 large bowls · small bowl · liquidiser or food processor · saucepan · 2 medium bowls · wire whisk · wooden spatula · fine sieve · charlotte mould, 16cm *(6¼ in)* in diameter · pastry brush
To serve: serving dish and a sauceboat

Preliminary preparations

Drain the pears over a large bowl to catch the syrup. Place 4½ tablespoons of the syrup in a small bowl and reserve for painting the sponge.

278

Cut 3 of the pear halves into thin slices and reserve. Cut the remaining 5 pear halves into large pieces and place in a liquidiser or food processor. Peel, quarter and core the fresh pears. Add them to the liquidiser with the lemon juice and blend to a purée. Measure the purée and add enough of the syrup in the large bowl to make 450ml (¾ pint).

The pear cream

Place the pear purée in a saucepan with the vanilla pod. Heat the purée, make the pear cream and cool it, as described for the strawberry cream in the Strawberry Charlotte (see p.256), using the measurements given here.

To line and assemble the charlotte

Line the charlotte mould with the lady's finger sponge as described for the Strawberry Charlotte. Paint the pastry with the reserved pear syrup (the pear taste may be intensified by adding the *eau-de-vie de poire* if desired).

When the pear cream is cold, whisk it perfectly smooth. Beat the egg white with 1 tablespoon of sugar until very stiff, then fold it into the pear cream.

Using the pear cream and slices of pear, assemble the charlotte in layers as described for the Strawberry Charlotte. Chill for at least 7–8 hours.

The raspberry sauce

Purée the raspberries in a liquidiser or food processor and strain into a sauceboat, rubbing and stirring the pips in the sieve with a wooden spoon to extract all the juice. Whisk in the icing sugar and reserve in the refrigerator until ready to serve.

To serve the charlotte

Turn out and serve the Pear Charlotte as described for the Strawberry Charlotte.

Suggestions

The raspberry sauce may be replaced by a blackcurrant or strawberry sauce, made as described above for raspberries, using the same quantities of fruit and sugar. The charlotte may also be served with a chocolate sauce (see Stuffed Pears Colette Dufour, p.248).

Note

Because the taste of this charlotte is very subtle and delicate, tell your guests to take only 2–3 spoonfuls of the sauce and to pour it around, not over, the charlotte, or serve it yourself in the kitchen. If served in this way, the sauce will bring out the taste of the pears; otherwise, the pear taste will be lost completely.

Wine

A Sylvaner.

Tarte Tatin
Tarte tatin

For 4–6 people

For the shortcrust pastry

¼ tsp	salt
3 tbsps	cold water
200g *(7 oz)*	plain flour
125g *(¼ lb)*	plus 2½ tbsps softened butter

For the apples

6	apples, weighing about 1.25kg *(2¾ lb)*
50g *(2 oz)*	butter
100g *(4 oz)*	caster sugar
¼ tsp	cinnamon
	crème fraîche (see p.290) (for serving; optional)

Equipment
small bowl or glass · mixing bowl (optional) · heavy metal tart tin or sandwich tin or round enamelled cast-iron gratin dish, 26–28cm *(10–11in)* in diameter and about 5cm *(2 in)* deep · rolling pin · pastry brush
To serve: large round serving dish

The pastry
Dissolve the salt in the water in a small bowl or glass.

Place the flour on a clean worktop or in a mixing bowl and distribute pieces of butter over it. With your fingers, pinch the flour and butter together rapidly until all the butter has been incorporated and a crumbly mixture has been formed – 1 minute of energetic pinching should do it. Add the salt water, mixing it in with the same pinching motion for about 1 minute more, then pack the pastry into a ball, cover with a floured cloth or aluminium foil and refrigerate for at least 30 minutes.

The apples
Peel and core the apples, then cut each one into 8 slices.

Place the tart tin over a moderate heat and melt the butter in it, add the pieces of apple, sprinkle with the sugar and cinnamon, and cook for 10–12 minutes or until the sugar begins to caramelise, turning the apples over with a wooden spoon. Remove the pan from the heat and arrange the slices of apple in circles or rows that cover the bottom of the tin in one layer.

To bake
Pre-heat the oven to 425°F/220°C/Reg. 7.

Roll out the pastry a little larger than the diameter of the baking tin.

With a dry pastry brush, brush any excess flour off the pastry. Roll the pastry on to the rolling pin (see Note), brushing off the flour from the bottom as you do so, then unroll it on top of the apples. Tuck the pastry in around the apples, folding the edges in to form a border; if there is too much pastry, cut some off with a knife.

Bake the tart at 425°F/220°C/Reg. 7 for 30 minutes, lower the oven to 350°F/180°C/Reg. 4 and bake for 15 minutes more or until the pastry is a rich golden brown.

Remove the tart from the oven and place it over a moderate heat on top of the stove for 1 minute.

To turn out and serve the tart

Remove the tart from the heat and place a deep serving dish upside down over it. With both hands (protect your fingers with oven gloves) lift up the tart tin with the dish on it, press the two together and flip everything over. Lift the tart tin off the tart.

Allow to cool for 5–10 minutes, then serve the tart warm, accompanied by a dish of *crème fraîche*, if desired.

Wine

A farm cider or a sweet wine.

Blackcurrant Tart

Tarte aux fruits-cassis

For 4–6 people

250g *(9 oz)*	puff pastry (see p.242) or shortcrust pastry (see Tarte Tatin, p.280)
3	eggs
75g *(3 oz)*	caster sugar
3 tbsps	ground almonds
	a pinch of cinnamon
350ml *(12 fl. oz)*	double cream or *crème fraîche* (see p.290)
275g *(10 oz)*	tinned blackcurrants in syrup, drained

Equipment

rolling pin · tart tin, 20cm *(8 in)* in diameter, or flan ring, about 4cm *(1½ in)* deep · large mixing bowl · wire whisk · ladle

To make and serve the tart

Pre-heat the oven to 425°F/220°C/Reg. 7. Lightly butter the tart tin or flan ring.

On a lightly floured worktop, roll out the pastry into a circle about 26cm *(10½ in)* wide. Brush off any excess flour and line the tin with the pastry. Press the bottom and sides of the tin lightly with your fingertips to eliminate any air pockets, then cut off any excess pastry. Chill.

Beat the eggs with the sugar, whisk in the ground almonds and cinnamon, then add the cream, whisking until perfectly smooth.

Pour the drained currants into the lined tart tin, spread them out evenly, then ladle in enough tart filling to fill the tart completely. Bake for 30–35 minutes or until golden brown on top.

Allow to cool for about 15 minutes. Serve warm, but not hot.

Wine

A red Burgundy with a fruity flavour, a cassis liqueur, or champagne, or another sparkling wine.

A Fine Apple Tart
Tarte bonne femme fine

For 4 people

300g *(10½ oz)*	puff pastry (see p.242)
3–4	medium apples, weighing 450g *(1 lb)*
2 tbsps	butter, cut into little cubes
3	generous tbsps caster sugar
	crème fraîche (see p.290) (for serving; optional)

Equipment
baking sheet · rolling pin
To serve: large rectangular serving dish and a sauceboat (optional)

To make
Pre-heat the oven to 450°F/230°C/Reg. 8. Lightly butter and flour a baking sheet.

Roll out the puff pastry into a rectangle about 38 × 23cm *(15 × 9 in)*. Trim the edges with a sharp knife, then place the pastry on the baking sheet, leaving a border about 2½cm *(1 in)* wide, and prick the pastry all over with a fork to keep it from rising too much.

Peel and core the apples, cut them in half, then cut them crosswise into extra-thin semi-circular slices. Place the slices on the pastry one at a time, laying them so that each one overlaps the preceding one almost completely, like the scales of a fish; cover the tart in this manner. Dot the apples with butter, sprinkle with the sugar and bake for 16 minutes. Lower the oven to 425°F/220°C/Reg. 7 and bake for 10 minutes more.

To serve the tart

Serve the tart as it comes from the oven, with *crème fraîche* on the side if desired.

Suggestions

Pears may be used instead of apples (but a pear tart will not keep), and short pastry (see the recipe for Tarte Tatin, p.280) can be used instead of puff pastry. If shortcrust pastry is used, roll it thinly and fold the edges up to make a border.

Wine

A rough cider, or Calvados.

Grape or Cherry Clafoutis
Clafoutis aux fruits frais

For 4 people

700g *(1½ lb)*	cherries or grapes
5	large or 6 medium eggs
90g *(3½ oz)*	caster sugar
	a pinch of cinnamon
	a pinch of salt
80g *(3 oz)*	plain flour
250ml *(9 fl. oz)*	milk
65g *(2½ oz)*	melted butter
2 generous tbsps	liquid honey

Equipment

mixing bowl · wire whisk · cake tin, 25cm *(10 in)* in diameter · large frying pan

The batter

Beat the eggs, sugar, cinnamon and salt together; sift the flour into the mixing bowl, whisk to combine, then whisk in the milk, little by little, and add the melted butter. Whisk until smooth.

The fruit

Stone the cherries or de-seed the grapes if desired (this is optional). Wash and dry the fruit completely if necessary.

In a large frying pan, heat the honey, add the fruit and cook over a high heat for 10–15 minutes to caramelise; the fruit will give out liquid, which will have to evaporate before it begins to caramelise. Stir the fruit as little as possible. Shake the pan from time to time to coat the fruit in the caramel once it begins to form. Be careful not to let it burn.

To bake and serve the *clafoutis*

Pre-heat the oven to 400°F/200°C/Reg. 6. Lightly butter the cake tin.

Whisk the batter and pour it into the cake tin, add the fruit, spreading it out evenly, and bake for 30–35 minutes or until the surface is golden brown.

Remove from the oven, allow to cool for 15 minutes, and serve warm.

Wine

A light white wine.

Walnut and Almond Chocolate Cake

Gâteau chocolaté aux noix et aux amandes fraîches

For 6–8 people

7 tbsps	softened butter
150g *(5 oz)*	caster sugar
1	large egg, separated
¼ tsp	salt
150ml *(5 fl. oz)*	milk
2 tbsps	unsweetened cocoa powder
150g *(5 oz)*	plain flour
2	drops of lemon juice
¾ tsp	vanilla sugar
125g *(4 oz)*	blanched almonds
125g *(4 oz)*	walnuts

Equipment

3 mixing bowls · wire whisk or electric mixer · wooden spatula · deep cake tin or loaf tin, 25cm *(10 in)* long
To serve: oval or rectangular serving dish

The cake mixture

Beat the butter and sugar in a mixing bowl until very pale and creamy, add the egg yolk and salt, then whisk in the milk little by little.

In another mixing bowl, mix the cocoa powder and the flour. Whisk this mixture little by little into the butter–sugar–milk mixture. Beat the batter vigorously until very creamy and smooth.

Add 2 drops of lemon juice to the egg white and whisk until very stiff. Begin folding it carefully into the batter; about halfway through, add the vanilla sugar, almonds and walnuts, and continue folding until there are no more bits of unmixed egg white in the batter.

284

To bake and serve the cake

Pre-heat the oven to 400°F/200°C/Reg. 6. Lightly butter a cake tin or loaf tin.

Transfer the mixture to the tin and bake for 30 minutes, then lower the oven to 350°F/180°C/Reg. 4 and continue baking for 40 minutes–1 hour. The cake is done when the blade of a knife inserted into the centre comes out clean and dry, and the cake begins to pull away from the sides of the tin.

Turn the cake out as soon as it comes from the oven and serve either barely warm or cold.

Note

The original recipe uses many more nuts and rather more flour to obtain a less rich but nuttier cake. If you want to try this, use fresh nuts, about 500g *(1 lb)* of each, 300g *(11 oz)* of flour and 300g *(11 oz)* of sugar, moistened with 300ml *(½ pint)* of milk. The remaining ingredients are the same.

Wine

Monbazilla, Jurançon.

Honey and Hazelnut Cake
Gâteau au miel et aux noisettes

For 6–8 people

4	eggs, separated
100ml *(4 fl. oz)*	liquid honey
65g *(2¼ oz)*	caster sugar
4 tbsps	softened butter
120g *(4 oz)*	plain flour, measured then sifted
150g *(5 oz)*	ground hazelnuts
2	drops lemon juice
2 tbsps	caster sugar (for the egg whites)

Equipment

2 large mixing bowls · wire whisk or electric beater · cake tin, 20cm *(8 in)* in diameter and 4–5cm *(1–2 in)* high
To serve: cake plate

To make and serve

Pre-heat the oven to 400°F/200°C/Reg. 6.

Beat the egg yolks, honey and sugar in a large bowl until pale and creamy. Beat in the butter, then stir in the flour and ground hazelnuts to make a stiff batter.

Beat the egg whites and lemon juice in a large bowl until they stiffen, then add 2 tablespoons of sugar and continue beating until very stiff. Fold a quarter of the egg whites into the batter, then fold in the remaining egg whites.

Lightly butter the cake tin, pour in the batter and bake for 40 minutes or until the cake is firm to the touch and a straw plunged into the centre comes out clean and dry.

Turn the cake out on to a cake plate when it comes from the oven, allow to cool for about 15 minutes, then serve.

Note
Walnuts or pecans can be used instead of hazelnuts.

Wine
Sweet white wine – Jurançon or Monbazillac.

Cigarettes
Cigarettes

For 24–30 cigarettes

2	egg whites
75g *(2½ oz)*	caster sugar
60g *(2 oz)*	butter, melted
70g *(2½ oz)*	plain flour

Equipment
small saucepan · wooden spoon · large mixing bowl · sieve · baking sheet · flexible spatula · cake rack

Preliminary preparations
At least 24 hours before baking, make the batter in the following way. Using a wooden spoon, beat the egg whites and sugar together for about 2–3 minutes, then beat in the melted butter little by little. When it has been perfectly mixed in, sift the flour into the batter, stirring as it is being added, then beat the batter until smooth. Cover the bowl with aluminium foil and refrigerate for at least 24 hours.

To bake and shape the cigarettes
Pre-heat the oven to 450°F/230°C/Reg. 8.

Lightly butter a baking sheet with melted butter. Place a teaspoon of batter on the baking sheet and spread it out with the back of the spoon to make a biscuit about 8cm *(3 in)* wide and as thin as possible (you should be able to see the baking sheet through the batter). About 8–9 biscuits can be placed on one baking sheet. Bake for 4–5 minutes or until browned to a pale cinnamon colour.

Using a wide, flexible spatula, remove a biscuit from the baking sheet; do not hesitate to push the spatula hard to remove the biscuit and don't be surprised if it forms pleats. Straighten it out, place it on a table, and set a pencil or the handle of a wooden spoon down on one edge of the biscuit (the spoon end of the spoon should stick out over the edge of the table). Roll the biscuit round the handle to form a tube, then slide it off and place it on a cake rack to cool. Keep the remaining biscuits warm by leaving them in the oven with the door open. Since they become brittle very rapidly, the biscuits must be removed from the baking sheet and shaped one by one.

Serve with coffee or dessert, particularly sorbets.

Note
As this batter will keep for several days in the refrigerator, it is best to bake the cigarettes as you need them. If not serving them immediately, place them in a tightly sealed cake tin as soon as they have cooled or they will very quickly become soft.

Financiers
Financiers

For 24–30 *financiers*

160g *(5½ oz)*	butter
4	egg whites
125g *(4½ oz)*	caster sugar
50g *(2 oz)*	ground almonds
50g *(2 oz)*	plain flour

Equipment
small saucepan · wooden spoon · mixing bowl · 24–30 oval moulds, about 8 × 5 × 1½cm *(3 × 1¾ × ½ in)* (2-tbsp capacity) (see Note) · cake rack

Preliminary preparations
At least a day before baking, make the batter. Heat 150g *(5 oz)* of butter in a small saucepan until it just begins to smell of hazelnuts and stops sizzling (do not allow to burn). Skim off the foam on the surface with a spoon and allow to cool.

With a wooden spoon, beat the egg whites and sugar together, then sift in the ground almonds and flour. Stir to make a smooth batter. Carefully pour the lightly browned butter into the batter little by little, lifting the batter with the spoon to incorporate air as the butter is being added. Be careful to leave any milk solids in the bottom of the saucepan as you add the butter.

When all the ingredients are well combined, cover the bowl with aluminium foil and refrigerate for at least 24 hours (the batter will keep for several days in the refrigerator).

To bake the *financiers*

Pre-heat the oven to 450°F/230°C/Reg. 8. Lightly butter each mould.

Beat the batter with a spoon to soften it. With an ordinary teaspoon, take a walnut-sized lump of batter and transfer it to one of the moulds with another spoon. When all the moulds have been filled, bake them for 10 minutes or until golden brown; the buns should rise and split down the middle as they bake.

Turn the little buns out as soon as they come out of the oven. Leave to cool upside down on a cake rack for about 10 minutes. Serve warm with dessert or coffee.

Suggestions

Ground hazelnuts or walnuts, ground in a blender or food processor, may be used instead of almonds. Or desiccated (grated) coconut can be used instead of nuts.

Note

The shape of the moulds is not important, but the capacity is: the moulds should hold 2 tablespoons. Barquette moulds or madeleine moulds give equally good results.

Spiced Palmiers
Palmiers épicés

For 10–12 *palmiers*

2 tbsps	caster sugar
½ tsp	ground cinnamon
⅛ tsp	ground allspice
⅛ tsp	Chinese five-spice powder
125g (4½ oz)	puff pastry (see p.242)
	caster sugar (for dipping the *palmiers*)

Equipment

bowl · rolling pin · baking sheet · flexible metal spatula · cake rack or clean baking sheet
To serve: serving plate

To roll out the pastry

Mix the sugar, cinnamon, allspice and Chinese five-spice powder together in a bowl.

Sprinkle the top and bottom of the puff pastry with some of the spiced sugar and sprinkle a little on a worktop. Roll out the pastry into a rectangle approximately 13 × 28cm *(5 × 11 in)*, sprinkling it and the worktop with the spice mixture as it is absorbed into the pastry until you have used all the sugared spice.

Starting at one of the short ends, roll the pastry towards the middle until it almost reaches the centre of the rectangle, then roll the other short end towards the middle until it touches the first. Place the pastry on a plate, cover with aluminium foil and refrigerate for 20 minutes.

To cut, bake and serve the *palmiers*

Pre-heat the oven to 425°F/230°C/Reg. 8. Cover the bottom of a plate with caster sugar.

With a large, very sharp knife, cut the pastry into 10–12 slices, about 1cm *(⅜–½ in)* thick. Place each slice in the icing sugar, turn it over to coat both sides, then set it down on a lightly buttered baking sheet. Leave plenty of space between the *palmiers*: they spread a great deal while baking.

Bake the *palmiers* for 5 minutes, then turn them over with a flexible metal spatula and bake for 5 minutes more or until golden brown and caramelised.

Slide the *palmiers* on to a cake rack or a clean baking sheet to cool for a few minutes. Cover a plate with a white napkin and serve the *palmiers* warm, piled up on the napkin.

Brandied Prunes 'Rénaudie'
Pruneaux Rénaudie

For 1-litre *(1¾-pint)* jar

4 tsps	tea
500ml *(17 fl. oz)*	boiling water
450g *(1 lb)*	large prunes, cooked
60g *(2 oz)*	caster sugar
250ml *(9 fl. oz)*	cognac or vodka

Equipment
teapot · 1-litre *(1¾-pint)* preserving jar

To make and serve the prunes
Place the tea in a warmed teapot and add the boiling water. Cover and allow to steep for 3–4 minutes.

Place the prunes in a sterilised preserving jar with the sugar and alcohol. Strain the tea into the jar, wait for 15 minutes, then close the jar tightly. Place in a cupboard for 2 weeks before serving.

Serve the prunes after dinner, about 3 per person, in small glasses with a few spoonfuls of alcohol from the jar.

Crème Fraîche
Crème fraîche

For 325ml *(11 fl. oz)*

300ml *(½ pint)*	double cream
3 tbsps	buttermilk (active culture)

To make
Place the cream and buttermilk in a saucepan, heat over a low heat until lukewarm to the touch, then remove from the heat and allow to stand in a warm place, covered, for 6–10 hours. Gently stir the cream to see if it is ready – if a thick layer has formed on top, but the cream is still liquid underneath, it is done (do not let it thicken too much or it will sour). Place the cream in a jar, stir to mix well, cover and place in the refrigerator overnight before using. The cream will finish thickening in the refrigerator and can be kept for up to a week before it starts to sour.

Note
Crème fraîche is simply double or whipping cream in which the natural lactic acids it contains are allowed to act until the cream has thickened considerably. It is usually then pasteurised. In most recipes, double cream may be used instead of *crème fraîche*; when there is a choice, this is indicated. If *crème fraîche* alone is given in the ingredients list, then it must be used, as its nutty taste and thick consistency are essential to the preparation involved. *Crème fraîche* can be found in some supermarkets but it tends to be very expensive, so it is worth making it yourself.

When making *crème fraîche*, use fresh pasteurised or unpasteurised, *not* ultra-pasteurised, cream. The chemical substances in ultra-pasteurised cream tend to slow down the thickening process and give the *crème fraîche* a slightly unpleasant metallic taste.

Chocolate Truffles
Truffes au chocolat

For about 20–25 truffles

1 tbsp	milk
2 tbsps	whipping or double cream
1½ tbsps	caster sugar
125g (4½ oz)	semi-sweet dark chocolate, *(Chocolat Menier* is ideal), broken into pieces
1 tbsp	Scotch whisky
50g *(2 oz)* approx.	unsweetened cocoa powder

Equipment
small saucepan · bowl · pastry bag with 1.5cm *(½-in)* nozzle (see Note) · large flat dish or baking sheet
To serve: serving plate

The truffle cream
Place the milk, cream and sugar in a small saucepan and bring slowly to a boil. Remove from the heat, add the chocolate and stir until it has melted completely. Add the whisky and stir until perfectly smooth. Pour into a bowl and place in the refrigerator, stirring occasionally with a wooden spoon, for about 35 minutes or until the mixture has stiffened to the consistency of thick chocolate icing.

Making the truffles
Beat the truffle cream with a wooden spoon to make it smooth. Spoon it into the pastry bag and squeeze it out on to a large flat dish or a baking sheet, making mounds the size of a small walnut. Place in the refrigerator to harden for 30–45 minutes.

Place the cocoa in a soup plate.

When the truffles are stiff, detach them from the plate with the tip of a knife and roll them in the cocoa, one at a time. Roll them rapidly between the palms of your hands to make them perfectly round, then roll them in the cocoa once more. Put the finished truffles on a clean plate and refrigerate for at least an hour before serving.

Suggestion
Instead of whisky, cognac or any fruit liqueur (raspberry, strawberry, plum, and so on) may be used.

Note
Instead of using a pastry bag, the mounds may be made by taking a teaspoon of truffle cream and pushing it on to the plate or baking sheet with a second spoon.

Chocolate-coated Orange Peel
Orangettes chocolatées

For 4–5 people

2	oranges
250ml *(9 fl. oz)*	water
225g *(8 oz)*	caster sugar
6 tbsps	Grand Marnier (or other orange-flavoured liqueur)
150g *(5 oz)*	semi-sweet dark chocolate *(Chocolat Menier* is ideal), broken into pieces

Equipment
saucepan · cake rack or drum sieve · double boiler · baking sheet
To serve: serving plate

The oranges
Wash the oranges in warm water and dry them. With the tip of a pointed knife, slit the skin into quarters. Peel the skin off, being very careful not to break it. (The fruit will not be used in this recipe, so keep it for something else, such as a fruit salad.)

Cut each piece of peel in half crosswise and trim the edges so that each half forms a rectangle. Discard the trimmings. With the knife, remove as much of the white part of the skin as possible, then cut each rectangle into 4 strips.

Place the strips of orange zest in a sieve, rinse under cold running water and drain.

To cook
Place the water, sugar and Grand Marnier in a saucepan, stir until the sugar has dissolved, bring to the boil, add the orange zest, lower the heat and simmer for 2 hours. (After 1 hour and 15 minutes, check the syrup; if it has become very thick, add 6 tablespoons of water, stir and continue cooking.)

Lift the strips out of the syrup with a fork and spread them out on a cake rack or drum sieve, making them as flat and straight as possible. They should not touch each other. Allow to cool completely and dry for at least 3 hours (or leave them overnight).

To coat with chocolate
In the bottom of a double boiler, heat a little water until it just simmers. Place the chocolate in the top of the double boiler and set it in place over but not touching the water. Melt the chocolate; this should take about 5–6 minutes, and the water should never boil.

Stir the melted chocolate until smooth, then remove the double boiler from the heat.

Place a large sheet of aluminium foil (or 2 smaller sheets) on the worktop. One by one, drop the strips of candied zest into the chocolate, turn them over with a fork, and lift them out, allowing the excess chocolate to drip off. Place them on the aluminium foil, as flat and straight as possible, and without allowing them to touch.

When all the pieces of zest have been coated, allow to cool for 10 minutes. Refrigerate them for 25–30 minutes, lift them off the foil and arrange them on a plate. Keep them refrigerated until ready to serve.

Suggestion
The zest of a grapefruit can be used instead of 2 oranges.

Tile-shaped Almond Biscuits
Tuiles aux amandes

For 12–15 *tuiles*

2	egg whites
60g *(2 oz)*	caster sugar
60g *(2 oz)*	butter, melted
35g *(1 ¼ oz)*	plain flour
	a generous 60g *(2 oz)* slivered almonds

Equipment
small saucepan · wooden spoon · large mixing bowl · baking sheet · flexible metal spatula · rolling pin · cake rack

Preliminary preparations
At least 24 hours before baking, make the batter in the following way. Using a wooden spoon, beat the egg whites and sugar together for about 2–3 minutes, then beat in the melted butter little by little. When all the butter has been completely mixed in, sift the flour into the batter, stirring as it is being added. When smooth, stir in the almonds, cover the bowl with aluminium foil and refrigerate for at least 24 hours.

To bake and shape the *tuiles*
Pre-heat the oven to 450°F/230°C/Reg. 8.

Lightly butter a baking sheet with melted butter. Drop a generous teaspoon of the batter on to the baking sheet and spread the almonds evenly throughout to make a thin round, about 6–8cm *(2½–3 in)* wide. Approximately 6 or 7 biscuits can be made at once on a baking sheet. Bake for 4–5 minutes or until the edges have browned to a cinnamon colour – the centres will be paler.

Use a spatula to remove the *tuiles* from the baking sheet. Lay each one on a rolling pin and, protecting your hand with an oven glove, press the biscuit around the rolling pin to shape it. (Keep the remaining *tuiles* warm by leaving them in the oven with the door open. They harden quickly and will become too brittle to bend if you take too many from the oven at once, so remove only as many as you can shape at a time.)

Place the finished *tuiles* on a cake rack to cool. Serve with coffee or dessert.

Suggestions

A little finely chopped lemon or orange zest may be added to the batter, or the amount of almonds can be increased, if desired.

Note

As this batter will keep in the refrigerator for several days, it is best to bake only as many *tuiles* as you need at one time. If they are not being served immediately, place them in a tightly sealed cake tin as soon as they are cool, as they will very quickly become soft.

Index

298

7